Julian M. Sturtevant

**Economics - Or the Science of Wealth**

Julian M. Sturtevant

**Economics - Or the Science of Wealth**

ISBN/EAN: 9783337035006

Printed in Europe, USA, Canada, Australia, Japan

Cover: Foto ©Suzi / pixelio.de

More available books at **www.hansebooks.com**

# ECONOMICS

OR

# THE SCIENCE OF WEALTH

BY

JULIAN M. STURTEVANT, D.D., LL.D.,

PROFESSOR OF POLITICAL ECONOMY IN ILLINOIS COLLEGE AND
EX-PRESIDENT OF THE SAME.

εἰ τις οὐ θέλει ἐργάζεσθαι, μηδὲ ἐσθιέτω.

PAUL.

---

NEW YORK

G. P. PUTNAM'S SONS

182 FIFTH AVENUE

1879.

# PREFACE.

I HAVE been induced to undertake this work by a conviction, the result of many years of experience as a teacher, that, to a considerable extent, the definitions in use in the science of which I have attempted to treat are indeterminate. Especially has it seemed to me, that while in all our treatises the subject matter of the science is assumed to be wealth, that word is either left without any satisfactory definition, or if a valid definition is given, it is not applied to the whole group of phenomena embraced in it. The words labor and capital also seem to me to have been so loosely defined, as to give an aspect of indefiniteness to the whole science. I can hardly be mistaken on this point. I have constantly seen the evidence in each successive class, and whatever text-book I have employed, that intelligent minds are aware of this indefiniteness, and their interest in the science is diminished by it. The same thing is apparent in the general public. Many intelligent minds either deny that any science of Economics exists, or if they admit its existence, they regard it as so vague and indeterminate as hardly to deserve to be called a science. I am compelled to admit that these complaints are not altogether groundless. If I am right in this admission, the ground of such objections can only be removed by more accurate definitions, and a more logical method. Such definitions I have attempted to frame; such a method I have sought to pursue. I have endeavored to present the whole science as a logical development of a single law of nature. Such I am sure it is, whether I have succeeded in so presenting it or not. If I have failed in what I have attempted, some other one more fortunate will surely succeed. With this frank statement of the motives which have induced me to write this treatise, I submit my work to the candid judgment of the American public. Surely no people ever had more urgent need of sound economic knowledge than we have at the present time.

J. M. S.

ILLINOIS COLLEGE, Sept. 3d, 1877.

# CONTENTS.

*N. B. The figures refer to the sections.*

## INTRODUCTION.

### FIRST PRINCIPLES.  PAGE 1

Fundamental natural law, 1. All ownership acquired by labor, 2. Two distinct sciences evolved from the same fundamental law, 3. Definition of Wealth, 3. Definition defended, 4 and 5. Definition of Labor, 6. Labor divided into two classes, 6. Name of the Science, 7. Definition of Economics, 7. Science consists of three parts, 8. Social and moral conditions assumed by the Science, 8a.

## *PART I.—Production.*

### CHAPTER I.

#### STIMULI TO LABOR.  11

A rational soul, 9. Impulse of appetite, 10. Need of clothing, shelter, etc., 11. Love of acquisition and ownership, 12. Love of the beautiful, 13. Love of humanity. 13. All men's powers must be brought into use, 14. Satisfaction of artificial wants, 15. Necessity of Government, 16.

## CHAPTER II.

#### CAPITAL.        PAGE 19

Love of gain insatiable, and why, 17. Definition of Capital, 18. Subdivisions and other definitions, 18. These definitions explained and justified, 19. Sole function of Capital, 20. How Capital aids Labor, first sustains the laborer, second furnishes tools, third provides machinery, 21. All human beings laborers, 22. Wealth not national, 23. Aid rendered by Capital to Labor unlimited, 24. Partial limitation in Agriculture, 25. Land the fixed Capital of Agriculture, 25.

## CHAPTER III.

#### CAPITAL A UNIVERSAL PATRIMONY.     30

Principle proved, 26. Illustrated by the estate of A. T. Stewart, 27. Individual gratification the compensation of the capitalist, 28. Promotes improvement in architecture, 28. How men become public treasurers, 28. Public treasurers unfaithful, 29. Public liberality, 30. Recapitulation, 31.

## CHAPTER IV.

#### DIVISION OF LABOR.     37

Diversity of natural endowments necessary to society, 32. Law of habit, 33. Definition of division of Labor, 33. Origin of do., 33. Extension of the principle in modern manufactures, 34. Economic advantages of it, 35. Increases skill, 35. Saves time in learning trades and in adjusting tools and adjusts compensation to skill, 35. Limitations of division of Labor, viz., Nature of the process, Want of sufficient capital, and Demand for the product, 36. Division of labor not national, 37. Combination of labor, 38. Other classifications of labor, 38a.

CONTENTS. vii

## PART II.—*Exchange.*

### CHAPTER I.

#### VALUE. PAGE 49

Definition of Exchange, 39. Importance of definition of value, 40. Definition of Competition, 41. Definition of Value, Do. of Cost, Do. of Price, Do. of Supply and Demand, 42. Relation of Cost to Value, 43. Competition the only test of Value, 44. Objections to Competition as a universal test of Value. 45.

### CHAPTER II.

#### FLUCTUATIONS OF VALUE. 58

Two causes of fluctuations of Value. First cause, variation of cost of production, by improvement in machinery, by increased facilities of communications 46. By changes in the cost of material, 47. Second, variation of the ratio of Supply and Demand, 48. Ratio of Supply to Demand may be increased or diminished temporarily or permanently, 48. When Supply can be increased without increased cost, 48. When Supply cannot be increased without increased cost, 49. When Supply cannot be increased, 50.

### CHAPTER III.

#### MONEY. 68

Money the tool of Exchange, 51. Not the invention of a single mind, 52. Definition of Money, 53. Money mercantile fixed Capital, 53. Gold and Silver suitable for Money, Universal desirableness; scarce and obtained by great labor, One suited for large Exchanges the other for small. Capability of minute division, 54. Little subject to fluctuations of Value, 55. Money cosmopolitan, 56. Indications of designing mind, 57.

## CHAPTER IV.

### THE RELATION OF THE GOVERNMENT TO THE MEDIUM OF EXCHANGE.     PAGE 78

Chimerical theories, 58. Right of the Government to prescribe a legal tender, 59. Notes of the United States made legal tender, 60. Why? 60. Government may not interfere with contracts, 61. Should never make its own promises legal tender, 61. Obligation to redeem greenbacks, 62. Greenbacks a depreciated currency, 63. Produce great fluctuations, 63. No natural limit of their amount, 64. Value varies inversely as the amount, 64. An elastic currency impossible, 65. Communism, 65. Unstable currency injurious to trade, 66.

## CHAPTER V.

### CREDIT AND PAPER MONEY.     90

Credit founded in human nature, 67. Always present in the relation of capital to labor, 67. Definition of credit, 67. Banks of deposit, 68. Facilitate exchanges, 69. Credit cosmopolitan, 69. Banks of loan, 70. Banks of issue, Paper money, 71. Convenience of paper money, 71. Unstable, 72. Credit and legislation, 72. National currency, 73. Security for its redemption, 73. Not a satisfactory solution of the banking question, 74. Depends on the credit of the government, 74. No security for the payment of deposits, 74. Credit should be left to its natural development, 74. Why not a national bank, 75.

## CHAPTER VI.

### FUNCTIONS OF CREDIT.     102

Great influence of credit, 76. Quickens exchanges, 76. Unites skill and capital, 77. Diminishes the amount of money

needed, 78. By book accounts. By checks and drafts, 78.
By bank notes, 78. The real advantage of paper money
79. Will facilitate our return to specie payments, 79.
Power of credit to control prices, 80. Dangerous element
80. Financial crisis of 1837, 80. Binds the whole civilized world together, 81.

## CHAPTER VII.

### MONOPOLIES.   PAGE 110

Foreign exchanges not international, 82. Definition of monopoly, 82. What monopolies are defensible, 83. The monopoly of protection, 84. The word protection used unfairly, 85. Competition the enemy of no legitimate business, 85. Tends to the perfection of the product, 86. General principles of the science adverse to "protection," 87. Human race one family, 87. Theoretical and practical, 88.

## CHAPTER VIII.

### FREE TRADE, OBJECTIONS CONSIDERED.   119

Definition of free trade, 89. Variety of industry said to be a condition of national prosperity, 90. Not universally, 90. Which is cause and which effect, 90. In the beginning of society variety of industry impossible, 90. Free trade only opposed to unprofitable industry, 91. Protection said to be necessary for infant manufactures, 92. Free trade said to deprive land of manure, 93. Free trade said to be destructive of national independence, 94. What is national independence, 94. Dependence of nations mutual 95. Free trade tends to universal peace, 96. It is said free trade should be reciprocal, 97. Self-destructive retaliation, 97. Protection said to encourage skilled labor, 98.

## CHAPTER IX.

#### OBJECTIONS TO PROTECTION CONSIDERED.     PAGE 135

Aim of protection, Means inadequate, 99. Injurious to public morals 99. Constructs the economic fabric on a false principle, 100. Corrupts our national legislation, 101. Destructive of statesmanship, 101. In its own nature unsocial, 102. Dangerous to our future, 102. Self-contradictory and self-destructive, 103. Raises the price of protected articles 103. Benefits no class, 104.

---

## *PART III.—Distribution.*

### CHAPTER I.

#### PRELIMINARY PRINCIPLES.     145

Exchange and distribution distinguishable, 106. Distribution defined, 106. Controlled by competition, 107. Recapitulation, 107. Two-fold division, 108.

### CHAPTER II.

#### WAGES DETERMINED BY COMPETITION.     150

Wages defined, 109. Labor and capital often in the same person, 109. Employer and employé, 110. Location of the conflict, 110. Wages not controlled by the employer, 111. Both parties controlled by competition, 112. Needle-women cannot be relieved of competition, 113. Wages above the rate of competition injurious to employés, 113. Minimum and maximum of wages, 114.

## CHAPTER III.

### WAGES AS AFFECTED BY COMBINATION.   PAGE 160

Combination of laborers, 115. Of capitalists, 115. The competing unit individual not social, 115. Strike defined, 116. When it can and when it cannot succeed, 116. Trades-unions, their objects, 117. Often monopolies, 117. Consequences if successful, 118. Success impossible, 119. Cannot control all workmen, 119. Will arrest accumulation, 120. Employers cannot resist competition by combination, 121. Must have the reputation of paying fair wages, 121. Violence must not be used, 122.

## CHAPTER IV.

### VARIATION OF THE RATE OF WAGES.   170

Causes of the varying results of competition, 123. First cause, change of the number of laborers in proportion to capital, 124. The greater the capital the greater the demand for laborers, and vice versa, 124. When both labor and capital vary wages depend on the ratio of one to the other, 125. Employers and employés not natural enemies, 125. Labor-saving machinery another cause, 126. Increases the demand for labor, 126. Chimerical expectations, 127. Exception for agricultural labor, 128. Wages vary with the cost of living, 129. Not merely with the cost of the necessaries of life, 129.

## CHAPTER V.

### CAUSES OF THE VARIATION OF WAGES FOR PARTICULAR PERSONS AND CLASSES.   180

First cause, diversity of natural gift, 130. Profits of eminent professional men, 130. Second cause, cost of acquiring skill, 131. Wages proportioned to skill, 131. Third cause, amount of confidence reposed, 132. Honor of position reduces wages, 132. Numerous causes, 133. Excessive competition in certain occupations, 134. Competing unit, 134. Living of some of the competitors not at stake, 134. Obscure and subtle causes affect wages, 135. Vicious celibacy, 135. Science not opposed to marriage, 136. Alleged injustice of the wages of women, 137. Said to receive less wages for the same work, 137. Why not pay women the same wages as men, 138. Competition a guide to one's proper occupation, 139. Applicable to the Christian Ministry, 139.

## CHAPTER VI.

### OWNERSHIP OF LAND.    PAGE 192

Two parties in distribution, 140. Ownership of land must depend on a natural law, 141. Case of land different from that of air and water, 142. Nations own water on which they bestow labor, 142. Ownership of land acquired by labor bestowed, 143. Not merely temporary, 143. Government title not procured by purchase from savages, 144. Savage tribes not nations, 145. Higher law, 145. What shall be done with the Indian, 146. Origin of the government title, 147. Right of political jurisdiction, 147. Objection to this view. Labor of subduing land said to be over compensated, 148. Not true, 148. Not relevant if true, 148. Another objection. Prospective enhancement of value, 149. Allowed for in rent, 149.

## CHAPTER VII.

### INTEREST.    204

Gains of the capitalist are either interest, rent or profit, 150. Interest defined, 150. Consists of two elements, 150. Why interest must be paid, 151. Legislative interference with, 151. A violation of ownership, 151. Controlled by competition, 152. Various causes of fluctuation, 153. Tenure of land affects the rate of interest, 153. Different rates in different countries, 154. Declines with the progress of civilization, 155. Stationary condition of capital not to be apprehended, 156. Demands for capital inversely as the rate of interest, 157. Cosmopolitan nature of capital sustains the rate of interest, 158. Also labor-saving invention, 158.

## CHAPTER VIII.

### RENT. PAGE 213

Rent defined, 159. No risk in rent, 159. Rent less than interest without risk. Reason why, 159. Ricardo's theory of rent stated, 160. Rent in new settlements, 161. Reason why, 161. Progress of cultivation, 162. Fallacy of Ricardo's theory, 163. Why rent rises with the progress of society, 164. Law of diminishing returns, 165. Rent an element in the cost of agricultural produce. 165a. Abolition of rent impossible, 166. Rent offset by transportation, 167. Fawcett's admission, 168. Same fallacy applied to minerals, 169.

## CHAPTER IX.

### PROFIT. 232

Profit defined, 170. How differs from interest, 170. Rate declines with advancing civilization, 170. Competition the supreme law, 171. Rate different in different occupations, 172. Each occupation has its natural rate of profit, 172. Combinations of capital to resist competition, 173. Free Trade the best antidote, 173. Particular combinations. Petroleum, 174. Great Railways, 175. General Railway law, 176. Wisdom of the managers not a sufficient public protection, 177. Question complicated and difficult, 178. No effectual protection against such combinations, 178. Great advantages of large combinations of capital, 179.

## CHAPTER X.

#### UNDERLYING CONDITIONS OF FREE COMPETITION. PAGE 245

Three conditions, 180. First condition, freedom of exchange, especially in land, 180. Required by the law of ownership, 181. Limitation of it injurious to both parties, 181. Desire of the agricultural laborer to own land, 182. Life hopeless without it, 182. Relative profit of large and small farming, 183. Comparison of English and American tillage, 184. Land more valuable in small proprietorships, 184. Why the number of holdings in England is diminishing, 185. Difficulty of the question, 185. Second condition, intelligence in both parties, 186. Competition impossible without it, 186. Relation of our science to public education, 187. Proper limits of public education, 187. Public education of itself not sufficient, 188. Agricultural population of New England, 189. Third condition, moral integrity, 190.

## CHAPTER XI.

#### POPULATION. 261

Malthus' theory of population, 191. False in practice, 192. Two results of free competition, 192. First result, universal dissemination of civilization, 193. This law recently developed, 193. English colonization, 193. Why this law was little known in antiquity, 194. Not manifested in some modern nations, 194. Depends on quality of emigration, 195. True economic lesson, 195. Law applicable to capital, 196. Second result, human race propagated from best specimens, 197. Four strata in civilized society, 197. First and second contribute little to population, 198. Fourth class contributes little, 199. Population chiefly derived from the third class, 199. Conditions most favorable, 199. Propagates the highest civilization, 200. The law of wages beneficent, 200. Darwin's natural selection, 200. Future of the human race secured, 201.

## CHAPTER XII.

**ECONOMIC CONDITIONS OF GENERAL PEACE.   PAGE 273**

Economic importance of the peace of the world, 202. Degraded masses dangerous to internal tranquillity, 203. Dangerous to international harmony, 204. All must demand and expect the comforts of life, 205. Strong to repel invasion, weak for aggression, 205. The one condition of general peace, 206.

## CHAPTER XIII.

**SUBSTITUTES FOR COMPETITION. SOCIALISM.   280**

Public mind unquiet. Coöperation, 207. Socialism, pure and simple, 207. A denial of our fundamental law, 208. Modified socialism 209. Relies on competition while it rejects it, 209. Dispensing with the services of middle men, 210. Allowing laborers a share of profits, 211. The true agricultural coöperation, 211. Education not sufficient, 211. Laborers should be stockholders, 211. True coöperation not kindred to socialism, 212. Competition the only hope for the laborer, 212. Abolition of private ownership of land, 213. National bankruptcy and anarchy, 213. Logical consequence of unjust laws of land tenure, 214. Should government find employment for the unemployed, 215. Abolition of the right of property, 215.

## CHAPTER XIV.

**TAXATION.   295**

No logical place for it, 216. Government a partner in all production, 216. Protection of person and property not the only political function, 217. Postal service. Streets, thoroughfares, etc., 217. Local taxation, by whom levied, 217. Expense of public education, 218. Limits of, 218. Care of the unfortunate, 219. How far gratuitous, 219.

State must protect its own existence, 220. Its promises bind individual conscience, 220. Abuse of the power of taxation, 221. Mode of taxation, 222. Revenue duties, 222. Should not interfere with trade, 222. Taxation of debts, 223. Creditor should pay, 224, to the State that protects, 224. Dangers of excessive taxation, 225.

## CHAPTER XV.

#### PAUPERISM. PAGE 312

An anomaly. No logical place for it, 226. Always attends civilization, 226. No modification of economic law can provide for it, 227. Moral forces require consideration. Inadequate, 228. The economist insists on two prohibitions. No ownership without labor. Men must not be relieved from the fear of want, 229. Out-door relief to be avoided, 230. Relief establishments should not undersell in the market, 230. Objections to out-door aid, 231. Tend to increase pauperism, 231. Paupers should not be voters, 231. Relief establishments should be reformatories, 232. Vicious self-indulgence should be restrained, 232. If society countenances vices it should support the pauperism they produce, 233.

## CHAPTER XVI.

#### WASTEFUL EXPENDITURE. 324

Supplementary topics, 234. Necessary and disposable products, 235. Stimulants and narcotics, 236. In great demand, 236. No reasons to justify this vast expenditure, 237. Eminently dangerous, 237. Economy enters no protest against the love of the beautiful, 238. False modes of ornamentation, 238. Fashion, 239. Peculiarly potent in democratic society, 240. Subject worthy of the consideration of the wealthy, 240. Adverse to correct taste, 241. Under freedom the people arbiters of their own destiny, 242. Relation to national character, 242. The wealthy not to lead useless lives, 243.

## CHAPTER XVII.

### PUBLIC LIBERALITY.     PAGE 334

Love of social prosperity a natural impulse, 244. Laws of exchange not adequate to supply all social want, 244. Governments cannot supply them, 244. Low rate of interest favorable to public liberality, 245. Intelligence of the community important to capital, 246. The rich should be voluntary public treasurers, 246. Public charities not to hold land by inalienable tenure, 247. Higher Institutions of education should be controlled by the highest culture, 248. Government inadequate to it, 248. Tendencies of democratic peoples to lavish expenditure, 249. Public liberality the remedy, 249. Capital so used not withdrawn from the aid of labor, 249.

# INTRODUCTION.

## FIRST PRINCIPLES.

§ 1. THE science we are about to expound, is the logical development and application to a special group of phenomena, of a single law of nature, as truly as physical astronomy is the logical development and application to the phenomena of the solar system, of the law of gravitation. The law of nature to which we refer may be thus enunciated:

*Every man owns himself, and all which he produces by the voluntary exertion of his own powers.*

Every science must assume something. Ours must assume that the idea of ownership is perfectly clear and intelligible to every one. It is a simple intuition, which originates in the spontaneous action of every human mind, and is therefore undefinable. It ranks in this respect with the idea of personality, of moral obligation and of causation. As the being we call self is conscious of its own wants, and exerts its own powers to supply them, it necessarily discerns the idea of possession, and begins to understand the meaning of possessive pronouns and learns correctly to apply them.

§ 2. This is our only idea of ownership. You cannot convince any human being, that another person may properly claim the possession of any thing as exclusively his own, unless his claim can be traced back to an origin in the natural law just enunciated.

If it can be so traced back, no man in his senses will call in question its validity. The ownership may have passed by voluntary gift or exchange, the nature of which transaction will hereafter be explained, through many hands; but if the ownership really exists, it must have been originally acquired by the exertion of some one's individual powers, to render the thing claimed serviceable to human well-being. The human mind instinctively discerns that in this way absolute ownership is acquired, and that the acquisition of any real ownership in any other way is impossible. The powers of nature are the free gift of God to all, and cannot be possessed. All those objects whereby man's wants are capable of being supplied by his own superadded efforts, are given in impartial liberality alike to all. The air, the water, the land, the spontaneous productions of the earth, the primeval forest, the game, the wild fruits are free to all. It is only when man has put forth his own efforts to render that helpful to human well being which was not so before, that the idea of ownership arises. Man's indisputable claim to the results of his own exerted powers carries along with it the material substance which by his exertion has been made fit for human use. The wild fruits as they hang upon the bush can be owned by no one. He who gathers them, by gathering becomes their owner. The nugget of gold that lies on the surface in some sequestered gorge of the mountains has no owner, any more than the atmospheric air which circulates around it. He who has made a journey to those unfrequented regions of desolation, discovered and picked up the precious thing, and carried it to the haunts of men, has become its owner, however great its value, just as he owned the ripe blackberry as soon as he had plucked it from its native bush. He who has entered on land never before subjected to human culture, has acquired the possession of all which by his own toil he has subdued and rendered capable of producing food for man. The savage who for generations roamed over it in pursuit of game, and lived on its spontaneous productions, acquired no ownership, because he did nothing to increase its capability of supplying human want. We do not expect to obtain full credence for these propositions without further proof than we can give in these preliminary statements. As we proceed in the development of the subject, there will be occasion more fully to illustrate and substantiate the principle. It is only appropriate here to give it its place among the fundamental principles of the science.

*All ownership of material things consists essentially in our unquestioned claim to possess and enjoy the results of that labor which we have expended upon them.*

§ 3. Two distinct sciences result from the development and application of this natural law. The being that owns these powers is capable of moral obligation, and is a subject of moral law. To point out the moral laws to which he is amenable in the exercise of these powers, is the sphere of the science of ethics. To develop the same fundamental law in the direction of the multiplication and exchange of objects fitted to satisfy human desire, and the distribution of them among all those who coöperate in their production, is the sphere of the science we are proposing to expound.

In constructing a system of science, it is necessary first to draw its extreme bounding lines. This can only be done by forming a comprehensive concept, which shall embrace precisely and only all the phenomena with which the science is to deal. We think that writers on our science have often failed to do this, and that much of the vagueness and indefiniteness with which it is charged is due to this cause. For the expression of that comprehensive concept we select the word wealth. We propose to write a treatise on the science of wealth. We must therefore define that word.

At the present stage of our inquiries, we can scarcely afford space for any controversy with those who think with Professor Perry, that it is impossible to frame any definition of wealth which will render the word fit for scientific use. Professor Perry has written a book which contains much clear thought and instructive suggestion. But it greatly lacks the scientific character, precisely for the reason that, instead of applying his acute mind to the definition of wealth, he has written about it without defining it. It is of no avail to say that the meaning of the word is unsettled. That only shows that it is necessary to settle it. The science itself will always be to a greater or less extent vague and indefinite, unworthy to be called a science, till the precise meaning of that word is determined by accurate definition. If the word wealth cannot be defined, then the science of wealth is simply impossible. Nor do we escape the difficulty by adopting Archbishop Whately's definition of the science,—"the science of exchange." We must still meet the question, what is wealth? for to wealth only is exchange applicable. We give therefore the following:

DEFINITION, *Wealth is anything which can be owned and exchanged for an equivalent.*

This definition embraces,

First, All human powers to adapt the materials of the world to the satisfaction of human desire by voluntary effort; for these are owned and can be exchanged for an equivalent. A man can exchange his power to produce such changes, for a day, for a year, for a life-time, for so many dollars, or for so much of any other desirable thing as may be agreed on between himself and the other party to the exchange.

Second, All tools, instruments and machines by which human labor is assisted.

Third, All objects which have been rendered capable by human effort of gratifying human desire, which remain at any time unconsumed, whether the process of fitting them for human use is completed, or in progress. Into precisely these three classes all wealth is divisible, and into one of them every thing of which the science properly treats will naturally fall.

§ 4. If to this definition it is objected that the word wealth is not ordinarily employed in so comprehensive a sense, the fact is admitted, but it is denied that this is any valid objection to the definition. In many sciences we are under the necessity of employing technical terms as comprehensive concepts of the phenomena with which any science has to do, which terms do not agree in the extent of their meaning with any terms which are in popular use. The popular mind has never formed that precise group of ideas with which the science has to do, and therefore has no term which expresses it. In every such case we have our choice of two expedients, either to select a new term not in popular use, more commonly derived from the storehouse of classical learning, or to choose a word in popular use which comes nearest to the desired meaning, and then limit it by a definition to a precise technical import. In the moral and social sciences we have for the most part pursued the course last indicated. Thus in Psychology the term perception is almost never used in popular speech in that precise meaning in which it is employed to express the acquisition of a knowledge of the material world through the senses. We have in this case selected a word from popular speech, and by a definition invested it with a precise technical meaning which it does not bear in common use. Precisely such liberty has been taken with the word wealth in our definition. Such a use of words finds innumerable justifications in all the moral and social sciences.

§ 5. If it is further objected to our definition of wealth, that it arranges in the same class things that are incongruous, that it embraces in the same genus things which have no generic likeness, as for example the wealth produced and the powers by which it is produced, our answer is, that the things referred to are not incongruous, that they are united by true generic resemblances. They are alike in the two generic characteristics, that they are capable of being owned and capable of being exchanged. The reason why so much difficulty has been experienced in defining this word is, that men have failed to notice that these are the true characteristics of the genus, and that they pertain alike to all which we have comprehended in our definition. Nothing is more common than such an occurrence as the following. One man has accumulated results of labor which he wishes to employ in trade. But he is infirm with age or otherwise incapacitated for exerting the active force which the business requires. He is therefore quite willing to enter into a partnership, on equal terms, with some one who possesses the requisite business efficiency, regarding the active powers of his partner as a full equivalent for the accumulated results of his own previous activity. One partner is just as rich in present active power, as the other is in accumulations of wealth. The two are regarded as perfectly homogeneous, and the one is freely exchanged for the other. If one of them is properly called wealth, why not the other? Examples involving and demonstrating the same principle are innumerable.

§ 6. The word labor will be of frequent occurrence in this treatise. We therefore propose the following:

DEFINITION, *Labor is the exertion of man's natural powers, for the purpose of producing such changes as conduce to the gratification of human desire and the supply of human want.*

All labor is divisible into two classes, viz:

First, That which is employed in constructing the implements and machines by which labor is aided and rendered efficient, and,

Second, That which is employed in producing changes whereby desire is directly gratified.

§ 7. The science of which we propose to treat is usually called Political Economy. To this name there are grave objections. We cannot help thinking that the continued use of this name is a standing proof, that the aim of the science has been to a certain extent misdirected. The name seems to suggest the idea, that the object of the science is to promote the wealth of the nation, that it always has special reference to the political divisions of the world, to those lines which are the conventional boundaries of nations. Some such idea seems to have been in the mind of Adam Smith, the father of the science, and to have induced him to choose for the title of his great work, "The Wealth of Nations." A recent writer on the subject, Professor Bowen, has chosen for the title of his book, "American Political Economy." In just so far as this idea of nationality has possession of the mind of the writer, it tends to a distorted and erroneous view of the subject. All this is as inappropriate as to speak of national Ethics, or American Astronomy. Science is not national or political. It is Universal. It is Human. Economy means, the law of the household, the family. There is a Human Family. "All ye are brethren." The Science of which we are to treat embraces that whole family, as truly as Ethics does, as truly as Astronomy gives us the science of the heavenly bodies, however separated from each other in immensity. We claim for the science its place among the universal sciences, like Ethics, Esthetics, Physics. Following the analogy according to which these names are constructed, we claim for our science the name ECONOMICS. We give the following:

DEFINITION, *Economics is the Science of Wealth.*

§ 8. As all wealth is either power to labor or the product of labor performed, and as power to labor is profitless unless it is exerted, our first inquiries will be, —what are those forces in human nature itself by which man is excited to exertion, and what are those devices and arrangements by which his natural powers are aided and rendered efficient? The first part of our science is concerned with these inquiries, and is called Production.

As it will appear in the progress of this work, that for the most part one man produces only one or at most a very few things, and must therefore supply his own multifarious wants by exchanging his products for the products of other men, it will be necessary to show how the law of exchange grows out of the law of ownership, and to explain the principal arrangements by which exchange is facilitated, and the natural law according to which it is conducted. This second part of the science is called Exchange.

As the whole human race is employed in greater or less degree in producing wealth, and must have a share in the wealth produced, or perish, we must expound those natural laws by which it is determined in what proportion the wealth of the world is distributed among all those who are concerned in its production. The third part of the science is devoted to the consideration of these laws, and is called Distribution.

To these it is customary to add a fourth part called Consumption. In it are explained the principles which regulate the application of wealth to the gratification of human desire, and the promotion of human wellbeing. But logically regarded, this fourth part of the science opens up the whole science of ethics. To pursue the subject exhaustively, we must inquire what is the destiny of man, for we cannot judge what man needs except in view of the destiny for which he was made. Having settled this question, it would next be incumbent on us to inquire by what application of his powers, he may most surely and completely attain this destiny. To pursue these inquiries by an exhaustive logic, would be to construct the science of ethics.

§ 8 *a*. In affirming that the Science of Economics is only a development of the single law enunciated above, we are not to be understood to assert, that the science so constructed is comprehensive of all the actual economic phenomena of the world as it is; but only that, if the laws of human nature were uncounteracted, either by government or vicious custom, and thus left free to work out their own proper results, those results would be in perfect conformity with the science thus evolved. This distinction is constantly recognized in this treatise, and if in any instance it is not formally stated, it is to be regarded as assumed and implied. It is our business as economists, not to point out a law which actually does regulate the economics of all peoples, but to show how the laws of human nature, when not viciously counteracted, would regulate them; and as far as may be, in cases where abnormal results exist, to discover the causes by which the mischief is wrought, and to suggest the needed economic remedies.

The enlightened economist will be quite ready to admit, that there are conditions of the successful working of the economic forces, which lie quite outside of his science. The intellectual and moral soundness of the individuals and the communities working these forces are such conditions. If we have to do with masses of men, in whom the intellect is deeply clouded by ignorance and superstition, and the moralities of life disregarded or unknown, economic science is impossible. That science always implies men, not brutes in human form,—civilized men, not barbarians,—men that know and obey the moral laws of human life. When we assert the universality of economic laws, we are not to be supposed to deny, or to be forgetful of these truths. But the existence of these truths can in no degree modify the development of economic laws, or detract any thing from the universality, or from the dignity or importance of the science.

# PART I.

## PRODUCTION.

### CHAPTER I.

*Stimuli to Labor.*

§ 9. It is the object of this chapter, to inquire what that is in the constitution of man that makes him the only laborer that inhabits this world. The lower orders of the creation cannot be said with any propriety to labor. All labor implies intelligent purpose. Man does not merely catch or gather his supplies. For the most part he makes them. He imparts to the materials which nature provides qualities which they did not possess before, and thus fits them for his use. By the combined agency of the atmosphere, the sunshine and the land, he produces the materials of food and clothing. Nothing but air and water and sunshine is found in a condition fit for his use. All else he makes fit by the exertion of his powers under the control of a rational soul. All the lower animals use nature as they find it. They gather, some of them store up, but they never fit it for their use. Man begins where all other animals end. He, like them, takes from nature what she furnishes, but unlike them, he fits it for his use by rational effort. This only is labor. *The first condition then of the performance of labor is the existence of a rational soul.* Labor is not mere effort, it is rational effort.

§ 10. The second stimulus to labor which we notice *is the impulse of the appetites of hunger, thirst and sex.* The two former have for their object the preservation of individual life and health; the latter, the perpetuation of the race. So important are these two objects that they are provided for by implanting in our very constitution impulses of appetite, so strong as to insure the end, without any experience or consideration of necessity. Men are driven to the satisfaction of these appetites without any thought of the necessity of such gratification to the preservation of their own lives, or the perpetuity of the race. So imperative are they that they compel a certain amount of labor even from the most indolent and degraded savage.

Men work, not like the bee or the beaver, from a direct impulse to work, but from a perceived necessity of working that they may have something to eat. The beaver is impelled to build his dam just as the man is impelled to eat his food when it is made ready to his hand. The bee and the beaver will work though relieved from all necessity. Relieve man from the pressure of the necessity of working that he may escape starvation, and he would never work at all. This is a law of human nature of which the economist must never lose sight.

§ 11. Another stimulus to labor is found in *certain needs of the human body which man learns only by experience.* These are the need of shelter from the storm, from the cold of winter, and from the burning sun of summer, and of clothing suited to the season of the year. These wants are not like those of the bodily appetites constant and regularly recurring, but vary indefinitely with climate, season and weather; and are provided for by no impulse of appetite. We are driven to provide for them only by experience of their urgency, and the more human nature is cultivated and developed, the more urgent and cogent these needs become. They are a no less natural stimulus to labor than the impulse of appetite. Apparently the only reason why they are not provided for by such special impulses, as in the case of the bird, is that in all man's vast variety of circumstances and conditions, no impulse acting by a uniform and unvarying law, like the appetite of hunger, could have answered the purpose. Such an appetite would have been too strong in one climate, and too weak in another.

§ 12. Another very important stimulus to labor is found in man's *love of acquisition and ownership*. It is difficult fully to conceive the power of this principle in our constitution, and its fitness to qualify man for his social destiny. Even in an isolated and savage existence, man's condition without any accumulation of the results of labor would be exceedingly precarious and wretched. But it is only when we view man in the social condition to which he is destined, that the importance of this provision becomes fully apparent. Without vast accumulations of wealth civilization is impossible. The most superficial inspection of any civilized community will convince any one of this. Farms under high cultivation, tools and machines for facilitating labor, roads, ships and railways are only a few of the conditions of civilization which depend for their existence on vast accumulations of wealth. There is a very close analogy between the strong love of ownership implanted in man's nature as a provision for this great social want, and the appetites already considered as a provision for the preservation of the individual man and of the race. Perhaps men might have accumulated wealth from a mere conviction founded on experience of the necessity of it to social well-being; but in that case the conditions of society must have been very uncertain, and its progress very slow and toilsome. We sometimes denounce the greed of gain, and perhaps not without reason in particular cases; for nothing can be meaner than a life spent under the supreme control of the love of money. But on the whole the desire of gain is not too strong in human nature. It is one of the most beneficent provisions of the Creator, and the economist should be foremost to condemn all arrangements which tend to restrain the freedom of its action.

§ 13. Another stimulus to labor is *the love of the beautiful*. This is a factor in our science of the importance of which many writers have not been fully aware. Some men who ought to know better inveigh against those artificial wants which men experience in civilized life, as though all which is expended in satisfying them, were so much withdrawn from the wealth of the community. This is simply objecting to all which distinguishes civilized man from a horde of savages, or human society from a herd of brute animals. What such men have to say about natural in distinction from artificial wants probably has reference to those wants which pertain to the support of life and the perpetuity of the race. They only are provided for by appetite and animal instinct. If these only were considered and their gratification provided for, there could be no science of economics. The condition of a gregarious herd of animals, or the lowest stage of barbarism in savage life would be all that man could attain to. Here is no field for social science. What are called the artificial wants of men are no less natural than those to which we are impelled by natural appetite. They differ from them, not in being less indicated by nature, but in being discoverable only by the rational use of the intellect.

Another stimulus to labor and the highest of all is *the love of humanity*. It is often disguised and overlaid by the appetites and the love of gain, until it seems to have quite disappeared from the human soul. But it is only in appearance. It is as truly an original and universal law of human nature as the appetite of hunger, and in proportion as man individual and social is developed and cultivated, it exerts a greater and more apparent influence on all human activities. It is the organic force in all society, and to give it controlling power over the individual man is the end to be aimed at in the formation of character. It is therefore not only entitled to a place, but to a foremost place among the stimuli to human labor.

§ 14. In order that man may feel the full stimulus to labor which exists in his constitution, it is needful that his whole nature should be brought into active development; not only those appetites which he shares with the brute creation, not only the consciousness of those needs which are common to him with the savage, but those propensities which belong to him as a being capable of foresight and calculation, and those tastes which raise him to the dignity of an esthetic and a moral being.

The economist must meet the question how human labor can all be called into the most energetic demand. Otherwise men will be more indolent but certainly not richer. Let us suppose that the only mode of employing human labor were for the supply of the bare necessaries of life. In such a case, a large portion of man's power to labor would remain forever uncalled for and unexerted. The human race is not constituted for such a mode of life. Man has vast powers and capabilities for which, in such a mode of life, he would have no use, and from which he could never derive any advantage. Nearly the same result will follow, if a large portion of the community do not enjoy and have no hope of enjoying any thing beyond the same bare necessaries, though a favored few do enjoy all the advantages of a civilized existence. Obviously the demand for labor in such a community would fall below its natural intensity, by the precise amount of all the labor which must be exerted to supply the unsupplied wants of all those who are reduced to the necessity of subsisting on bare necessaries. It may indeed be true, that these depressed classes may, as in certain classes of laborers in England and still more in Ireland, find their labor all demanded in producing something which is to find a market in other lands. But in that case it is only necessary to remember, that wealth is not a national but a human phenomenon. It will then become apparent that, over the whole earth, the stimulus to labor is impaired just in proportion as any portion of the human race, no matter within what nationality, is reduced to the necessity of subsisting on bare necessaries.

§ 15. Hence it appears evident that the stimulus to human labor throughout the world will be increased or diminished, *according as a greater or less proportion of the human race attain to the satisfaction of those wants which are commonly called artificial,* i. e., those wants of which we become conscious only through an active and cultivated intellect. All which adorns and beautifies life is of this character.

This perfectly agrees with the observed facts of human experience. The savage does not labor because he has no artificial wants. His love of the beautiful aspires to nothing higher than the gaudiest feathers which he can pluck from the birds he kills for food, or a few daubs of paint derived from the colored earths he chances to discover in his wanderings. The coarsest food and clothing and the rudest shelter from the sun and the cold are the only gratifications to which he aspires. Neither does he furnish any market for the beautiful products of more civilized peoples. If America were reduced to the condition in which Columbus found it, England herself would find no buyers for a large portion of what she produces, and must recede in wealth and prosperity far back toward the condition in which she was three hundred years ago.

Communities which are separated from the rest of the world by an insular position or by barriers of mountains, often acquire very slowly a knowledge of the progress of invention in the arts which adorn and beautify society. Such communities do not advance in wealth more but much less rapidly than those nations which are always abreast of the progress of invention, and enjoy all its refinements and beauties. If you would quicken the activity and increase the prosperity of such an isolated community, you must multiply their artificial wants. The theory that profuse consumption is the source of prosperity is absurd and mischievous enough, and yet it has in it an element of truth which many economists have sadly overlooked.

A sound and true culture of the whole nature of man is a most important condition of the highest activity of human labor. It is also of great importance that the civilizing forces should be applied to all portions of the community instead of being limited to a favored few. The economist is most intensely interested in so constructing society, that as far as possible, every portion of the human race shall aspire to and actually enjoy a civilized life, that there shall remain no out of the way places, no dark corners where barbarism can be hid away and concealed amid surroundings that are all radiant with beauty. How far this ideal of the economist can be realized in the actual condition of society, we shall not be prepared to judge, till we have considered those great natural laws which determine the distribution of wealth among those who are concerned in producing it.

§ 16. It is obvious that none of these stimuli to labor can have much beneficial influence, unless men can in fact own and enjoy the products of their own labor. It is also evident that in all communities, there are men who would rather live by theft, robbery and fraud, than by their own honest labor. Our science therefore recognizes the necessity of the existence and all pervading influence of just, equitable and enlightened civil government, to protect every man in the enjoyment of the results of his own labor, against the violence and fraud of every other. Without the pervading presence and active efficiency of such a government, there can be no effective stimulus to labor and economic prosperity. Just in proportion as the laws of any country respecting property or the taxation of property are in contravention of the natural law or ownership, as it has been already expounded; or the government fails to protect the individual in the full enjoyment of the products of his own labor, and of all the property rights which he has acquired in harmony with that law; just in that proportion will its stimulus to labor be diminished, and the increase of wealth be retarded. It is to be feared that governments often fail to appreciate the delicacy and sacredness of this function, and by inconsiderate legislation crush out that prosperity which it is their business to cherish and encourage.

## CHAPTER II.

*Capital.*

§ 17. MAN labors that he may satisfy the cravings of desire. But he has certain cravings that never can be satisfied. The reason is, that the aims toward which they are directed can never be fully attained. They are needed as perpetual stimuli of man's effort to attain that which he is always attaining but never attains. One of these is the love of gain. It is easily seen why this is insatiable. If all the laws of man's individual and social nature are obeyed, the progress of human society has no assignable limit. It is capable of an indefinite growth in numbers and in all the elements of a true civilization. It is certain indeed that there is somewhere a limit to the possible increase of the materials of human sustenance which our planet can produce. But that limit is so far removed beyond anything which man has yet achieved or conceived of, that it is to us as though it did not exist.

The insatiable character of the love of gain is correlate to this capability of limitless progress in society. It is a provision in the constitution of man for the indefinite accumulation of the products of human labor, to supply the wants of a civilization perpetually advancing in population and in the successful efforts of inventive genius. It is set over against all the other desires of the soul, to limit their gratification. All the other desires consume the results of labor in their gratification. This one is gratified by saving. Hence life is a constant compromise between the desire of gain on the one hand, and the tendency to spend in the gratification of other desires on the other. As the former preponderates there is an approach to one extreme, which we will call the extreme of frugality. When the desire of gain is feeble, and the other desires preponderate, there is an approach to the other extreme, the extreme of prodigality. In the former case, other things being equal, accumulation will be rapid, in the latter it will be retarded, or in peculiar circumstances altogether cease.

§ 18. There is then in the human constitution, a provision for the unlimited accumulation of the results of labor for future use. Our present inquiry is,—in what relation do these accumulations stand to the economic system? To what uses do they minister? Before however we enter on these inquiries, it is necessary to define a word which must be frequently used in all our subsequent discussions. That word is capital. We propose the following

DEFINITION, *Capital is every thing produced by previous human labor which still remains unexpended.*

We have previously included all that can be owned and exchanged under the generic concept wealth. By a definition also previously given we have embraced in a species under that genus all human power to labor, and called the species labor. By the definition just given we have appropriated to the only remaining species of the genus the name capital. Wealth therefore expresses the content of the science, and the two words labor and capital are its extent. In order that the whole subject may be presented at a single view we give in this place two or three other definitions.

All capital may be subdivided into two classes, viz., Fixed Capital, and Circulating Capital.

DEFINITION, *Fixed Capital is that which is employed to aid labor and render it efficient.*

DEFINITION, *Circulating Capital is that which is prepared to be used in gratifying human desire.*

Fixed capital is capable of a three-fold subdivision,—the Real, the Mechanical and the Mercantile.

DEFINITION, *Real Fixed Capital consists of land and all its improvements.*

DEFINITION, *Mechanical Fixed Capital is that which is used in producing and regulating momentum.*

DEFINITION, *Mercantile Fixed Capital is that which is used to assist exchanges.*

§ 19. We are not sanguine enough to expect that the definitions given in the previous paragraphs will be accepted without questioning and without argument. We prefer however to leave the confirmation of our positions to the subsequent discussion and development of our system, rather than enter on any extended argument at this point. A few things however must be said rather in the way of explanation than of argument. It has been usual to divide all accumulated wealth into two portions, one portion comprehending all that which is devoted to the gratification of desire, the other portion comprehending that which is devoted to the farther production of wealth. To the latter portion only the word capital has been applied. Our reflections on the subject have led us to the conclusion that it is not possible to render this distinction clear and definite for scientific purposes. Scarcely any thing tends so much to confusion of thought, as attempts at distinction when the things to be distinguished from each other are not separated by any boundaries which can be exactly drawn and defined. It seems to us that the distinction here attempted is of this character, and that it has introduced a great deal of confusion of thought into the whole subject.

We have chosen therefore to neglect this distinction altogether, and to regard all human beings as laborers, and the support of all who are supported, in such degrees of expensiveness as they actually attain to, as ne cessary to the maintenance of the labor by which the economical machinery of the world is worked. It is true that nearly half the human race are in infancy and childhood, and as yet not only unable to perform any labor, but requiring the whole labor-power of one parent to rear and care for them. But it is as necessary that the wants of children should be supplied in order that the ranks of efficient laborers should be kept full, as it is that a power-loom should be built before one can weave with it. You might just as well contend that a power-loom in process of construction is not capital, as that a healthy new-born infant is not a laborer, or that the man who is making a power-loom is not a laborer, as that the mother who is rearing that infant is not a laborer. Whatever therefore is expended in rearing children is as truly capital employed in supporting labor, as the wages given to the laborer of to-day for the work of to-day.

Many are incapacitated for labor by disease or the decrepitude of old age. These must be supported in consideration of the work they have done, or would do if they were able. In our arrangements for the support of labor, we must not forget our social nature. Mutual support is as necessary to the working of the economical machinery of the world as individual support. It is as necessary that the laborer should sustain his decrepid or disabled parent, child, brother, sister, as that he should eat or wear clothes.

§ 20. It is true that many live more expensively than is absolutely necessary to the performance of labor. But we have already seen that in the view of the economist it is very desirable that all should do so. The principles of a true economy abundantly recognize it as fit and wise that the support of the laborer should imply not only such a supply of the bare necessaries of life as will keep the machinery of bones, sinews, muscles and nerves in working order, but all the conditions of a proper human life.

If it is still asserted that, beyond all that these considerations embrace, there is a vast waste of the wealth of every community; our reply is, that the true economist will acknowledge this, and unite with all good men in deploring it. But all he can do about it is to wish that men may become wiser and therefore happier. Their lack of wisdom however cannot modify his science. If all which is expended in the gratification of human desire, is not the fit and proper reward of labor, the reason is to be sought, not in the structure of the economic machine, but in the follies of men.

We are justified therefore in the position, that <u>for all the purposes of our science</u>, *the sole function of all accumulated results of human labor is to support and assist labor and render it efficient. It is therefore properly all to be regarded as capital.*

§ 21. Let us next inquire how this is accomplished.

First, *Every laborer has immediate wants which must be satisfied while he is performing his labor, and waiting for the mature results of it.* The supply of these must come from the results of pre-exerted labor. Man is not like the bird of the air that makes a breakfast of the insect, the worm or the seed it has even now picked up. He must for the most part live to-day on the results of the labor of previous days, and the labor of to-day must supply the subsistence of coming days. This is one of the reasons why he is made capable of foresight and accumulation. The first function of capital is to sustain the laborer while he is doing his work.

Second, Man can do nothing without a tool. The savage must have his bow and arrows. Every tool is a product of a rational soul. Human life is impossible except as man employs his rational powers in devising and executing contrivances by which he engages the forces of the material world to aid him in accomplishing his ends. Every tool, from the bow and arrows of the savage upward, is such a contrivance. No man can have a tool to aid the work of the moment, except as the product of some previous labor. Of all the millions who are to-day performing the labor of the world, very few could be found who had not tools in their hands, without which the results they are aiming at, either could not be accomplished at all, or if at all not without greatly increased difficulty. The amount of wealth invested in such tools at any one time is enormous.

The second function of capital is to *supply each individual laborer with necessary tools.*

Third, The time is past in which the needs of society can be supplied by those simple tools which have for the most part sufficed for past generations. The demand has now become imperative for those complicated machines for increasing the efficiency of labor, the use of which is one of the grandest characteristics of this modern age. In principle a machine does not differ at all from the simplest tool, as a knife, spade, or hammer. Both are alike arrangements for rendering the natural forces around us the helpers of our toil. The difference is only in the scale on which this is accomplished. The machine is often as complicated and costly as the tool is simple and inexpensive. It is only when we contemplate the vast outlays of wealth demanded by modern manufactures and locomotion, that we begin to form a just conception of the importance of capital to human well-being. It is doubtful whether the wealth of the Roman Empire in its palmiest days would have sufficed to construct the railways of the United States.

The third function of capital is *to encourage the inven-*

tion and provide for the construction of the complicated machines which have become a necessity of civilization.

§ 22. We have no difficulty then in discerning the purposes which capital is intended to accomplish in the economic system. *Every human being is intended to be a laborer, to affect more or less of changes which should be conducive to human well-being.* Every laborer is intended in nature's plan to receive such a support from the results of his labor as will enable him to lead a true and proper human life. All labor is to be assisted by such tools as human genius can invent, for rendering natural forces to the utmost possible extent helpful of human effort.

It must also be kept in mind that man's power to labor is applicable, and is designed to be applied to the entire development of a perfected humanity. He who exerts his God-given powers in aid of the true culture of the intellectual, social, esthetic or moral nature of man is no less a laborer in the view of a true economy, than he who makes corn to grow, where without his labor none would have grown. To aid, encourage and reward such labor is no less included in the true function of capital than to aid in tilling the soil. A true system of economics has no more difficulty in finding a place for the labors of a Raphael, or a Michael Angelo than for the building of a railway or a steam engine.

§ 23. Nor will our view of the subject be adequate without a full recognition of the principle, that both labor and capital are quite independent of the nationalities, the political divisions of the earth. In the grand aggregate, wealth in all its forms is a God-given patrimony of the human family. In the present condition of economic science, it is not to be expected that this proposition will be believed, unless it can be proved, but we think the proof is easy. This is certainly not the stand-point from which economists are accustomed to view the subject; but is it not the stand-point from which it must be viewed, to be seen truly? The question which to a great extent writers have had in mind is,—how may a nation grow rich? We claim that the true question is,—how may men grow rich? How may any man of any nation increase in wealth most rapidly? If we have a science of economics it must be universal. If it is a science it will develop an economic system, in accordance with which all men of all nationalities will most successfully supply their wants and increase their wealth.

That this is the true stand-point from which to view the subject, is demonstrated by many facts that admit of no denial. There is no privilege which the world regards as more sacred than the right of every man who possesses power to labor to exert that power wherever he can receive for it the highest compensation. For example, the world is before an American laborer. He may go and exert his powers in any spot on the face of the earth. National lines have no necessary relation to the matter. The only question he is concerned with, is, not how his labor can do most to enrich the United States, but where on earth it is most wanted, as indicated by the fact, that in that spot it will command a higher compensation than in any other. His labor is a part of the world's wealth, and not of American wealth; and where he finds the world most wants it, he will spend it. Labor is then a human and not a national patrimony. No American thinks of complaining because labor of American birth and training is found in almost every nation under heaven. This is just as it should be.

The same is true of capital. No man in his senses would think of confining the capital of England to her own island. It is a part of the universal patrimony. It is only necessary to convince an English property-holder, that an investment in a canal across the Isthmus of Suez, or in a railway in India, or across the Rocky Mountains, will pay better than any he can make in England, to secure such an investment without delay. Capital has in itself a sort of consciousness that it is cosmopolitan, that it has and can have no nationality. English capital and Irish and German labor build American railways and American cities, and American capital runs a line of steamers far up into the heart of China. The fact that both capital and labor have in themselves such a consciousness of their human and universal relations and destiny is surely a sufficient reason why the science that treats of them should be universal also.

§ 24. *There is no assignable limit to the possible increase of the efficiency of labor by the aid of capital.* As long as there is any surplus above bare necessaries, there will always be some tendency to convert circulating capital into fixed capital. Men will always seek to accomplish their ends with the least possible exertion of their own powers. If one performs with his own hand the labor he needs, he will find it irksome, and be always looking around him for the means of making it easier. If he employ the labor of others, he will wish to use as little as possible, in order that his own gain may be greater. Any means therefore will always be in demand, by which a given desired result can be attained by less labor. Some men will therefore find inducement to devote themselves to inventing and constructing fixed capital. As these men must, like every other human being, live on circulating capital, they are engaged in changing circulating capital into fixed capital.

In a general view of the case, it would appear that the result of this must be two-fold, and it will appear from a thorough examination of the whole subject that this view is correct.

First, *It will increase the efficiency of existing labor, and render the surplus of circulating capital above bare necessaries greater than before.* This will increase the motive to convert circulating into fixed capital; for there will be more circulating capital than is needed, and some of it must be converted into fixed capital, or be useless. No one can assign any limit to this process.

Second, *Such a continually increasing supply of circulating capital as must result from this, must render the satisfaction of all human want easier, and mankind richer, and, if they are wise, happier.* Other questions however here arise. Will not this render the capitalist in a great measure independent of the laborer, diminish the demand for labor, and thus reduce its wages? Will not this progressive increase of fixed capital set the extremes of society more remote from each other than ever? Will it not make the rich man richer, and the poor man poorer? Will not the owner of a powerful labor-saving machine be able to dictate wages to his laborers, and prices to his customers? Will not society be divided between boundless wealth and abject poverty?

To answer these questions belongs to Distribution, and the consideration of them must therefore be deferred for the present. If our science cannot at the proper time return a satisfactory answer to them, it is surely a prophet of evil and can afford us very little comfort.

§ 25. To this indefinite increase of fixed capital, there seems however to be one very important exception, at least in respect to labor-saving machinery. It can have no such indefinite multiplication in the department of agriculture as in many other branches of industry. The reason is found in the nature of the case. In manufacturing industry, or in locomotion, a machine may be kept in constant use, and thus yield a constant income. In agriculture no machine can be used for more than a portion of the year, most machines only for a few days of the year, and must not only be quite useless for the remainder of it, but involve expense to protect them from injury. If the machines used in manufacturing could be employed but three weeks in the year, and must be furnished with house room for the rest of it, most of them would be quite worthless. This is an inevitable and a nearly fatal drawback to the profit to be derived from agricultural machinery. It is admitted by those practically acquainted with the subject, that most of the agricultural machines now in use do not much diminish the expense of the processes to which they are applied. They are chiefly important, because it is impossible to command a sufficient number of laborers to accomplish certain processes in the season of them. There doubtless are some machines of which this is not true. But even in respect to them, the fact that they must be useless for ten or eleven months in the year detracts so much from the profit of using them, that they become, as compared with manufacturing machinery, of small importance, and can never very greatly affect the cost of tillage.

The fixed capital of agriculture is land itself, subdued and fitted for cultivation, and its improvement must consist chiefly in the discovery and application of better methods of increasing its fertility. But as wealth and population advance, a vast outlay of capital will be justified and required for subduing new lands, and subjecting them to cultivation. The subject of rent is to be examined hereafter. It is necessary to say at this point, that the cause which extends the area of cultivation with the progress of capital and population, is the fact that an increased demand for food and a lower rate of interest will render increasing outlays of capital in subduing land not hitherto brought under cultivation profitable modes of investment. It is always costly to remove the obstructions which naturally stand in the way of cultivation. The greater the demand for food, and the lower the rate of interest, the greater will be the expenditure of capital for this purpose. On the Atlantic slope of this continent are many millions of acres of land, which in their present condition will never yield anything. But should our population be very greatly increased, and our rates of interest decline to such rates as are now paid in England, these lands would justify and reward a sufficient outlay of capital to render them highly productive.

## CHAPTER III.

### *Capital a Universal Patrimony.*

§ 26. THE principle implied in the heading of this chapter has been already asserted, though without any argument in confirmation of it. On the other hand the fundamental law of the science already enunciated subjects all possible wealth to an exclusive individual ownership. How can it be made to appear that these two principles are possibly consistent with each other? It is quite necessary that we answer this inquiry, or retract one or both of our previous assertions. Our answer is contained in the following proposition, viz:

*By the law of individual ownership, the use and benefit of all existing capital is more perfectly secured to the whole human family than it could be under any other conceivable arrangement.* The very nature of ownership insures this result, not only in respect to capital, but in respect to both forms of wealth. This proposition occupies a very central position in the science of economics, and must be clearly established.

Regarding every man's power to labor as an element in the world's wealth,—or if we for a moment assume that it may be so—we should readily admit, that the first use to which the results of his labor should be applied would be self-support, to preserve himself in working order, to save his power to labor from being impaired or extinguished. We should admit this if we had reference to the general good only, just as we should admit that the first use to be made of the profits of a steam flouring mill should be to keep the mill in perfect repair, in order to render it as useful as possible to the public. Such a use of the first products of labor would, on the supposition we have made, be in perfect accordance with the law we are proposing to substantiate. Let us now make the additional supposition, that the laborer in question produces a surplus above self-support; he owns that surplus and will of course employ it according to his own judgment, for his own advantage. There is but one way in which he can use it for his own advantage. He must use it to assist labor. The product of his labor will thereby be increased, and as he does not himself need that which will be produced by the additional labor which he will thus be able to perform, he must and will employ it in producing that which somebody else wants. His own highest advantage will be secured by producing that which is more wanted than anything else within his power. He is compelled by the very nature of ownership, as the only possible means of securing the gratification of his own desires, to produce precisely that which the world most needs, or at least believes that it most needs. By the very law of ownership, the addition which he has made to his own wealth must also be an addition to the common patrimony of the human race. He can only use it as his own, by using it in producing that which will supply the want of which the world is most conscious. It may be that that want exists on the opposite side of the globe, and that to get the advantages which he is to derive from his newly acquired wealth, he must send the products of his labor to China or Japan. He will dispose of them in the spot where he finds the greatest conscious need of them to exist. To make his capital most his own, minister most to his own advantage, he must be the servant of mankind.

§ 27. Let us now apply this principle to such a vast estate as that of the late A. T. Stewart. There are questions with respect to the relations of such an estate to general economic interests, which we are not prepared to meet at this stage in the development of our subject. It is asserted, not perhaps without reason, that such great accumulations of capital under the control of a single mind are capable of being so used as to suspend, at least temporarily, the natural law of competition. We must defer any inquiry into such a liability, till the law of competition shall have been unfolded, as it will be in a subsequent part of this treatise. Waiving that question for the present, it is plain that such an estate may be conceived of as divided into two parts, one of which shall consist of all that portion of the estate which the proprietor used for the gratification of other desires than that of gain, the other and very much larger portion of it which he employed as an investment, for the increase of his wealth. It is obvious in respect to the part last mentioned, that it was made, through his ownership, strictly a portion of the world's common patrimony. Mr. Stewart was the treasurer of it, to manage it for the benefit of mankind. There may have been no philanthropy at all in his intentions. He may have been wholly governed by the hard, cold greed of gain. But he could gain nothing from it except by employing it in supplying the wants of mankind; and he could make the greatest possible gain from it, only by using it in providing a supply of those wants of which the great human family was most intensely conscious. The success of his vast enterprises would of necessity have been directly and exactly proportioned to his sagacity in discerning what and where that greatest conscious want was. He meant not so perhaps, neither did his heart think so, but the very law of ownership compelled him to be, to the full extent of all which he employed for the purposes of gain, simply and only a treasurer, and as skillful a treasurer as possible for the general good of the race. The law of ownership and the love of gain with which he was endowed combined to compel him to manage that great estate for the benefit of his fellow-men. So far therefore as the capital of the world is employed by its owners for the gratification of their love of gain, it must be used both to aid and reward labor, and to employ that labor as efficiently as possible in producing that which mankind are most consciously in need of.

§ 28. Let us now see how the case stands in respect to that part of his property which he used for the gratification of his own taste and desires other than that of gain. We must in the first place bear in mind that Mr. Stewart was no less a laborer than the clerks that stood behind his counters. It was no contemptible service which he performed for mankind, in managing for their benefit a property of many millions of dollars. If his vast property had been owned by a joint-stock company, the stockholders would have been only too glad to pay a very large remuneration to a man of such financial talent as Mr. Stewart possessed, to act as their manager. The labor which he performed was of a kind which always commands the highest compensation, according to a natural law of wages to be hereafter explained. In that view alone it would be difficult to prove, that the compensation which he received for his labor was at all extravagant. The most careful examination might show, we think it would show, that he managed that whole vast property for the supply of human want for a very small remuneration.

Again it must be borne in mind, that those persons who use large means for the satisfaction of their own desires, are, like the rest of mankind, esthetic beings, and will therefore expend much upon objects of beauty. Many of those objects will be open to the view of all the world, and can be enjoyed by millions as well as by the owner. Mr. Stewart's late residence, for example, on the corner of Fifth Avenue and Thirty-fourth Street, is an object of interest to every visitor of New York from whatever land he comes. But for the large income of men of wealth, the beautiful domestic architecture which is more and more adorning, not only our cities and large towns, but even our villages and farms, would never have any existence. What intelligent man does not rejoice that there is a provision in nature's economic system for thus thickly strewing over the face of the earth the glorious charm of beauty? What man whose memory runs back to fifty years ago would willingly consent that our domestic architecture and landscape gardening should be put back again to the condition in which they were at the beginning of that period? Does not every one feel that it would be a sad loss to the whole community? Such would be the fact, if men of wealth had not the means of gratifying their love of the beautiful. All things considered, it would be difficult to show that the outlay for such purposes is at all in excess of what a regard for the general welfare would require.

Even in respect to those objects of beauty which adorn the interior of a rich man's dwelling, though they are covered from the view of the million, they are yet seen and enjoyed by multitudes, and through their influence become instruments of general culture and happiness. The existence of such objects of beauty is therefore by no means valueless to the whole human family. We cannot however forbear expressing in this place our disapprobation of all those usages in society which tend to exclude the multitude from the enjoyment of whatever is beautiful in natural scenery, landscape gardening and architecture. It is to be hoped that in our country high stone walls will never shut out not only the feet but the eyes of the multitude from those combinations of natural scenery, artistic ornamentation, and elegant architecture by which men of wealth seek to gratify their love of the beautiful.

We have therefore sustained our proposition, that by the very nature of ownership the possessors of this world's wealth are made to hold their property as the treasurers of the human race. Some of them may have become treasurers by fraud and robbery. Our science has no smile of approval for them, any more than for other usurpers of positions of place and power. But all those who have acquired their possessions by fair and legitimate means have been made treasurers, not by popular election or by appointment from any of the higher powers of the earth, but by their wisdom, industry, and skill in affairs, or in other words by proving their fitness for the high trust. If at any future time they become reckless and improvident, or transmit their estates to children who are so, their wealth will slip from their hands; they will be forced to abdicate their treasurership by showing their unfitness to discharge the trust reposed in them.

§ 29. It may be said these treasurers are often unfaithful and abuse the trust committed to them. This cannot be denied. But human imperfection mars all the works of man. If any one thinks he has a valid objection to this order of things, it were well for him very seriously to consider, whether he can suggest any other arrangement, which would afford as good security as we have under the present system of individual ownership, that the wealth of the world would be faithfully applied to the supply of human want. Doubtless rich men might often manage their affairs much better for their own good, and much better for the general good than they do. But for the mismanagement of the great common patrimony which really occurs, the masses are far more responsible than the few rich men that own most of the property. The masses often fatally misjudge of their own real wants, and demand that the capital of the world shall be employed in supplying wants which are imaginary and false, and the supply of which is not beneficial but hurtful; instead of furnishing those things which tend to the promotion of real well-being. Of this the enormous trade in alcoholic stimulants furnishes a very sad example. When the people learn rightly to estimate their own wants, this trade will decline from its present enormous magnitude to very small dimensions.

§ 30. This view of the functions of capital would be quite defective if it did not embrace one further consideration. A treatise on the science of Economics has nothing to do with questions of duty. But it is not inappropriate here to remark, that there are great public interests which can be provided for only by the munificence of the wealthy; and that in all the countries of modern Christendom, such interests have been largely so cared for. Every wise man, if by the possession of capital he is made one of the world's treasurers, will recognize it as one of the privileges of his high position, that he may enjoy the luxury of practicing an enlarged and generous philanthropy. The more society is cultivated and morally improved, the more will men of wealth become the benefactors of the human family, not only from necessity under the impulse of the love of gain, but also from the promptings of a philanthropic spirit.

§ 31. In our examination of the functions and uses of capital, we have therefore found good solid foundations for the following positions; that the one object of all capital is to reward and assist labor; that it is not national or political, but universal and human in its function and destiny; that it is a common patrimony given to the human race by the Creator, compelled to be so used by the law of ownership and the nature of man; that its owners are the world's treasurers, designated to their high trust by having given evidence of possessing such skill and wisdom as fit them to discharge it; and that there is in the nature of man and his relation to things around him, provision for its indefinite increase to supply the growing wants of a progressive civilization.

## CHAPTER IV.

### *Division of Labor.*

§ 32. MAN was made for society, and society is rendered possible only by the mutual dependence of those who compose it. Division of labor is the necessary result of this great social law of our constitution. The most primitive and fundamental manifestation of it is found in sex, creating the necessity of marriage and the mutual relations of husbands and wives, parents and children. In this most natural of all societies, each member has his function, and each is happy not by his own independent efforts, but by the mutual helps and services of all. Such in principle is all human life. The man who should emancipate himself from this dependence, do all for himself and nothing for others, would sink lower than savage life; he would become a solitary wild beast. A flock of sheep or a herd of buffalo could teach him lessons of civilization.

Two well established principles of human nature combine to the same result. First, *Individuals are very differently constituted as to their powers and capacities.* One man has strength of muscle, and power of endurance. Another has tact, pliancy of muscle, delicacy of touch, and exactness of adaptation. Another still has peculiar mental endowments, such as insight, the power to analyze the most complicated wholes into their simplest parts, and to combine many parts into new and beautiful or eminently useful wholes. The more men are civilized, developed, cultivated, the more these differences become apparent and the more they are multiplied. Each of these natural endowments constitutes a fitness for doing some things, and often a corresponding disqualification for doing other things. Those natural endowments which perfectly qualify woman to perform her function in the domestic society, disqualify her to sustain those severe labors by which a family is fed and clothed and housed in circumstances of comfort and abundance. Every human society is in like manner a whole made up of very dissimilar parts all conspiring to a common end. Every man and every woman is to be made happy, not by doing every thing for self, but by performing well some very limited function, and depending for all the rest on many other persons performing their limited functions also.

§ 33. Second, The other law of human nature referred to above is *the law of habit.* What one does frequently, he acquires the power of doing easily and skillfully. When therefore one devotes himself exclusively to the doing of that for which he has some natural fitness, he acquires such dexterity in doing it, that any one who wants that thing done can far better afford to pay him for doing it than to do it for himself; and the skilled man can accomplish so much more in doing that one thing where his skill lies, that he cannot afford to do any thing else. In order therefore that labor may be in the highest degree efficient, it is necessary that every one should so devote himself to some one line of employment, as to acquire the skill which habit confers, and that each should as far as possible employ his labor in doing that in which he has greatest skill.

Arrangements suggested by these two laws of human nature have perhaps accomplished more to render human labor efficient than labor-saving machinery itself. These arrangements are described by the phrase Division of Labor. Of this term we propose the following

DEFINITION, *Division of labor is such a distribution of the labor by which the wants of men are supplied, that each individual may devote himself exclusively to some one or to a very few processes.*

Let us now suppose that in a community devoted to the cultivation of the soil, every man were accustomed to build his own houses and barns, to make his own hats, shoes and clothes, his own household furniture and agricultural instruments, shoe his own horses, in short, to carry on every branch of mechanical labor sufficiently to supply all his own necessities, it is apparent at once that such a community would be almost entirely deprived of all the advantages which are derived from skill. Every one's farm must be greatly neglected and could yield only scanty products. All other wants would be very imperfectly and inadequately supplied. A civilized life would be impossible. Every family would be poorly fed because farms were poorly cultivated, and they would be very badly housed and clothed, and very scantily furnished in every department, with the comforts and conveniences of life. Every thing men ever did in such a community would be very rudely done, without any skill, and consequently at a ruinous cost of time and labor. Life would be barbarous and wretched. There would perhaps be more equality than in more civilized communities, but it would be equality in poverty and wretchedness.

Let us now suppose that a sufficient number of men leave farming entirely, and devote themselves to the various mechanical trades, to supply all the wants of that whole community. Families will now be provided with all the comforts and conveniences of life. Farmers will be farmers only, and furnish all the products of the farm in such abundance, that they can supply their mechanics with all they need of what the farm produces, and still have enough for their own families. Every mechanic will devote himself to his own trade and thus acquire the highest skill and dexterity in it of which he is capable, every thing will be produced at the smallest possible cost of labor, and all products will be as cheap and as perfect as they were before costly and rude. A complete revolution has been effected. Before, every thing was done without skill, now nothing is done without skill, and every one has the benefit of skill.

As wealth and population increase, what was originally a single trade will be subdivided into many. Builders will be subdivided into carpenters, masons, plasterers and painters; and other trades after the same manner, so that each man may devote himself more exclusively to those processes for which he is naturally best fitted, and may have opportunity to acquire the highest possible skill in the single process which he has chosen for his specialty. In all progressive civilization, this subdivision of trades and professions is constantly going on and indicates constantly increasing skill in the various departments of labor.

§ 34. The progress of modern manufactures has developed an application of division of labor till recently little known. It is a subdivision of the processes of the same trade. When for example the working of metals had been divided and sub-divided until the making of pins was recognized as a distinct trade, it might seem that the limit of possible division had been reached. But the making of a pin is itself divisible into many distinct processes. The wire must be drawn, straightened, polished, and cut into pieces of proper length. Each pin must be sharpened and headed, and placed upon the paper. Each of these processes might be assigned to an operative, who should conduct it, and do nothing else. At one stage in this branch of manufacture this arrangement was carried out we believe, in practice. Since the introduction of modern machinery, this principle has been enormously extended, and with an astonishing increase of the efficiency of labor. Mechanical invention itself has scarcely accomplished greater results than this skillful distribution of labor among many operatives acting in harmony for a common end. The results thus attained are among the economic wonders of this modern age.

§ 35. It remains to point out the reasons of the great economic advantage thus obtained.

1. The principle has already been stated that when one devotes himself exclusively to a single process, he acquires much greater skill in it than is otherwise possi-

ble. The simpler the process the greater the skill acquired. If a common mechanic were to attempt to do a day's work in heading pins, it is likely he would finish but a small number. But when a man heads pins and does nothing else, the rapidity of his execution becomes something wonderful. It is like the dexterity with which the accomplished pianist fingers his keys. A person who has not the skill looks on with astonishment.

2. If all the processes of a given manufacture must be performed by the same individual, he must take time to learn them all. Perhaps to accomplish himself in all parts of the trade he must serve an apprenticeship of seven years. But if the trade is divided into seven distinct processes, and each process allotted to a single operative, he need learn but one of the seven, and can therefore accomplish himself for his trade by an apprenticeship of a single year. Six-sevenths of the time required to learn the trade and six-sevenths of the material wasted by the unskillfulness of the learner would thus be saved.

3. It is also said that much time is saved which would otherwise be spent in passing from one process to another, especially if tools are to be adjusted, or a furnace is to be heated up. Some recent writers claim, that Adam Smith over-estimated the importance of this advantage.

4. Another advantage is certainly real, and important. When the fabricating of a given product is thus analyzed into its distinct processes, all these processes will not be found to require labor of the same grade of skill and efficiency. Some will require the highest order of workmanship. These may be assigned to workmen who receive the highest compensation. Other processes may require labor of only the lowest grade, and therefore receiving only the lowest rate of compensation.

By division of labor each process may be compensated according to the grade of workmanship which it requires. But if one man must perform all parts of the work, he must be paid for his highest skill and efficiency, though employed in processes in which the cheapest labor would suffice. Thus division of labor greatly reduces the cost of the matured product.

It is also important to mention, that in this way division of labor furnishes suitable employment to many persons who would otherwise have no employment at all, because they are quite inadequate to the more difficult parts of the work. Much labor is thus rendered productive which would otherwise remain unemployed. Women and their special advocates often complain that modern economics do not properly reward women's work. This subject will be discussed in its proper place. It is evident however at this stage of our discussion, that to division of labor they are to a great extent indebted for the fact that they have any employment at all, outside of the domestic circle.

§ 36. Division of Labor is in its possible application subject to several important limitations, some of which are the following:

1. *The nature of the process.* When any work to be done has been so analyzed as to divide it into the greatest possible number of distinct processes, and each of these processes has been allotted to an individual operative, division of labor can be carried no further. If more laborers are to be employed, the number employed must be some multiple of the number of processes into which the work has been divided. But no further division of labor can thereby be accomplished.

2. The application of division of labor may also be limited by the *want of sufficient capital.* If a man has only sufficient capital to support himself and supply the

tools which he must himself use, he must of course perform all the work with his own hands. This is the reason why so little division of labor is used in the ruder stages of society, when little capital has been accumulated. The savage whose only capital is his bow and arrows can have no division of labor, and he must advance many stages on the road to civilization before he can make any considerable use of it. This is the reason why manufactures cannot be successfully conducted till large accumulations of capital have been made. No single man and no combination of men which can be effected in the earlier stages of a people's progress can command for the purpose a sufficient amount of capital to procure the necessary machinery and to support the requisite number of laborers and the requisite variety of skill. Peoples that are in such a condition can never compete with those whose capital is abundant. The attempt to do so is only the farce of the child playing the man.

3. The possible application of division of labor may also be limited by the demand for the product, to the fabrication of which it is to be applied. If one man working by himself can supply the whole existing demand, he cannot afford to resort to a division of labor. It may be that two men dividing the work between them might produce three times as much product as one man working alone. But as there would be no demand for two-thirds of the product thus furnished, there would be no advantage in producing it. For this reason also, division of labor can be little used in the ruder states of society. Population is sparse, capital is scanty, and therefore the demand for most products is so small that it can be supplied without much division of labor. As population multiplies, capital increases and facilities for communication between remote districts are made abun-

dant and cheap, the demand for all articles of comfort, beauty and luxury will be constantly multiplied, and division of labor will be more used, and higher skill in every department of production will be attained. All men will be more skillful in their work, all products more abundant and of better quality, and the whole community more civilized, richer and happier.

§ 37. It is stated by many writers that the principle of division of labor is applied between nations as well as between individuals. This is certainly not scientifically accurate. Nations are not, in the economic sense, laborers. It is not easy to see that they have any economic function, except to secure to all their subjects freedom to exert their natural powers without any molestation, and the most perfect enjoyment of their own products. In the proper place it will be shown, that for this service they are entitled to the loyal support of all who live under their protection.

Division of labor is not, however, naturally limited within any national lines. Like every other element of our science it is human, not national. Those laws of human nature from which it springs act without the slightest reference to the boundaries of nations. The law holds good everywhere, that every man should use the products of the highest skill and the greatest natural advantages for the supply of his wants wherever they may be found. Not to do so, tends not to the advancement of civilization, but to the perpetuity of barbarism. Division of labor however occurs in all cases, not between one nation and another, but between individuals of every nation irrespective of nationality. We send our products to the north and the south, to the east and the west in search of the best market which the world affords; and we receive in return the fruits and spices of the tropics, the manufactures of England and France, and the furs of Russia and Sweden. If we are wise we shall procure every thing where it can be procured most cheaply, and in greatest perfection. Such a division of labor among all the inhabitants of the earth is accordant with the intention of the Creator as indicated in the constitution of man, and a beautiful illustration of the brotherhood of the human race. Any nation incurs a most serious responsibility by interfering with these fraternal relations, except for reasons of the most cogent necessity. Whether such necessity exists, we shall inquire in the proper place.

§ 38. Some writers are inclined to attach a good deal of importance to what they have called the Combination of Labor. This is either simple or complex. It is simple when several laborers combine their strength to do the same thing. This takes place when something is to be done for the doing of which the powers of a single individual are insufficient. He naturally provides for combining the efforts of other laborers with his own, and thus securing sufficient strength to accomplish the end he has in view. Such combination is a very common occurrence in every civilized community, and is so perfectly simple and natural, and so much a matter of course, as not to require any special attention in this place.

Complex combination of labor is the coöperation of many individuals conducting different processes, in accomplishing a common result. Thus the cotton planter in Louisiana, the cotton spinner in Manchester, the carrier who transports the cotton from the planter to the manufacturer, and all persons engaged in fabricating machinery, and probably many other classes of laborers, all combine their labor to produce a single yard of cotton cloth. But this is only division of labor viewed under another aspect. If the movement of thought is from the circumference of the circle towards the centre where the result is completed, it is combination of labor; if from the centre towards the circumference, it is division of labor. The combination of labor sustains the same relation to the division of labor, that the distance from New York to Boston does to the distance from Boston to New York.

§ 38*a*. Writers have insisted on several classifications of labor which have no scientific significancy, and therefore embarrass and confuse the student rather than instruct him. Ours is not a science of mere classification, but of causes and laws; and no generalization is of any value in it which does not aid in the discovery or the definition of causes and laws. Of this character is the distinction of labor as that of the body, from that of the mind. All human labor, even the simplest, is in greater or less degree the labor of the mind. It cannot be performed without the constant exertion of human intelligence. No brute animal can be trained to the simplest processes, not even to gather and pile stones. Mind dominates over it all. It is true indeed that some kinds of labor require much higher intelligence than others, and some processes are purely mental, as those of discovery and invention. But this is a consideration of no special economic significancy.

In like manner, the division of laborers into the three classes,—discoverers, inventors, and operatives, conducts to no important results, and does not extend our knowledge of the forces with which we are concerned. A man seldom confines himself to either of these departments. Operatives have sometimes made the most valuable inventions, and inventors have often been discoverers also. Much the same may be said of the division of industry into the three departments of agriculture, manufactures and commerce. Those forces and causes which have already been explained as stimulating and aiding production, alike pervade and dominate them all, and account for the phenomena which they present. We think therefore that by insisting on these distinctions we should perplex and confuse rather than instruct the student.

# PART II.

## EXCHANGE.

### CHAPTER I.

*Value.*

§ 39. IN our discussion of the forces concerned in Production, it has been all along assumed that laborers must to a very large extent exchange their products with each other. A man that makes hats must have food and clothing for other parts of his body than his head. If he makes nothing but hats, he must supply other people with hats, and receive from them in return other things which he needs; or his hats, except an occasional one for his own wear, will be of no use to him. We have now reached that point in the development of the subject, where it is necessary to explain the nature of exchange, and the laws by which it is governed.

DEFINITION. *Exchange is the voluntary transfer of the ownership of some item of wealth for the ownership of something else regarded by both parties as equally desirable.*

It is believed this definition will be found to be accurate and exhaustive, and in perfect consistency with our definition of wealth. It matters not whether the exchange be of labor for labor, or of labor for some product of labor, or of one product of labor for another, or what the nature of the products to be exchanged may be. It is in every case an item of wealth for another item of wealth, regarded as equally desirable, with the voluntary consent of both owners.

§ 40. As soon as one finds himself in possession of something which he desires to exchange for something else of which another person is the owner, the question at once occurs to him,—how much of mine must I give for what I desire of his? If I make hats, and wish to exchange them for wheat, the question is,—how much wheat for a hat? That for which one is inquiring when he asks this question, is expressed by the word *Value*. What is the value of a hat? What is it worth? We can proceed no further in the development of the science till we have defined this word. Nowhere else has so much confusion of thought found its way into the discussions of economists, as in respect to the meaning of this word. There can be no science of Economics without an exact and scientific definition of value. If we succeed in framing such a definition, the remaining part of the task which we have undertaken will be comparatively easy and plain. If we fail in the attempt it were better to prosecute the undertaking no further, for it can result in nothing but confusion and endless controversy.

§ 41. We cannot however give the needed definition of value, till we have introduced to the reader's notice another great law of nature of which we have hitherto said nothing. We refer to *the law of competition*. Through the remaining portion of our science, this law must be our constant guide.

The law of competition results directly from the fundamental law, out of which we said in the outset the whole science should be developed. Every man owns himself and all which he produces by the voluntary exertion of his own powers. What he owns he not only may, but he always will use as he desires. It follows of course that what he does not want himself, but desires to exchange for some object of desire owned by another, he will so exchange as to obtain for it as much gratification of his own desires as he can. If he wants to exchange hats for wheat, he will inquire what is the largest quantity of wheat which any one will give him for a hat, and with the man that offers him the largest quantity he will exchange in preference to any other. He will refuse to make any exchange at all till he thinks he has found the man that will give him more than any one else, or at least as much. It is as much a law of nature that exchanges should be conducted in this way, and not in any other, as it is that the planets should move in elliptical orbits, and not along the bounding lines of a square or parallelogram. When men conduct exchanges thus, they are not acting meanly or selfishly, but they are obeying a law of nature, as truly as a heavy body obeys a law of nature by falling when it is unsupported. This law of nature is competition. We propose the following:

DEFINITION, *Competition is that law of human nature by which every man who makes an exchange will seek to obtain as much as he can of the wealth of another for a given amount of his own wealth.*

It is to be kept in mind that we are not teaching ethics. We do not say that a man has a right to buy as cheaply as he can, and sell as dearly as he can, but that by a law of his nature he not only will but must do so. It is not a case of moral choice at all. Where two objects of desire do not differ at all in kind, but only in quantity, it is as natural for us to accept the greater rather than the less, as for a stone dropped from the hand to fall to the ground. We do not mean of course, that the buyer will bring every sort of influence true or false to bear on the seller's mind, to induce him to sell cheaply, or that he will seek to exert upon him any influence at all. All this our science turns over to the teacher of ethics. Competition simply assumes that every man knows his own mind, and that he who has any thing to exchange inquires who will give most for it, and that he who wishes to get something by exchange inquires who will sell it most cheaply, and buys and sells accordingly.

If any one says this is not a law of nature, that a man will often sell to one man more cheaply than he will to another, the answer is, that if such a case occurs, it is only because the seller has some special regard for the man with whom he prefers to exchange, and is willing to take as a part of the gratification which he is to get by the exchange, the satisfaction of doing him a favor. It is no exception to the universality of the law. He still gets as much gratification by the exchange as he can.

It matters not whether the thing to be exchanged is the product of the owner's personal labor, or of some other one's labor of which he has obtained the ownership by gift or exchange, or whether he wishes to exchange his labor for some other man's labor, or his labor for some product of the labor of another. In either case the law holds in all its force. In competition we have a law which is as pervasive of the whole science of economics, as the law of gravitation is of the science of physical astronomy. He who is engaged in endeavoring to construct an economic system from which competition shall be excluded, has on his hand an attempt which is just as absurd and impossible, as to construct a machine from which all influence of gravitation and friction shall be excluded. But more of this hereafter.

§ 42. DEFINITION, *Value is relative desirableness as ascertained by competition.*

Value in its technical use is always a relative term. Nothing has intrinsic value. It is an absurdity in terms. In popular language, we speak of the intrinsic value of a thing without impropriety. We mean of course its utility. But utility does not imply value in the strict sense. What is more useful than atmospheric air? But it has no economic value. It will bring nothing in the market. When we speak of the value of a thing in the technical sense, we mean that for which it can be exchanged. If it will bring nothing in exchange, no matter how much labor has been laid out on it, no matter how useful it is, in the strict sense of the word it has no value.

There are certain words with the use of which it is impossible to dispense, which it is necessary to employ with technical accuracy. Before proceeding further we will therefore define them.

DEFINITION, *Cost is the amount of labor and capital expended on any product.*

DEFINITION, *Price is the value of any thing as compared with some specific thing, regarded as a fit standard by which all other values are supposed to be measured.*

That specific thing in comparison with which price is estimated is money, of which we shall speak hereafter.

DEFINITION, *Supply and Demand are correlative terms, indicating,—the latter, the desire that exists for any article of exchange as manifested by readiness to offer other things for it, and the former, the amount of the article demanded which is ready at any time to be exchanged.*

§ 43. Economists have been much at variance respecting the relation of value to cost. It is therefore necessary to examine that question. Value has no necessary relation to cost at all. Cost has no power to control or determine value. Capital and labor will render nothing valuable except as they make it capable of gratifying human desire. But men will expend labor and capital only in producing that which they themselves regard as more desirable than the labor and capital expended, or which they believe others will so regard. One can command nothing in exchange for any product merely in consideration of the cost of it. The milliner who has a large supply of ladies' bonnets, will plead in vain in justification of her high prices the cost of her wares, after the fashion has changed. But nothing will continue to be produced which for long periods is found to be of less value than the cost. Men are not fond of laboriously throwing away either labor or capital. On the other hand, nothing can for long periods maintain a value which is above cost, for somebody will always be found ready to produce it at cost. Competition will therefore always insure the gravitation toward cost of the value of all the great permanent utilities of life. If a sudden demand springs up for any article exceeding the supply, its value will be raised, and of course its price enhanced. Labor and capital employed in producing it will be more remunerative than usual, and more of both will be invested in increasing the supply. This will go on till the supply and demand are equalized. The enhancement in price however will in most cases not be permanent, for reasons which will be explained hereafter.

§ 44. *No test of value other than that furnished by competition is possible.* As in mechanics weight is our only available test of quantity of matter, so in economics competition is our only test of value. The proposition to determine what a thing is really worth without reference to what it will command in exchange, is an absurdity even in terms. Men may have a judgment of the value of a horse without offering him for exchange, but if it is worthy of any confidence it must be founded on what it is known other horses of equal desirableness have been sold for. It must go on the assumption that people will regard another horse as equally desirable with those which have recently been sold. But one can never know it till the test of competition has been appealed to. The price current is not the judgment of any man however sagacious, what the commodities mentioned in it ought to be worth, but the record of the fact, what they were actually exchanged for.

It is true that valuable property may be offered for exchange, in circumstances in which no one desires it at the price which is usually paid for a like article. And yet the owner may have so strong a desire to obtain something else in exchange for it, that he would be glad to part with it at almost any price which any one will give him. It may in that case be said that he exchanges his property for much less than its real value. But if the language has any meaning, it is only that the usual value is greater than that at which he exchanged it, and that the belief is confidently entertained, that at a not distant day, the demand for it will increase so that it will command in exchange more than was received for it. That however does not show that the present value was not precisely what was obtained for it. The anticipated future value of it may differ greatly from the present. Probably the purchaser did not want it for his own use, and was only induced to purchase it, because he believed it would command more in exchange at a future time than now. He purchased for the sake of gain by a future exchange, and not to satisfy any present want. Its present value is what it will exchange for now, its future value will depend on what it will exchange for at a future time.

§ 45. It may seem to some a valid objection to the universality of the law of competition, that many transactions of exchange are regulated by custom or law and not by competition. If for example I employ a licensed hackman, the price which I must pay him is regulated by law. Rents in many different countries are regulated by custom, which has been handed down through many successive generations, and with which competition does not interfere. The rate of interest on money has been and is regulated by law. In these and many other cases, competition has apparently and in some of them really, no place. This is not the place to consider some of the questions involved in the examples just given. Rents and interest on money belong to another part of the subject. But it will be shown in the proper place, that whenever rent is regulated otherwise than by competition, it is because the fundamental laws of our science have been utterly disregarded. An immemorial custom is a law. In such cases the nominal proprietor of the land is only the partial owner of it. The tenant is also a partial owner. The proprietor owns the right of disposing of one-half or one-third of the produce, not the right of treating as his own and disposing at his pleasure the land and all its utilities. The tenant is also a partial owner. He has a right to appropriate a certain share of the profits of the land. Our science has nothing to do with such an order of things. Those natural forces with which it has to do have no opportunity to act. The laws of human nature are superseded by a custom which originated far back in ages of barbarism.

Much the same may be said of laws regulating the interest on money. They are in direct conflict with the law of ownership. So our science must regard and treat them. They assume to forbid the owner of property to enjoy and appropriate the full benefit of it. The economist can not deal with them in any other aspect. We must however add that for the most part they are a dead letter on the statute book, quite disregarded in practice.

As to the case of the licensed hackman, he has made a contract with the municipal government to carry passengers at given rates, and has paid for the privilege, and is therefore bound to fulfill the contract he has made. If he will surrender his license and the city endorsement which that gives him, he may then regulate his charges by competition without any interference of the law.

The founder of a science becomes illustrious in succeeding ages, and justly. Yet it is often true, that the reason why the foundations of the science were not laid and its superstructure reared in previous generations, is found in the fact, that in that age for the first time the conditions of the possibility of the science had existed. Physical astronomy was not possible, till the labors of Tycho Brahe and others had furnished a vast accumulation of observations, and Kepler had discovered the laws of planetary motion. For like reasons our science was scarcely possible before the time of Adam Smith. Labor and capital were not sufficiently emancipated from the despotic interference of governments, and the tyranny of immemorial custom, to manifest the laws by which they are governed in a free system. From that barbarism of the earlier ages, many economic elements have not even yet emerged, or if at all, only in a few favored countries. Some of the examples given above are illustrations of this remark. It is only in countries in which the private ownership of land is understood and recognized by the laws regulating exchanges and inheritance, that the theory of rent can be successfully studied; and the natural laws which govern interest are never very apparent, except in countries where the government is wise enough to abstain from interfering with it, or else the people intelligent enough to treat the statutes which interfere with it as a nullity. In this view of things, it is perhaps not wonderful, that the science of economics has not reached its perfection in the first century of its existence.

## CHAPTER II.

### *Fluctuations of Value.*

§ 46. THE general aspect presented to the unthinking mind by those fluctuations of value which are always going on around us, is, very analogous to the impression made upon us by the wanderings of the moon, or the varying directions and strength of the atmospheric currents, which we daily experience. In the previous chapter we explained the law of competition, and showed that it is the force which always controls and measures value. It is our intention in this chapter to show how competition explains and accounts for the seemingly capricious fluctuations of value which are constantly going on around us. As in the commercial world all values are estimated by comparison with a common standard, money, and as the value of any article estimated in money is called its price, we shall in this chapter conform to this popular usage, and employ the word price instead of value.

All the fluctuations of price which can occur are the results of one of two causes, viz.

1. *Variation of the cost of Production.*
2. *Variation of the ratio between Supply and Demand.*

The cost of Production may be *diminished* in various ways.

First, By rendering labor more efficient. This may be done by *improvements in machinery, more perfect division of labor, or better methods of applying it.* The result in all these cases must be to reduce the price of the product. If a single producer could introduce any of these improved methods, and confine the use of them to his own operations, he might appropriate all the advantage derived from them to himself, by exchanging his product at the same prices which others receive, who do not use the improved methods. But such secrets cannot be kept, and society offers to the inventor of any such improvement a sufficient inducement in the form of a patent right, to disclose it to the general public. Competition then begins at once to perform its office, and reduces prices till cost and value are equalized. There will never be wanting those who will be eager to produce a commodity at a price equal to the cost of production.

The consequence must be the *cheapening of the commodity whose cost of production has been thus diminished* to the general public, and thus all men will share the benefits of every new invention by which the efficiency of labor is increased. The reduction of the price of the commodity will proportionally increase the demand for it. The reason of this may easily be rendered obvious. While the price was high none but the wealthy could afford to use it. As its price is reduced the wealthy themselves will use it more freely and for purposes for which it was not before employed, and persons in moderate circumstances will be able to afford it. The poor and those of limited means are always many times more numerous than the rich, and as by reducing the cost of production any commodity is cheapened, it finds its way into the homes of thousands and perhaps of millions who, at its former high price, would have been entirely forbidden its use. Competition reduces price, till what used to be confined to the homes of the rich, becomes abundant in the humble dwellings of the comparatively poor.

It should however be remarked in this place that such changes in value as those described in the preceding paragraph have not hitherto in the history of the world occurred, *except in relation to commodities which must be considered rather as luxuries than as necessaries of life.* Should they ever occur in respect to such commodities as strictly necessary food and clothing, the occurrence would produce a revolution in the fundamental conditions of human life which it is not likely can ever take place. We have already shown in a previous chapter that from the very nature of the labor employed in agriculture, it is highly improbable that its efficiency can ever be increased by invention in any such degree as has already been attained to in other departments of industry; and from agriculture the necessaries of life are chiefly obtained. This subject will be further considered in connection with the subject of Rent.

Second, The cost of producing any commodity in any given place may be diminished *by increasing the facilities of communication with the rest of the world.* The cost of any commodity at any particular place is the cost of producing it added to the cost of transportation.

If by means of increased facilities for transportation, the producers of any commodities in remote places are able to bring their products into the market at a less cost than that of producing them in the immediate vicinity, they will be able to undersell the near producers, and reduce the price of the article.

Increased facilities for bringing into any market the products of distant regions may be provided, by removing either *artificial* or *natural* obstacles. It may be that the laws of a country have hitherto been such as to prohibit the introduction of foreign products. The removal of these prohibitions will of course enable foreign producers to compete with those at home, and reduce the price of the commodities in the market. Thus the repeal of the English corn laws enabled all the corn-growers of the world to compete with those of England in her markets. If the result has not been the reduction of the price of grain in England, it is only because the increase of her population has been so rapid as to create a demand for the additional supply thus furnished, and keep the price nearly stationary. It may yet happen, that the pressure of foreign grown grain upon the markets of England may be such, as actually to reduce the price of the food of her people.

The same result may be secured by removing *natural obstructions and providing the means of cheaper and more rapid transportation.* This is abundantly illustrated by the history of transportation in our own country. As a consequence of our greatly improved modes of transportation, the productions of regions a thousand miles in the interior of the continent are offered in the markets of the Atlantic sea-coast, at prices which are often below the cost of producing them in the immediate vicinity of those markets, and the price of agricultural products in the markets of Great Britain is to a considerable extent controlled by the competition of the products of the interior of North America and even of the Pacific Coast. The price of grain in our Atlantic cities and in the markets of England and Europe can never again depend on the resources of their immediate vicinity, but on the productions of the whole earth. Practical economy is becoming, like the science itself, universal and human. The competition of the world controls the markets of all civilized countries.

§ 47. There are various causes by which, in particular cases, the cost of production *may be increased*. They may however be summed up under the single statement that it may become necessary to derive supplies for human want from sources involving a greater outlay of labor and capital. For example, a mineral may be needed, the supply of which comes only from mines the working of which is constantly becoming more costly; or if new mines are discovered, they may be in reginos so remote from the place of consumption, or so difficult of access, that their products cannot be cheaper than the product of the mines before known. The case may occur that no new mines of gold and silver may be discovered for a long time to come, and that within a generation or two, the rich surface mining of California, Australia and the Rocky Mountains, may be quite exhausted, so that the future supply of gold and silver must be derived from deep mines, requiring an immensely greater expenditure of labor and capital. In this way it may happen that the supply of gold and silver, the cost of which has been greatly diminished by the discoveries of the last thirty years, may for generations to come be obtained at constantly increasing cost. The point of lowest depression in the value of gold and silver may soon be reached, from which point onwards for an indefinite future, constantly increasing cost may cause steadily advancing value of the precious metals. The effect of such changes in the value of gold and silver will be discussed in connection with the subject of money.

§ 48. It remains to point out the *influence of a variation of the ratio of supply and demand on prices.* In speaking of the ratio of supply and demand we of course mean, not that demand or desire can sustain a ratio to that which supplies it, but the ratio of the quantity ready to be exchanged to the quantity requisite in order that all may be supplied who are able and willing to offer the equivalent.

First, The ratio of supply to demand may be increased either temporarily or permanently. If the commodity in question is one of permanent utility and desirableness, the effect will be only temporary. As the supply exceeds the demand sellers will underbid each other and prices will fall. The effect of this will be two-fold. Fall in price on the one hand will increase demand. Those who would not purchase at the higher price, will be ready to purchase at the lower. This will tend to equalize supply and demand. On the other hand if supply is still in excess the motive to produce is diminished. Production will be slackened. Capital and labor will be withdrawn from the trade, until supply and demand are equalized.

If the demand is dependent, *not on any permanent utility or desirableness,* but on some caprice or fashion, supply and demand will become more and more unequal, the demand will rapidly decline until the production of the supply entirely ceases, and the commodity is removed from the market altogether.

Second, The ratio of supply to demand may also be diminished either *temporarily or permanently.* If the fluctuation is only temporary, it will be re-adjusted by the law of competition acting precisely in the manner just described. But if it results from permanent causes, three distinct cases arise, each of which must be considered by itself. One thing is common to all three of the cases. The demand constantly tends to exceed the supply. The first case is that in which the supply can be increased without increasing the cost of production. This is the case of most manufactured articles. All that is necessary to an indefinite increase of the supply of these is to employ for the purpose a greater amount of labor and capital. Under the conditions in which the demand for manufactured articles is steadily increasing, both labor and capital are increasing also, and seeking new modes of employment. There is therefore in the economic system, a provision for the increase of the supply of such commodities to respond to any demand which may ever arise, without increase of cost. It is true that such an increase may raise the price of materials, but the cost of the material in most cases bears so small a ratio to the whole cost of the product, that a considerable increase of the cost of the material would scarcely affect the cost of the product appreciably. On the other hand a constantly growing demand will facilitate production upon a larger scale, and therefore with increasing economical advantage. It will also stimulate invention to devise better methods of assisting and applying labor, better machinery and more perfect economy in every department; and these advantages will probably much more than compensate for any increase in the cost of raw material. Nature's provision is therefore perfect for furnishing a supply of the comforts, conveniences and beauties of life to any increase of population.

To this view of the case there might seem to be *one objection*. It may seem probable that in so great an increase of manufacturing industry, the supply of some article of essential importance to the process may fail, or become so expensive as greatly to increase the cost of the product. For example should the English coal fields approach exhaustion, the cost of coal might be so much advanced as seriously to increase the price of manufactured articles. But it must be borne in mind, that our science is not English but universal. The effect of such an occurrence would be only to transfer the manufactures affected by the change to other localities where fuel is cheap and abundant. Whenever in any country the conditions of cheap manufacturing no longer exist, its manufactures will no longer be able to compete with those of other countries in the markets of the world, and it will soon be obliged to deliver over the trade to others who possess the requisite conditions.

§ 49. *The second case to be considered is that of products the supply of which can not be increased, except at an increased cost of production.* The reason is that some of the conditions of production, perhaps all of them, must be derived from sources of supply requiring a greater amount of capital and labor to be employed in working them. This case therefore is identical with that examined in § 47. Mr. Fawcett claims that the principle stated in that section holds good in respect to all agricultural and mineral products. With certain modifications in his modes of statement, which will be pointed out when we come to speak of Ricardo's theory of rent, this might be true of a single country like England, already far advanced towards maturity of her civilization, on the supposition that she could receive no supplies from the rest of the world. But considering England simply as a small part of the world, and her people only as a fraction of the human race, the view has no approximation to correctness. The agricultural productions of the United

States have been doubled within a few years, without any appreciable increase, we suspect indeed with an absolute diminution, of the cost of production. They are apparently capable of being increased by a much greater multiplier within a few years to come, and still without increased cost of production. The quantity of agricultural products offered in the markets of England may be increased in the same manner, to an extent to which no one is at present able to assign any limit. Areas of fertile land in comparison with which the whole surface of Britain is simply insignificant, exist both in this and in other countries, which are now quite uncultivated, and which will only remain so till they can be brought into cultivation without depressing the price of agricultural products below the rates which prevail at present. Any nation which like England opens its ports to corn produced in whatever nation, need have no apprehension of any increased costliness of such agricultural products as can be brought to her from beyond the seas. Her increasing population may find it more advantageous to trace back the lines along which food finds its way to her shores, and make their homes amid the fields where it is produced, than to remain crowded together in her island homestead, dear as it justly is to all her children. But either at home, or in the lands from which her supply of bread comes, her people have little reason to apprehend scarcity of food, or much enhancement of its price.

§ 50. *The third case is that of desirable products which from the nature of the case are limited in amount, and can in no manner be increased.* To this class belong paintings and other valuable productions of masters who are no longer living. The price of such works is limited only by the desire to possess them, and ability to purchase them. As long as the love of high art continues to increase, and the works of any master continue to rise, or do not decline in the relative estimation in which they are held; and the wealth of the community, or of the highly civilized nations of the world continues to increase, the works of such a master will be likely to rise in price beyond any assignable limit. The love of the beautiful in human nature is sufficiently strong to insure a high valuation of the works of genius.

The same considerations are applicable to all commodities and all exchangeable values, the supply of which is limited and incapable of being increased. To this class belongs the land on which a great city is built, embracing a considerable area around it. It is needed for purposes of the greatest importance, and no other land can be substituted for it. As the population and wealth of the city increase, its desirableness increases also, and men of wealth in increasing numbers, compete with each other for its possession, and it is difficult to set any limit to its increasing value, so long as the growth of the city continues. The constantly advancing price of land in all countries of rapidly growing wealth and population participates more or less of the same character. It performs a function in the economic system which nothing else can perform; the importance of that function is growing with every successive generation, and no outlay of labor or capital can render any other land capable of performing that function. Prices must therefore be steadily advanced till the increase of wealth and population is by some cause arrested. On the supposition of the simultaneous and persistent application of the forces of civilization to our whole planet, the whole surface of the earth must ultimately be subjected to this law. Land must every where advance in price under the influence of increasing wealth and population till its entire productive power has been brought into use, and the ultimate limit of the possible increase of the human race attained. The time however at which such a result would be reached is so remote in the distant future, that the apprehension of it can make no modification of our present economic system.

---

## CHAPTER III.

### *Money.*

§ 51. IN no stage of the development of the science of Economics, can we ever be far removed from some great law of human nature. This holds of exchange as of every other branch of the subject. *Brutes use no tools, man does nothing without tools.* No brute is capable of such a comparison of the desirableness of two things, as to qualify him voluntarily to accept of one of them as an equivalent for the other. Man's life is not only filled up with such exchanges, but, true to his rational nature, he has invented and used through the ages a tool by which such exchanges are facilitated and assisted. That tool is money. By means of the tools which we employ in the production of material wealth, we avail ourselves of some natural force, to assist our labor, as by the water wheel we employ for this purpose the momentum of falling water. By means of the tool of exchange, we make use of the desire of all men for certain rare, brilliant and beautiful objects, to facilitate the exchange of all other objects of desire which have value.

§ 52. *This tool is not however, like the steam engine*

*or the electric telegraph, the invention of any single mind.* It must have come into use gradually through the like experience of many persons, and been brought to its present perfection in the progress of many ages. All exchanges must have originally been exchanges in kind,—mere barter. Such exchanges always involve great inconvenience. He who has anything to exchange has great difficulty in finding some one who desires what he has to part with, and will give him for it what he wants. The exchange is therefore long delayed, and during this delay that which he wishes to exchange yields no profit, and much time is wasted in trying to make the exchange, which would otherwise have been employed in production. If what he has to exchange is of considerable value, as a horse, or a yoke of oxen, it is very difficult to effect such a division of it as to procure many small articles which he needs. In order to accomplish it, he is forced to make many exchanges instead of one. He at length discovers, in the course of his experience, that there is some one species of wealth which nearly every one desires, and at all times and in any quantity large or small. It immediately occurs to a sagacious man, that by exchanging what he has to spare for what he finds almost every one is in want of, he can with that object of general desire procure without difficulty whatever he wants. He adopts that method of exchange, and finds great advantage in it. Other men easily make the same discovery, and resort to the same method of exchange. This renders the object of general desire still more desirable. Every one will be eager to get it, because he can easily exchange it for anything which he happens to want. Thus without any one's invention, without any formal agreement, this object of general desire has become an accepted medium of exchange,—money. It may be any thing which happens to be regarded as universally desirable, in the particular community that uses it. If that community is so isolated that it has no exchanges with the rest of the world, it will be a satisfactory money, as long as it continues to be an object of universal desire.

§ 53. It can only however perform its function satisfactorily, so long *as that community continues to be a world by itself, unless it is also regarded as universally desirable by the rest of the world, as well as by the people of that particular community.* It would not in the least facilitate outside exchanges. If for example some isolated people had so great a fancy for certain rare sea shells found on their coast, either as articles of ornament, or because they believed them to be a peculiarly acceptable offering to make to their gods, that everyone always desired to procure them, and was willing to give in exchange for them whatever he desired to part with, those shells would do well enough for money, while they had no intercourse with any other people; but they would procure nothing in exchange from any portion of the world where no such fancy prevailed. They could not even be money to that people themselves, unless, for some such reason as we have supposed, they were objects of universal desire. No agreement, no enactment even, can ever fit any substance to become a universal medium of exchange, unless it is an object of desire wherever in all the world exchanges are to be carried on, so that whoever desires to procure anything from us may know what he must offer in exchange for it, and that whatever we may wish to procure from abroad we may know an equivalent by which we may be sure to obtain it.

DEFINITION, *Money is some product of labor which in every region of the earth to which exchanges extend, is desired by all men, in all quantities, and at all times.*

Perhaps it may be thought that this definition is too comprehensive. There may be—there are some, savage tribes with whom occasional visitors from the civilized world may make some trifling exchanges, who know nothing of the value of the money which we use. But no people can gain admittance into the economic brotherhood without some degree of civilization. The world of our science is everywhere sufficiently civilized to carry on something like regular trade. In so far as any portion of the human race is in the savage state, it can have no place in social science.

In connection with this definition it is proper to refer again to the logical division of capital which has already been given. Fixed capital was sub-divided into three species—the Real, the Mechanical and the Mercantile. *Money is the mercantile fixed capital, the labor-saving machine of exchange.* It just as truly assists the labor which is employed in exchange, as machinery assists the labor of the manufacturer. The negotiation of exchanges is just as truly labor as the spinning of cotton, and just as truly needs to be assisted by invention. Professor Perry says all labor consists in " moving things." This is quite too narrow a view of labor. A great deal of labor is performed without moving things at all. This is true of much of the labor of exchange.

§ 54. In the two metals gold and silver we have substances which possess to a degree quite wonderful the essential quality of money — universal desirableness. They sustain such a relation to human taste and use, that they have been universally desired all along in the world's history, from the earliest antiquity of which we have any authentic record. Nor is there any reason to suppose that in the future, however distant, they are to be supplanted from that place in human regard which they have always occupied. The taste of all men for the brilliant, the beautiful and the permanent has made gold and silver to be money for many ages and over a large portion of the world. They are the ornaments of kings, of their palaces, their persons, their crowns and their thrones, and their carriages of state, of the temples and of the altars of divinity, of the wealthy and the great, and of female beauty and loveliness. It is this relation to human taste, that has so long made them the circulating medium of the civilized world, and will probably fit them to perform that function in the distant future.

They have also other qualities which combine with their brilliancy and beauty to increase their fitness for that function. Their *scarcity* and the *great amount of human labor necessary to procure them* and introduce them into the markets of the world, are such as to render a small quantity of either of them of great value. Nothing, it has been shown, will continue to be produced, unless its value for long periods equals its cost. As the cost of these metals is high, their value must be high also. A small amount of gold and silver will procure by exchange a large amount of other objects of desire. One can therefore, by converting what he has for exchange into gold and silver, compress great purchasing power into very small bulk and weight. This very greatly increases the usefulness of these substances as money.

It is however possible that a substance may be *of too high value* to be used in exchanging articles whose price is small. This is true of gold. When so minutely divided as to represent very small values, the pieces become so small as to be easily lost, and incapable of being counted or handled with convenience. It is therefore a great advantage that we have another metal fit in other respects to be used for money, which is much less valuable, and therefore much better suited to small exchanges. Gold coins of less value than one dollar would be very undesirable, and are never made. The sub-divisions of the dollar are always coined from silver. Even silver is too costly for the minutest divisions which are found convenient. For these copper is therefore employed in its stead.

*Capability of minute division without loss of value is another great advantage* which gold and silver possess, without which they would be ill-adapted to some of the uses of money. Diamonds, like gold, have great value in very small compass, but are incapable of division without loss of value. A large diamond is greatly more valuable than an equal weight of small ones. They are therefore unfit to be divided into pieces sustaining definite relations of value to each other, nor can they receive any impress by which their value can be indicated to the eye.

§ 55. Another quality is exceedingly important in that which is to perform the functions of money. *Its cost, and therefore its value must be as invariable as possible.* This introduces to our consideration another function of money not hitherto mentioned, which is of the greatest importance. We have already shown that any substance universally desired originally becomes money only because the convenience of exchange requires it. But any substance by becoming the universal medium of exchange, also becomes of necessity (*the universal measure of value.*) If there were no medium of exchange, there could be no generally recognized standard by which values could be estimated. No general estimate could be formed of the wealth of a man, or of a community. You could only give a catalogue of existing possessions, for example, so many horses, so many oxen, so many sheep and so on. There could be no accurate comparison of the value of the things exchanged for each other, and only a very rude approximation to true equivalency.

But as soon as there is any accepted medium of exchange, it of necessity becomes also a standard of value. All values are estimated by comparison with the circulating medium, and can therefore be directly compared with each other. A horse is not worth so many oxen, or so many sheep, but so many dollars. It thus becomes easy to estimate the entire amount of any one's wealth or of the wealth of a community or a nation.

This function of money becomes very important in the case of time contracts. If one contracts to pay one hundred bushels of wheat in twelve months the next harvest may be a very bad one, and he may therefore be under the necessity of paying one hundred bushels when a bushel is worth twice as much as when the contract was made. This makes the transaction inequitable, and such a liability will make men averse to all time contracts, and throw a grave impediment in the way of the working of the natural law of exchange. The subject of credit will be considered in another place: it is sufficient to say of it in this place, that the use of credit in exchanges is an outgrowth of our social nature, and if our instrument of exchange is not suited to it, great inconvenience must follow. A medium of exchange will always be a standard of value, and if it is liable to great fluctuations of its own value, it will be a barrier nearly insuperable to all negotiations of exchanges which involve the element of time.

*The precious metals are eminently fit to perform this function of money.* Of course their value is not strictly invariable. The discovery of new and more productive mines than were before known sometimes sensibly diminishes the cost of the precious metals, and therefore diminishes their value as compared with all other objects of desire. But history clearly shows that this variation has been less than in the case of any other product of human labor. There have been, so far as history informs us, but two instances in many centuries, in which there has been a change in the value of these metals which was appreciable, without extending the comparison over long periods of time. Those two instances were of course the discovery of America, and the opening of the mineral resources of California, Australia and the Rocky Mountains. The effect of this last great monetary revolution is not even now fully developed. But nothing has yet occurred to weaken the assertion, that the value of the precious metals is less fluctuating than the value of any other product of human labor. Just so far as that proposition remains true, they are of course preeminently fitted to be the standard of value for the commercial world.

§ 56. We have here another illustration of the *cosmopolitan character of our science*, and of the importance of always keeping it in mind. It is exceedingly desirable that whatever we use as the standard of value and the medium of exchange, in one country, should be so used in all other countries to the extreme limits of the economic world. If the same substance is used for these purposes everywhere, that circumstance alone has a very important influence in preventing fluctuation of value. If our country only had used the precious metals for money, and all the rest of the world had used a different medium of exchange, the gold which has been obtained from our recently discovered mines would have mostly remained at home. Its effect on the standard of value would have then depended on the ratio existing between it and the amount of gold which would have been in circulation among us, had these mines never been discovered. The effect must have been to produce a depression in the value of gold which must have greatly disturbed the prices of all other commodities. But in the present order of things, gold being the money, not of a single country only, but of the world, the effect produced on the standard of value is regulated by the ratio of the recently produced gold to the whole amount previously existing in the world. Great therefore as the amount of recently produced gold is, the fluctuation of value occasioned by it, is comparatively small. A single heavy rain will raise the level of a mill-pond or of a small inland lake, so as to produce disaster, but it will have no appreciable effect on the ocean level. Gold and silver, considered as a standard of value, are an ocean flowing around the whole economic world, and very large additions at two or three points are immediately distributed to every part, like water which is poured into the ocean from a single river, can have no appreciable effect on its level.

§ 57. It is hardly possible to avoid being impressed with the thought of a *designing mind*, as we contemplate the relation of these two metals to the economy of the human family. Among all the materials of which the solid earth is composed two substances are found, each of which is so related to human taste as to render it an object of universal desire among all civilized nations, and thus fit to be everywhere without concert or any form of agreement, a medium of exchange and a standard of value. Both these substances exist in quantities so small and require so much labor to bring them into the markets of the world, as to insure their great value, and in a great degree to protect them from liability to fluctuation. They stand also in such relations of value to each other, as to fit one of them for large exchanges and the other for small. They are so easily transported, that by means of them the largest values may be carried to any requisite distance almost without expense; and thus a deficiency of them in any one part of the world may be very quickly supplied from parts where they are in excess. They are thus fitted and seem intended to unite the whole human family into one great economic world, around which they circulate as an ocean of liquid value, whose sea level is almost as invariable as that of the ocean of waters, and whose fluctuations scarcely exceed those caused by oceanic tides.

This comparative exemption from fluctuation is very greatly increased by the facilities of communication which recent invention has provided. Taken in connection with the small bulk of the precious metals in proportion to their value, these modern inventions give to the money of the world almost the fluidity of water itself. If wheat or iron or any other heavy or bulky substance were the medium of exchange, nothing of the kind could happen. All men do indeed need and desire wheat. But its bulk and weight are such, that to transport it from the point of abundance to the point of deficiency would soon consume half its value, or even in some cases its whole value. If therefore it were scarce in one region of the earth it would there rise in value without the possibility of supplying the deficiency, and bringing down the price to the common standard, by transporting it from regions of abundance. In that case there could be no ocean of value of a uniform level. One may, we think, in this view of things easily become satisfied that all theories of money must be fallacious and deceptive, which leave out of the account this oceanic character of the world's standard of value. Such theories cannot be expressions of the natural laws of exchange.

## CHAPTER IV.

*The Relation of the Government to the Medium of Exchange.*

§ 58. IN the present condition of the public mind, the subject indicated by the heading of this chapter is one of great delicacy, and yet of great importance. It is therefore necessary that it should be discussed with candor and thoroughness.

The fact that each piece of money as it is ordinarily used *bears a government stamp,* most commonly a stamp of the government under which it chiefly circulates, has been the occasion of much confusion of thought, and many erroneous conceptions of the subject. We hear in these days utterance given to many such crude notions, from men of respectability and intelligence, and even from some who aspire to be the rulers and legislators of the nation; as for example, that money is the creature of the government, that it circulates as money because the government has made it money by enactment, and that the government can make anything to be money which it chooses. At the present time our country is the hotbed of false and chimerical ideas on this whole subject. The reason why it is so, is found in the fact, that our whole history since the American Revolution has been a series of unsuccessful experiments on the currency, and the fact that some fifteen years ago an act of Congress was passed in direct violation of the first principles on which the monetary system of the world is founded, and that that law remains still in force. Our history in relation to this subject has certainly been unfortunate, and in that better time coming when the true principles of the subject shall be understood and reduced to practice, will be reviewed with wonder and sorrow. The whole financial system of the nation is unsettled and in confusion, and men's minds are filled with strangely wild and chimerical theories. Of the financial arrangements which originated during the war of the rebellion, under the pressure of military necessity, we shall speak in another place. But the nature of that power which governments exercise over money must be explained here. We have already shown that money originates, and the substance or substances to be used for money are selected in accordance with natural laws, without any intervention of the government whatever. Coinage is a mere arrangement for the common convenience. To determine the precise quantity of gold or silver in any given mass is difficult and troublesome, and considering the ordinary crude condition in which these metals are for the most part found, more or less alloyed with the baser metals, it would be in the ordinary transactions of business, impossible. The governments of the civilized world, in order to remove this inconvenience, undertake to reduce the precious metals to a recognized standard of purity, to divide them into pieces bearing such relations to one another as convenience is found to require, and to place on each piece a stamp which shall certify, on the faith of the government, the quantity of the precious metal contained in it. Coinage is in principle precisely like the arrangements of the government for furnishing invariable standards of length, weight and capacity. All these provisions are alike matters of mere convenience, and give the government no right of control or dictation in the matter, beyond what the common convenience requires. If one has had the accuracy of his half bushel certified, by having a government stamp put on it, that does not prove that the government owns the half bushel, instead of the nominal owner of it, but only that the owner has made it more trustworthy for his own use by the government certificate. The coining of money has the same significancy—no more—no less.

That this is a true account of the matter, is very apparent. During a considerable portion of our history as a nation, the specie in circulation was of Spanish and not of our own coinage. It consisted of the Spanish dollar and its half, quarter, eighth and sixteenth, and bore the image, not of liberty, but of the kings of Spain. The people had confidence in the soundness and honesty of that coinage, and were willing to accept it, instead of putting our government to the expense of re-coining it. We happened to have it, because at that time we produced little either of gold or silver, and received our supplies of them from Mexican and South American mines, then under the dominion of Spain.

If our government were to attempt to manufacture money out of baser metal, such money would be just as certainly and indignantly rejected by the creditor, if offered in payment of his debt, as it would be if it came from any irresponsible counterfeiter. Is it asked then—has not the government a right to enact what shall be legal tender? and may it not make one thing legal tender as well as another?

§ 59. *The right of the government to declare what shall be legal tender in the payment of debts sustains no relation whatever to the nature and functions of money.* It has already been shown, that it is a necessity of all men, that the civil government under which they live should protect them in their property rights. In the performance of this duty, the government must necessarily undertake to compel men to pay their fairly contracted debts. In order to do this, it must prescribe some plain and equitable rule, by which it shall be determined what constitutes payment. If for example A. has promised to pay

B. a certain sum, and it is not specified in the obligation in what it is to be paid, B. may perhaps insist on receiving it in some unusual product, which it is very inconvenient for A. to furnish. The legal tender law, as it existed before the war, provided, that in all such cases the contract shall be interpreted to require payment in the ordinary and recognized medium of exchange, gold and silver coin of the United States. The full extent of the power of the government to prescribe what shall be legal tender in the payment of debts, is its power to prescribe an equitable rule by which such contracts shall be interpreted, according to the clearly presumable intention of the parties. Till the great financial revolution growing out of the late war, no one ever imagined that the right to prescribe a legal tender had any other significancy or extent than this. Whence then the notion that under this right there is included a power to compel the creditor, whenever the government shall so enact, to receive paper or tin dollars instead of gold in payment of all debts? Such an idea is utterly groundless, and its prevalence among a people every man of whom casts his vote for the rulers and legislators of the nation, is dangerous in the extreme.

§ 60. *Was then the Act of Congress making the United States Treasury Notes, known as Greenbacks, legal tender for all debts, an act of injustice and tyranny?* To a question so directly ethical in its nature as this, it is not our business to respond. But it does come within our sphere to show as clearly as possible what was the real effect of that law on our economic system. When that law was enacted the value of a greenback dollar differed very little from that of the gold dollar, and it was probably hoped, and by many believed, that no great difference would afterwards arise. It was not therefore supposed that any great inconvenience was to be experienced from the working of the law, and little was therefore thought of the question of its justice or injustice. But within a few months after its passage it required two hundred and eighty-five dollars in greenbacks to buy one hundred in gold; that is a greenback dollar was worth only thirty-six cents in gold. Its power to procure by exchange all other objects of desire was depreciated in the same ratio. The practical working of the law was a reduction by Act of Congress of the value of all stated incomes in the ratio of one hundred dollars to thirty-six dollars. A provision for the support of a widowed mother and her children was reduced from a competency of ten thousand dollars, with an income of one thousand dollars, to the pittance of thirty-six hundred dollars, with an income of three hundred and sixty dollars. On the other hand the debtor that owed one thousand dollars in gold, could pay it with one thousand dollars in greenbacks worth only three hundred and sixty dollars.

*What motive*, it may be asked, *had the government for enacting such a law?* This is a very pertinent question and shall be fairly answered. It certainly was not because any one supposed or pretended, that in the ordinary conditions of national existence, any government had a right to interfere in this manner with the relations of a debtor to his creditor. It was well-known to be a flagrant violation of the fundamental law of ownership, and of a sound economy. It was justified only in consideration of the stern necessities to which the war had reduced the nation. Money could not be raised either by taxation or regular loan with sufficient rapidity to meet the expenses of the war. The government was compelled by inevitable necessity to put off its creditors for the present with promises to pay, which at the time she was utterly unable to fulfill. It was evidently very important to employ every practicable means to prevent the depreciation of these promises. It was therefore deemed advisable to make them receivable in payment of debts by all creditors as well as by the creditors of the government. By this measure it was hoped that their depreciation would be wholly prevented, or at least greatly retarded. Hence the legal tender clause in the law authorizing the issue of treasury notes.

§ 61. It is not within our province to express an opinion on the very grave question, whether so high-handed and anomalous an act could be justified even in circumstances so urgent. It is enough for us to say, that *our science knows nothing of any such control of the government over the world's medium of exchange.* The admission of the principle would be utterly destructive of the property rights of the creditor in his relations to the debtor. What the creditor might hope to receive would depend, not on what the debtor had promised, but on what the arbitrary will of the government might enact. The law of ownership can recognize no loans either to individuals or governments, except by the voluntary consent of the lender. For example A. owed B. one thousand dollars payable in gold; the government owed A. one thousand dollars expressed in a note of the Treasury of the United States. It required B. to accept its promise to pay one thousand dollars without interest, at that uncertain future period when it should be prepared to redeem its promise, as payment in full of A's debt of one thousand dollars in gold bearing interest. It was a requirement that B. should loan the government one thousand dollars in gold without interest, and wait till the government was prepared to pay the debt. It was a direct violation of the law of ownership. The government took the property of the owner without consent either granted or even asked.

It seems to be a very popular idea in the discussions

of the present, that the government ought indeed as soon as practicable to redeem greenbacks in gold whenever presented, but that they should by no means be withdrawn from circulation. This is simply a proposition to perpetuate without any pretense of necessity, this violation of a fundamental law which was originally resorted to under a plea of a necessity involving the very life of the nation. A government never can make its promises to pay a legal tender in the payment of private debts, without violating the fundamental law of all exchange, the free consent of both parties. It is of no avail to say that when the government redeems greenbacks with specie they will be at par with gold and silver. That may be true so long as the credit of the government is unimpaired. But if national disaster again comes, and a severe strain is brought upon the credit of the government, greenbacks will again be depreciated, and the injustice which the creditor has suffered in former years will be again renewed. It is no function of government to intrude its promises upon the creditor in payment of debts. It is not protecting the property rights of the citizen, but divesting him of his property without his consent. The practice of issuing treasury notes made legal tender may plead as a precedent the fact that the notes of the Bank of England are legal tender in the payment of debts. The example of England herself cannot justify the violation of a fundamental law of exchange. That provision in the charter of the Bank of England may work no individual wrong in times of national prosperity like the present, but calamity may yet again come upon England, and then the consequences of that law may be very disastrous. If at present it is harmless, it is also useless. Why not then abolish it, and let the future legislate for itself?

§ 62. One thing would seem too evident to require

any confirmation by argument. It is that *no obligation resting on our government can be more sacred, than the duty of repaying such a forced loan at the earliest possible day.* The whole amount of greenbacks in circulation is a forced loan, and if our government means to earn the reputation of being the protector of the property of the citizen, instead of openly and flagrantly violating it, too much haste cannot be made in redeeming the promise of the government which is expressed on the face of every greenback. It is no wonder that strange theories of money and finance are rife, when the government, during the twelve years which have elapsed since the war was ended, has scarcely taken a step in the direction of fulfilling these promises; while she is buying up her bonded debt at what it is worth in the market, by hundreds of millions, and that on the plea that it is desirable to diminish the amount of interest to be paid, and this forced loan is bearing no interest. An honest man is tempted to reply with some sharpness to such a plea, "it ought to be bearing interest. One would think it had been held without interest quite long enough." But with the morality of the question we are not now concerned. It is to be hoped that so strange an anomaly may soon be removed from our statute book, and that a precedent so full of danger may be eliminated from our legislation.

§ 63. It remains to point out the relation of this anomaly to the economic system. It affords a striking illustration of the phenomena which always attend a depreciated currency. By a depreciated currency is meant a national medium of exchange, which is in value below the standard of the rest of the world. The effect of the Legal Tender Act was, to give the people of the United States such a currency. All debts were payable in greenbacks. Of course as soon as greenbacks began to be inferior in value to gold, all debts were paid in them. It being at the option of the debtor to pay in which ever he pleased, he always chose to pay in the less valuable. Gold therefore ceased to circulate as money, and greenbacks became the sole medium of exchange and standard of value. They were always at par and gold at a premium, and all other species of property have advanced in price in the same ratio.

The natural consequences of a depreciated currency have been conspicuously exhibited. We have had most disastrous and seemingly capricious fluctuations of our standard of value. We do not purpose to give the sad history of the New York gold room for the last fifteen years. It is melancholy enough, and by no means creditable to our civilization. It is sufficient to say, that again and again fluctuations have occurred within a few days, sometimes even in a single day, of sufficient magnitude to reduce thousands from princely wealth to bankruptcy, and to raise other thousands from comparative poverty to great opulence. It is important to make the causes of these fluctuations clearly apparent. It has already been shown, that the stability of the medium of exchange is greatly promoted by its being the same throughout the world. The currency of the world thus becomes an ocean, the level of which cannot be raised in any part without raising the whole simultaneously. While therefore the currency of any country is the same as that of all the rest of the world, sudden fluctuation is impossible. But our medium of exchange has no connection with that of the rest of the world, and is therefore liable to rise and fall with any sudden and temporary impulse originating among ourselves. Increased or diminished confidence in the government, the success of one political party or another, a bad harvest, or any one of a multitude of other causes may any day occasion disastrous fluctuations.

As gold and silver were no longer money we had little use for them in any of the ordinary transactions of trade. The government had large payments of interest to make, and large collections of duties to be received, in gold. It had therefore constantly on hand a large amount of coin. But with that exception the precious metals were only kept on hand as merchandise, and the amount so kept was never very large. Merchants must however still pay duties and foreign balances in gold, and considerable dealings in gold were therefore inevitable. In these circumstances it was not impossible for combinations of speculators to obtain control of nearly the whole amount of gold in the market, and dispose of it only on their own terms. Panics of the most fearful character have been thus created, by which the whole nation was distressed, and thousands were ruined.

§ 64. Another and most important cause of fluctuation remains to be explained. No principle is better established, than that whenever any object of desire is thrown upon the market in greater quantities than the needs of the people, or their ability to purchase requires, the fact will be indicated by *a fall in its price*, and that reduction of price will go on as long as the excessive supply continues to be increased. Such fluctuations of price are in a normal condition of things certain to be arrested by the fact that the labor and capital employed in producing that which is in excess cease to receive satisfactory remuneration, and are withdrawn to some investment in which they are more needed. In a sound condition of exchanges, money is as much subject to this law as any other commodity. If for any cause it is excessively abundant, it will no longer be profitable to bring it in, and it will be profitable to carry it away. The equilibrium therefore cannot be much disturbed. But with such a medium of exchange as that which our country now employs, the quantity may be indefinitely increased or diminished without involving any change in the employment of either labor or capital. Its increase or diminution depends only on the greater or less activity of a single printing press. The necessities or the caprices of the government may expand or contract its volume indefinitely. If it is in excess, it is money no where except within our national lines, and has therefore no outlet. Increasing the quantity only diminishes its value, and the system provides no remedy for the fluctuation.

Various efforts have been made to discover *whether we have an excess or a deficiency of currency*. But such attempts are mere guess-work. We have no standard by which to judge. Accordingly the most widely opposite opinions are expressed. All are alike worthless. In one way only can the question be decided. Bring our medium of exchange to a par with that of the rest of the world. Open the communications between it and the great monetary ocean, and the question will soon be decided. If our medium of exchange is redundant, it will flow outward and the level will sink. If it is deficient it will flow inward, and the level will rise.

§ 65. Our statesmen and legislators have been much perplexed in trying to discover some means of rendering *our currency elastic.* By elasticity they of course mean a capability of spontaneously expanding and contracting its volume, according as exchanges are more or less active. It is even proposed that when money is excessive in the hands of the people, so that they are unable to find satisfactory modes of investing it, the government shall borrow it of them, and pay them interest for it, by issuing a convertible interest-bearing bond, which may at any time be given in exchange for greenbacks, and redeemed in greenbacks on the demand of the holder. If such a law is enacted the government should carry out the principle of it to its logical consequences. Consistency would require that when the people want work and cannot find it at satisfactory wages, the government should employ them at moderate wages, till they can find more lucrative employment elsewhere. A government that undertakes to find investment for all idle capital, should surely furnish occupation for all unemployed laborers also.

Such a medium of exchange as ours can have no such quality of elasticity as is so anxiously sought for. Indeed the quality needed is not elasticity but fluidity, and that can be provided for only by a free and open communication with the currency of the world.

§ 66. We are not of the number of those who think that the unsatisfactory condition of trade which has existed in this country for several years, is wholly referable to any one cause. Many causes have probably conspired to produce it. But of these *our unstable medium of exchange is doubtless one of the chief*. It has impaired men's confidence in the future and rendered them incapable of relying on any calculations respecting it. Excessive caution is the characteristic of the time, not greater indeed than the uncertainties which surround us justify, but such as to render energy and enterprise in trade dangerous and to a great extent impossible. It seems to every intelligent thoughtful man, that he knows not what shall be on the morrow. Confidence in men and in the order of things around us is one of the most potent elements in the economic world. That element is at the present time in this country singularly impaired by an unstable currency, and by the lack of any satisfactory proof, that the political forces that govern us can be relied on to relieve us of this oppressive burden, by which all the movements of trade have been for years overweighted and retarded.

## CHAPTER V.

### *Credit and Paper Money.*

§ 67. IF we would construct a true economic system, we must leave out of the consideration *none of the forces of human nature,* which have any influence on it. *One of these is credit.* It claims and will have its place in the system, whatever our theories about it may be. It is natural for every man to repose more or less confidence in his fellows. If it were not, society would be impossible, and solitude better than any human intercourse. Confidence always occupies a much larger place in the economic arrangements of the world than we are apt to suppose. Whenever any one has more capital than his own labor can employ, he is compelled to entrust it in some form to other hands; and in every possible mode of employing it, he is forced to place more or less confidence in those by whose labor his surplus capital is made productive. If he hires laborers, they are not mere machines, but rational free agents, and no superintendence can entirely secure him against liabilities to suffer from their unfaithfulness. Every laborer of whatever grade has a character, which renders his services more or less desirable to an employer, and either has the benefit of credit, or suffers from the want of it. Credit is an element which cannot be eliminated from any arrangement by which one man labors with the capital of another. All such transactions are more alike in principle than they seem to be. All use of capital requires not only the exertion of muscular power, but of mind power to direct it to its end. When one hires laborers to employ his capital, he exercises the mind force himself, as far as possible, and leaves as little of it to the laborer as he can. The laborer therefore only receives pay for his muscular force and such small exercise of rationality as is necessary to the common laborer. The compensation for the mind force the employer reserves to himself. Sometimes a laborer is hired in such a manner as to allow him a large scope for the exercise of his mind force, and greatly to relieve the employer from superintendence, and is paid accordingly. The element of credit enters much more largely into such a contract than into the employment of a common laborer. In still another class of contracts the owner surrenders his capital entirely, for a limited time, into the hands of another, and is quite relieved from all superintendence of labor, only exacting from the person to whom he entrusts it a promise to return it or an equivalent agreed upon, at a fixed time, with a stipulated compensation for its use. It is common to apply the word credit only to the case in which the owner entrusts his capital entirely to another for a limited time. But it is plain that it is applicable in various degrees to all the other cases, and can never be absent from any transaction in which the labor of one man employs the capital of another.

Credit is therefore one of the natural forces with which we must deal, and an economic system which should fail to find its true place would be radically defective.

DEFINITION, *Credit is the confidence which any one inspires by his integrity, energy and skill in affairs.*

The methods by which it becomes influential in economic arrangements, are very various and for the most part quite spontaneous, and are so simple and natural as to require no particular notice here. Some of them however are more artificial and complicated, and on account of the important relations which they sustain to the whole system of exchange, require a more particular explanation.

§ 68. One of the most important of these is *Banking*. This in all its varieties and modifications involves the principle of credit. Banks perform four distinct functions, and are known as *Banks of deposit*, *Banks of discount and exchange*, *Banks of loan* and *Banks of issue*.

In any community in which numerous exchanges are to be made, a *Bank of deposit is a necessity*. Any one who has many exchanges to make must necessarily keep on hand a considerable amount of the instrument by which exchanges are effected. An accumulation of money at any one place requires expensive precautions to protect it against robbery. It is no more expensive to furnish these safeguards for a large sum than for a small one. If therefore an individual or a company possessing in a high degree the confidence of the public provides such a place of safety, and offers to receive money for safe keeping on reasonable terms, many persons will gladly avail themselves of it. This can always be done without any expense to the depositors. For the managers of the bank, having a large amount in their hands deposited by many individuals, can always have the fullest assurance that it will not all, or even a very large proportion of it, be demanded at any one time. As taking one day with another, every man must receive as much as he pays out, it may be expected that each individual will deposit as much as he draws, and that while one man is drawing out, another will be depositing. The managers of the bank may therefore at all times lend a considerable portion of their deposits, receiving interest for the same. In this way they may easily and safely obtain remuneration for the expense and trouble of taking care of deposits, without any expense to the depositor. It must however be borne in mind, that much wisdom and integrity are necessary in order that such loans may always be restrained within the limits of perfect safety. A rash, imprudent, unscrupulous banker may and often does expose his customers to great loss. The managers of a bank of deposit have need not only to possess but to deserve the highest credit.

§ 69. A bank of deposit will almost of course and by necessity become *an important auxiliary in exchanges*. The counting and handling of money will by its assistance be almost entirely dispensed with. Any customer of the bank makes his payments for the most part by checks. Each check is charged to the account of the drawer, and credited to the account of the person in whose favor it is drawn. Thus the whole transaction, however large the check, is completed without the use of any money at all, merely by writing a few words in the books of the bank. The labor thus saved to a great trading community is immense.

The same things may be done with very little modification of the process, between individuals depositing in different banks, and even residing at a great distance from each other.

So extended and complete is the banking system of the civilized world, that payments between dealers in cities and countries however remote from each other are generally effected by checks and drafts, without any transfer of money, except the amount by which the purchases of one country or one city may exceed those of another. The extent to which the remotest portions of the earth are bound together by these invisible bonds of mutual credit, as invisible and yet as strong as gravitation, is highly honorable to human nature, and strikingly illustrates the vastness of the area of modern civilization, and of the economic system that pervades it.

The banks which perform this function are banks of exchange, and do not necessarily require any legislative sanction, or the conferring of any special privileges by act of the government. They need nothing in this regard except protection of every man's rights of property, and the impartial enforcement of the obligations of contracts according to their true intent and meaning. They are in no sense the creatures of legislation.

§ 70. *Banks of Deposit and Exchange* very naturally become to a certain extent, *Banks of Loan*. They lend so much of their deposit fund as is not needful to be kept on hand, to secure the entire safety of their depositors. The loaning of money is a business as truly legitimate as any other. The subject of interest on money will be discussed in another place. It is enough to say of it here, that there are many persons who have money which they cannot employ in active business. It is greatly to their advantage and to the advantage of the whole community, that all capital should be actively employed. It is better for its owners to live on the interest of their capital than to consume their principal, and it is a great advantage to persons having skill and power to labor, to obtain at a moderate rate of interest, the means of procuring tools and material, by which they can render their labor and skill available. Banks often render a very valuable service by collecting together such idle capital, and lending it to those who need it, and are able and willing to make reasonable compensation for the use of it. For the performance of this function, no legislative grant of peculiar privileges is at all necessary. It may be performed by a single individual, or by several individuals in an ordinary partnership.

§ 71. There is another banking function which requires a rather more detailed examination. *It is the issuing notes payable on demand to be circulated as a medium of exchange,* instead of gold and silver. Such bank notes are called *Paper Money.* They can be called so only by a rather violent figure of speech. No paper can be truly money. A bank note is nothing more than a piece of paper with a promise of some individual or corporation inscribed on it, to pay a given amount of money. To call such a promise money, is a use of language which strongly tends to that confusion of thought which is at present so prevalent in relation to the subject of money. Such a promise can only obtain general circulation in any community at its par value, on condition that the people have implicit faith that the promiser will on demand pay what he has promised. On this condition a bank note passes from hand to hand, not as money, but as affording to the holder an assurance that he can at any time obtain the money by demanding it. No one can deny that such promises to pay, when implicitly confided in by the people, have certain points of superiority for general circulation over gold and silver. If one has need to draw from a bank the sum of one thousand dollars, it is surely much easier and more convenient to take from the bank an assurance that the money will be paid on being demanded, and with that paper to obtain whatever one needs to purchase, than to carry away from the bank a bag containing one thousand dollars in gold or silver. If those with whom one wishes to deal have implicit faith in the assurance which is expressed on that piece of paper, it will be more agreeable and convenient to them to receive that paper in payment for what they sell than to be under the necessity of handling and caring for bags of gold or silver. It is in the nature of the case highly probable that for the sake of such a substantial convenience, men will always continue to use in the transactions of exchange some such expression of credit, to save themselves the inconvenience of handling and transporting the precious metals.

During a large portion of our history the advantages of some such use of credit have been so highly prized and so much insisted on, that a large portion of the money in circulation has consisted in such promises to pay. Banks were incorporated in great numbers by the legislatures of the several states. They were for the most part limited corporations, the stockholders of which were liable for the debts of the company only to the amount of their stock, and had a right to issue their notes payable on demand for general circulation. In the year 1856 no less than one thousand four hundred such State banks were in existence in the United States. In New England alone were five hundred and seven, with an aggregate capital of one hundred and fourteen million six hundred and eleven thousand, seven hundred fifty-two dollars. The losses experienced by the failure of such banks to redeem their notes were enormous almost beyond belief, and, before the outbreak of the war in 1861, had wrought in the minds of thinking men generally the conviction, that the system was radically unsound and untrustworthy.

§ 72. Perhaps it is not difficult to point out *in what the unsoundness consists*. Men's eagerness for substituting a paper currency for real money was a delusion, a sort of madness. Credit is abundantly capable of obtaining for itself all necessary expansion, without being stimulated by any artificial legislative helps and inventions. The active enterprise of an intelligent, industrious, commercial people will easily devise methods of supplying all the substantial conveniences of a paper currency, without acts of incorporation or the endowment of banking institutions with special privileges, to enable them to supply such a currency for the use of the people. The experience of a century, both in this country and in England, has demonstrated, that the demand notes of incorporated banks are a very untrustworthy medium of exchange. Credit should never be interfered with by legislation. If an individual or a private co partnership can procure so much credit in the community that their notes payable on demand will circulate as a medium of exchange, we know no reason why the law should interfere between them and the public. Each man may be safely left to take care of himself. But men who issue such notes should be held responsible for their redemption to the full extent of all their property. Men who are held to such a liability will be very cautious how they issue promises to pay on demand which they cannot perform. No advantages of a paper circulation can possibly compensate for the disasters which experience has shown to be inseparable from allowing banks of a limited responsibility to issue their notes as the circulating medium of a community. We do not believe that experiment will ever be tried again in the United States. "A burnt child dreads the fire."

§ 73. The war from 1861 to 1865 gave the United States a new monetary system which it is necessary to examine. That part of it which consists of Treasury Notes, called Greenbacks, we have already examined, in speaking of the legal tender law. The necessities of the government during that war were such as to compel it to resort to every practicable method of borrowing money. Out of these necessities grew our present novel system of national banks, which so far as circulation is concerned, has superseded the State banks in all portions of the country, except the Pacific Coast. The national banks are all organized under a law of the

United States. A bank is constituted by depositing the amount of its capital stock in bonds of the United States with the Treasurer of the United States, as security for the redemption of the notes which it issues. It receives back ninety per cent of the same in officially certified notes, which the bank issues to its customers, and it can circulate no notes not so certified. The notes of these banks thus secured and certified are receivable for all taxes except impost duties, and for all dues to and from the United States except interest of the national debt. They are redeemable on demand in lawful money of the United States, including of course greenbacks, so long as they continue to be by law legal tender. As long therefore as the banks redeem their notes on demand as the law requires, their value will be precisely equal to that of greenbacks. If any bank fails to redeem its notes as the law requires, its affairs will be wound up by authority of the government, its notes will be redeemed out of the Treasury of the United States, which will be re-imbursed by the sale of the deposited bonds of the bank to the highest bidder. So long therefore as the United States keeps its depreciated legal tender notes in circulation, the national bank notes will be a depreciated currency also. During the continuance of the war, these banks afforded the government great assistance in raising money, for many capitalists were eager to purchase the bonds of the United States for the purpose of using them in profitable banking.

In all the ordinary conditions of our national life, *the security for the redemption of national bank notes in legal tender of the United States is absolute.* The credit of the notes of every national bank issued according to law must be exactly equal to that of the government, for the faith of the government is pledged for their redemption. If a bank fails the government will redeem its notes. If hereafter the government shall do the tardy justice of redeeming its own long unfulfilled promises to pay, and shall remove from its statutes that anomalous law, which compels the people to receive the government's promises, however long unfulfilled, in payment of all debts, there will then remain no legal tender of the United States but gold coin ; and the national banks will be forced to redeem their notes in gold, or go into liquidation, and in the latter alternative the United States Treasury will redeem their notes in gold. A more perfect security for the redemption of national bank notes than would exist if the United States fulfilled its own promises, would be inconceivable. This will be admitted, we think, by all candid men.

§ 74. *Is then our national banking system to be accepted as a satisfactory and final solution of the question* so long and so fiercely agitated, *of banks and paper money?* We think not for the following reasons :

First, The credit of the banks under this system must always suffer, *when from any even temporary cause, the credit of the government suffers.* Unfortunately we cannot assume that a severe strain has been brought upon our country's credit for the last time, and should such an event occur again, while we have our present national banking system, the immediate consequence must be a depreciation of our whole currency in general use, which must greatly intensify the effect of national calamity. A medium of exchange, to be sound, must not rest on mere opinion in respect to the solvency of any government, but on solid permanent desirableness, as estimated by the whole civilized world.

Second, Though our national banks afford a satisfactory security for the redemption of their notes, they afford *no adequate security for the re-payment of deposits.* Formerly, in times of financial difficulty, the untrustworthiness of our banks manifested itself in their inability to redeem their notes. Under our present banking system, it has appeared in their inability to repay their depositors on demand. It matters not in which of these two ways the disaster comes, one is just as fatal as the other. Our national banking system affords no adequate security against destructive failure in this last form. It may be said, and with some truth, that perfect security against such failure is impossible. But this being granted as true, should effectually warn us against building up any such great artificial system of credit on the basis of special legislative provisions. Credit is one of the great natural forces of the world's economic system. But it is for that very reason a delicate thing for governments to meddle with. It is a dangerous experiment for a government to establish a vast net-work of banks to cover half a continent, to receive for safe keeping the spare funds of many millions of people, while the private property of those who are interested in founding and managing these institutions is not held responsible for the safe keeping of the funds which may be deposited with them. Let credit be free and unrestrained. Let any man who desires to receive the money of his fellow-citizens for safe keeping obtain as much of their confidence as he can on simple personal responsibility. Let all who choose commit their money to his charge. But let not the government provide any means by which any portion of his property may be exempted from responsibility to redeem his pledges to those who have trusted him. Let government interfere in no way whatever with the natural and spontaneous development of credit. Let it confine itself to its own proper function of rigidly enforcing all contracts according to the true intent and meaning thereof. The financial disasters which occur under such a system, may fairly be presumed to be unavoidable by any human wisdom or invention.

Third, In the nature of the case this system *can only last as long as our national debt remains unpaid.* If the time ever again comes when, as in former years, we are a nation without a national debt, there will be no national bonds in the market, which can be used as the basis of a national banking system. The banks now in existence must go into liquidation, because the foundation on which they are constructed will have ceased to exist. We shall then have no banks and no paper money, or we must construct a new monetary system on some other principle.

§ 75. Perhaps the ultimate and normal condition of the economic world in relation to this matter of paper money, will be found to be, that credit will everywhere be left to its own spontaneous development, according to its own natural laws, with no artificial contrivances to stimulate or to check it. It may be asked, why not adopt the plan of a great national bank like that of England, and those of other nations? That suggestion does not seem worthy of any special examination in this place. The efforts which we have made in that line have not resulted in such a way, as to encourage further experiments of the same sort. Past experience would suggest grave doubts, whether a great national bank like that of England can ever be amalgamated with our institutions and character. Why should we desire to experiment further in that direction? It must be obvious even now to all well informed persons, that those vast lines of confidence and exchange which rank among the grandest characteristics of modern civilization, are controlled by private bankers, who owe nothing to any legislative tinkering or favoritism. The natural development of credit over the economic world has produced private banking houses, that are fully adequate to be the fiscal agents of great nations, and even to negotiate the war-loans of all Europe. Why then should it be doubted that credit, without being aided or interfered with by any of the governments of the world, is capable of furnishing to the individual merchants and travellers of all countries, all the substantial conveniences and advantages which have ever been supposed to be derived from banks and paper money?

## CHAPTER VI.

### *The Functions of Credit.*

§ 76. FROM what has already been said it is obvious at a glance, that *the influence of credit on the working of the whole economic machine must be exceedingly great.* It has been shown that without it no man could ever find use for any more capital than his own hands could employ; for the moment he entrusted it to another hand to be used in production, the operation of credit would begin All mutual dependence, all mutual helpfulness, all human society inevitably implies credit. The unavoidable necessity of such uses of credit none will deny.

A little consideration will satisfy us, that the necessity of some of the more extended and seemingly optional forms of credit is scarcely less imperative. The first of these which requires to be particularly mentioned is its influence in quickening exchanges. The producer of any commodity, so soon as he has completed it, has need of the entire investment of labor and capital which he has placed in it, to be used again in further production. Perhaps his capital is small and is all invested in that one product. He must therefore either by sale procure it to be used again, or he must borrow the capital necessary to procure more material, and the means of living while he employs himself on some other product, or he must cease to work, and his means of present support must fail. If he could dispose of the product on hand to some one of good credit on the promise of payment at the end of six months, he could use the credit of the purchaser in addition to his own, and thereby procure the capital necessary to the continued prosecution of his trade. The man who purchased on credit may by means of that very purchase also have been enabled to prosecute a successful trade, and before his debt falls due, have earned the means of redeeming his promise. By means of that credit transaction therefore all the advantages of an immediate sale were realized. Had not the purchaser procured what he needed on credit, two men would have been reduced to the necessity of being unemployed, through the tardiness of exchange. Credit quickened the exchange, and procured for themselves and the community the benefit of their labor. What occurred in this case is constantly happening in all industrious communities. Credit affords great and much needed facilities for bringing all products into use as soon as they are ready for the consumer. Without this quickening influence of credit on exchanges, all industry must move heavily and slowly. It is a natural provision for bringing the producer and consumer as near together as possible.

§ 77. Another influence of credit is that *it gives to the energetic and skillful man without capital almost his only chance of acquiring it.* The world of trade is everywhere full of illustrations of the great advantage to be derived from the laborer owning the capital with which he works, and being therefore able to regard as his own all the benefits of his energy and skill. It is capable of working wonders. But if the skillful man who has no capital cannot obtain it on his credit, he must in most cases be a mere laborer on hire, till his best days of energy, invention and enterprise are past, and his best chances of a successful life gone. The capital which he uses only for the profit of another will produce much less valuable results than it would have done if he could have used it for his own profit. All society is thereby poorer. No man can calculate the loss to modern society, which would accrue from depriving it of all the productive power which credit in this way produces. Energy, invention, enterprise would become almost useless words. The man that began life in poverty, must almost of necessity end as he began, and even the rich would be much less opulent than at present. The greatest fortunes are apt to be amassed by those who began in their youth with a judicious use of their credit.

§ 78. Another function of credit is, *greatly to diminish the amount of money necessary to be used in the transaction of business.* Perhaps the simplest illustration of this is the case of two individuals, who have frequent exchanges with each other. Neither pays any money. What each buys is charged in the books of the seller. Perhaps at the end of six months they adjust their accounts. It turns out that the purchases of each are very nearly equal. A small balance only remains to be paid in cash, and perhaps even that may be charged over to a new account. And yet perhaps the amount of traffic between them may have been large. In this way credit transacts a large amount of business without any use of money whatever. And yet the existence of a recognized medium of exchange is just as important in these transactions, as though every purchase were made in money. It is by the fact that the value of every thing is estimated in a recognized medium of exchange, that these accounts can be kept with so much ease and accuracy. Money is just as important to us, when we do our exchanges without it, and the use of it in some cases enables us to substitute credit for it in many other cases.

In every case in which payments are made by checks or drafts, whether payable at sight or on time, credit is made a substitute for money, and by so much diminishes the amount of money needed to transact the exchanges of the community. This becomes quite obvious in the operations of a bank of deposit. If every man had kept his money in his own hands instead of depositing it with the bank, and paid by counting and handing over money, the whole amount of the deposits of the bank would have been no more than sufficient to effect the exchanges of the depositors. But when they deposit the same funds in the bank, and pay by checks, it is found that one third the amount will suffice, and the remaining two thirds can be placed at interest with entire safety. This fact demonstrates the great diminution of the money required to be kept in circulation, which results from making payments in checks.

The same tendency of credit to diminish the amount of money necessary to be used in the exchanges of a community is still more strikingly apparent in *the use of bank notes as a medium of exchange.* It is the received opinion that a bank whose specie on hand is equal to one half its notes in circulation is perfectly safe. If this is so, then the currency of any community might consist of one third real money, and two thirds paper money, and still be perfectly sound. But two dollars in every three of that currency would represent credit, and only one in three would be real money. Such a currency, could it be perfectly insured to remain such, would answer the purposes of exchange just as well as though it were entirely composed of gold, without any use of paper money. Credit would therefore diminish the amount of real money necessary to negotiate the exchanges of that community by two thirds.

§ 79. *This fact is the one truth which is to be found amid all the fallacies of paper money.* No method has ever yet been devised by which banks can be empowered to issue such a currency, and yet be effectually restrained from exceeding in its issues a prescribed and definite limit. Men cannot safely place confidence in such banks. Sooner or later their issues, or their indebtedness in some form, will not only transcend all prescribed limits but all limits of prudence and safety. Disaster has followed so often and spread ruin so widely, that the principle must be given up as an utterly unsafe foundation for a medium of exchange.

The truth however still remains, that by methods which are perfectly natural and safe, credit is to a vast extent made a substitute for money in conducting the exchanges of the world. This function of credit has certainly been greatly extended during the present century. Should the governments of the world at length become wise enough to leave the operation of credit without any interference, to the spontaneous development of its own laws, this function will yet be very greatly extended, and the efficiency both of capital and labor be much more aided by it, than hitherto.

The consideration deserves to be mentioned that this power of credit to diminish the amount of money needful in a given state of exchanges, *sustains a most important relation to our present great problem of a return to a sound currency.* It may readily be admitted that if that problem were actually to substitute gold for paper in transacting all the exchanges of the country, any speedy solution of it would be quite out of the question. Such is not the problem however. We have our national bank currency strictly limited by national authority so far as respects the ratio it sustains to the stock of the banks, and depending for its circulation, not on individual or corporate, but on national credit, and requiring only so much gold as will enable the banks to redeem their bills on presentation. In this state of things, with this extensive use of our national credit as a basis in part of our medium of exchange, the amount of gold needful to be employed will probably be less in proportion to the amount of exchanges to be transacted, than in any other country of the world, and a return to specie payments must be comparatively easy. This is clearly indicated by the fact that at this writing both greenbacks and national currency are reported at a discount of only about five per cent.

§ 80. Another very important influence of credit *lies in its power to control prices.* Such a power it must necessarily possess. Price we have already seen varies with demand, and evidently demand depends largely on the use which is made of credit. If no exchanges are made on credit, transactions must be limited to those who have money in hand. But if credit is employed with freedom, all who have good credit may be purchasers. The demand therefore will be increased by precisely the amount purchased on credit, which could not have been purchased if no credit had been used. This function of credit is very variable, depending very greatly on men's hopes or fears. In times of prosperity hope preponderates and credit is very freely employed. Prices as a necessary consequence are buoyant, since all commodities are in demand. In times of adversity men's fears preponderate, and the use of credit in exchanges is reduced to a minimum. As a necessary consequence demand diminishes and prices decline.

*This is the dangerous and critical element in credit.* In circumstances favoring its largest development, it is capable of so raising prices as for the time being to render even a sound currency almost useless as a standard of value, and when concurring with an unsound currency, of producing a sort of temporary madness in whole communities and even nations. About the year 1836 the public mind throughout our country became greatly excited in prospect of the rapid settlement of that vast area of fertile land which lies in the Upper Mississippi valley. It was foreseen that in the life-time of men then living several great States were to be founded in what was then a wilderness, each equal in wealth and population to a great nation. Men's imaginations were greatly excited. The sites of the great cities which were soon to be, were selected, and laid out on a scale of such magnificence, as the imagination stimulated by the hope of gain could suggest, where not as yet a human dwelling had been erected. Lots were offered for sale on terms requiring little cash, and giving long credits for the remainder. Those small payments of cash, a highly inflated currency rendered it easy to make, and about the future few had any misgivings. Tens of thousands hastened to make their fortunes by purchasing western city lots. The excitement was nearly universal, demand increased rapidly, and prices were advanced, being limited only by men's imaginations. Men believed that they had made an independent fortune in a single day, when those fortunes existed only in the imagination. After a few months the real began to assert itself. Men must return from this aërial flight to the actual world. Some men found they must have money, and began to press their debtors for payment. These urged others to pay who were equally unable. All turned to the banks; the banks were as unable as individuals. Their credit failed them, their paper money would no longer circulate, but returned upon them for redemption. They were quite unable to redeem them, and in a few months nearly all the banks in the country suspended specie payment, and universal disaster and almost bankruptcy followed. Western town plats were forgotten or remembered only in sorrow, and the nation wiser but sadder turned again to sober industry. There is in this power which credit possesses, an element of danger, which is inherent in its very nature, of which the foregoing narrative presents only one out of innumerable examples. We do not believe this danger can ever be entirely eliminated from the use of credit. It will be as small as possible when legislators have learned that credit is too delicate a thing for them to interfere with by their clumsy tinkering.

§ 81. Perhaps enough has already been said of that function of credit, by which *it binds the whole civilized world together* in one economic whole of mutual dependence and mutual helpfulness. It is a bond of universal attraction as invisible and impalpable as gravitation itself, and yet as irresistible and indestructible. The power of that universal attraction to bind the whole human race into a common brotherhood and a common civilization, is rapidly increasing. Every new improvement in the means of locomotion and inter-communication among the various populations of the world, extends the area of credit, and intensifies its attractive force. Theoretically the world is the field of our science, and the actual condition of the world is conforming more and more to the theory.

## CHAPTER VII.

### *Monopolies.*

§ 82. WE confess to having felt some perplexity *about the heading to be employed for this chapter.* The thought occurred to us to call it " International Exchanges." But the thing which is naturally suggested by this phrase has no existence in fact. Nations are neither producers nor exchangers. Both these are individual and not national functions. Why then talk of international exchanges, when exchanges, wherever the exchangers may happen to live, are inter-individual and not international. Individual Englishmen may exchange with individual Frenchmen, but this is not England exchanging with France. Let us call things by their right names, if we would have an understanding of their real nature.

What we wish to discuss in this chapter is, the economic character of certain restrictions on exchanges, which have been much practiced by the different nations of the world in its past history. It seems to us that those restrictions are common in their nature, design and working, and they are all fitly described by the word which stands at the head of this chapter—Monopolies.

DEFINITION, *A Monopoly is such a control of the supply of any desirable object, as will enable its holder to determine its price without appeal to competition.*

Some monopolies are conferred by the government, and are provided for by legal enactments. Others are secured by mere combinations of capital or labor or both. Some monopolies are entire, protecting their holders against all competition. Others are only partial, procuring for their holders exemption from competition only within certain limits. But protection to the holder against the competition to which other men are exposed is the common aim and result of them all.

Monopolies have certainly occupied a very prominent place in the arrangements of modern Christendom, and the principle of monopoly may still be easily discerned in the laws and institutions of most countries, nor can it be justly claimed that our own country is entirely exempt from them. It is therefore necessary, before leaving the subject of exchange, carefully to examine their nature, the grounds on which men seek to justify them, and their relations to the economic system.

§ 83. *Some monopolies are defensible on sound economic principles.* It has already been shown, that when labor has been expended in giving value to any material thing, the laborer thereby acquires the ownership of the substance upon which he has exerted his labor. If that substance was the property of a previous owner, in consequence of labor performed in producing it, the last laborer that works upon it must compensate the previous owner. But if it was without value when it came into his hand, he has gained the entire ownership of it, by the labor he has expended on it, and may exchange it in the form to which he has wrought it for any other value which he can obtain for it. Thus the possession of the material on which he has labored insures to him compensation for his labor according to its value. If a man of skill has made a table out of wood which was of no value, he is sure of being paid for his work; for no one can make a table of equal desirableness with less work, and tables are always in demand.

But there are products of great value, the producers of which have no such natural assurance of obtaining the reward of their labor. For example, an ingenious man invents a machine which is of great value to the labor of the world, and builds a model or exhibits a drawing of it.  Any ingenious mechanic may from that model or draft construct and multiply the machine indefinitely. The labor of the inventor was purely intellectual and not connected with the ownership of any material thing, by the sale of which he can secure his own reward.  As soon as his thought has been comprehended by another mind, it may be by that mind communicated to any number of minds or to the whole world, and thus pass from the inventor without any compensation whatever.  The public, the world, can well afford to give him as compensation for disclosing so valuable a secret, a monopoly of the manufacture and sale of that machine for a limited number of years.  A patent right confers precisely such a monopoly.  No right-minded man will hesitate to admit that it is good economy for the government, as the representative of the whole community, to give to the inventor of such a machine a monopoly of its sale, and faithfully to protect him in the enjoyment of it.  If it is an invention of universal utility, no government should refuse to grant the inventor a patent right on his application.  It should be granted equally to an alien as to a native born citizen.

The same may be said of the *copyright of books, and of the products of purely intellectual labor generally*, or more generally still, of any product of labor or skill the producer of which has no natural security for obtaining the reward of his labor.  The principle however does not apply to professional skill and talent, though it may be purely intellectual.  For example the function which the lawyer performs is one of urgent necessity for the protection of the rights of individuals.  No man can perform that function as well as he can, with less natural talent and less skill than he possesses, and no one can acquire the requisite knowledge of law and readiness in applying it to particular cases with less time and labor than he has bestowed upon it. He has therefore every assurance that men will be glad to pay him the full value of all the professional skill which he possesses, and can put in no valid claim to be protected by monopoly, to secure to him a fair compensation for the service he renders. The same is true of all properly professional labor.

There are a few cases in which *labor not strictly intellectual may be protected by a monopoly*. Such are the building of bridges, and the establishing of expensive ferries across rivers or straits, to accommodate public traffic. It might often be true, that no man would be willing to make the necessary outlay, unless he could be insured a monopoly of the carrying trade across the water in question, at least for a term of years. In such a case the community would often purchase the accommodation very cheaply by granting such a monopoly, and faithfully protecting the holder in the full enjoyment of it. All these are cases in which the holder of a monopoly renders to the community a full equivalent for the privilege conferred on him.

§ 84. But there is another class of monopolies of a very different character and which require a far more thorough and exhaustive examination. If we mistake not they can be justified by no plea of equivalent service rendered to the community. *We refer to monopolies granted to certain branches of industry in one country, to shield them against the competition of similar industries in other countries.* We find examples, in all exemption from competition granted to certain branches of manufactures, to shield them from the competition of like manufactures in foreign lands, by imposing discriminating duties on imported products. It may seem to some a mistake to class such arrangements under the head of monopolies. But it seems to us that they belong under that head in the nature of the case, and we have sought in vain to find any other head under which the discussion of them can be introduced, without an obvious violation of logical arrangement. No fundamental law of the science calls for any such limitation of competition, but all conspire together to protest against it. Economic principles can deal with such legislation only in the form of protest. In principle such legislation does confer a monopoly, not always entire, but if not entire at least partial. Its effect is to protect one person, or a particular class of persons from a perfectly natural competition, which they must otherwise encounter. It is true that the method in which the end is sought to be accomplished is not by absolutely forbidding certain products to be sold in this country, but by compelling all foreign producers to compete with the American manufacturer under such conditions of disadvantage, as to amount to prohibition. It is proposed to accompl'sh this by levying such duties on articles manufactured abroad, that the foreign producer cannot pay the duty and still compete with the American producer. It is assumed, that by thus driving the foreign producer from our markets, the home producer will be able to demand such prices as will render a business remunerative, which could not be profitable in presence of foreign competition. One would think the bare statement of the case might suffice, without further argument. No injustice can be done by calling such legislation a monopoly in favor of the American manufacturer. Such legislation abounds in this country at the present time, under the soft and taking pretense of "protecting home industry."

§ 85. *The phrase "protection of home industry" is most infelicitously and unfairly applied.* Protection is a precious thing, in which every good citizen believes. To protect the industry of every citizen, to secure to him the unobstructed pursuit of his legitimate objects, and the full enjoyment of all the products of his labor, is the most sacred function of civil government. The resources of our planet can never be fully developed and applied to the uses of human well-being, till every portion of it where man can dwell, is under a government that can and will protect the industry of every dweller on the soil. This is true protection. Let the phrase "protection of home industry" be used in this its only legitimate sense, and there will be no controversy about the matter.

But in the use that is made of the phrase by the advocates of what is called "Protection," it is wrenched away from this its proper and universally accepted meaning, and, without any even pretense of definition, applied to a device of their own, sustaining no relation whatever to the proper meaning of the word. Protection implies that the thing in behalf of which it is invoked, is in danger from some hostile force. In this use of the word the hostile force against which industry is to be protected is natural competition. The interposition of the government is invoked to shield certain people from competition in trade, in order that they may be able to set such prices on their wares as will be satisfactory to themselves. As they press their demands upon the government, they ask in tones somewhat lugubrious; will not our government protect the industry of our own citizens? *This assumption is always false. Natural competition is the enemy of no legitimate business.* It only determines, what all the world is interested in knowing, who can make a given product of the best quality at the cheapest rate. Whoever that person is, and wherever he dwells, it is cheaper to employ him than any one else, and any one who is permitted to own his own property, will employ him. Those who cannot compete with him will employ themselves in producing something else which they can produce in the face of competition. Let us suppose a case which is as clear as possible. Some man takes a fancy to produce coffee in Minnesota. No doubt by planting trees in hot houses, and supplying the requisite temperature and other atmospheric conditions, coffee might be produced. When the trees are grown, and have yielded their first crop, the proprietor of this hot house coffee plantation petitions the government for "protection of our home industry." He says the competition of coffee grown within the tropics is quite ruinous to me. Is competition this man's enemy? On the contrary it seems to be the only teacher that can give him wisdom, and make him see the folly of thus misapplying capital and labor. If he will heed its lessons, it will show him the necessity of employing himself in some more rational fashion. It never can be known whether a given commodity can be profitably produced in given circumstances of time and place, except by trying the experiment in presence of free competition. The competition which puts that question to the test of a fair experiment is the true friend of human industry everywhere. If you would know whether pig iron can be made as cheaply in Pennsylvania as in Scotland, try the experiment, and you will know. You never can know in any other way.

§ 86. *The freest and widest competition is the best friend of all industry in another way.* Let us suppose that manufactures have been recently established in any community, and are yet in their infancy. In what circumstances will those manufactures soonest reach their maturity and perfection? Obviously in the presence and under the full stimulus of the most perfect manufactures of the world. If the community in which they are situated were isolated by natural barriers from all the rest of mankind, the low demands of the community around them would be supplied, and nothing more would be aimed at. There would be little stimulus to improvement, and progress would be very slow. But if they were constantly in presence of the most perfectly manufactured fabrics of the world, the best models would be always in sight of their managers, and the strongest inducements would stimulate them to bring every process to the highest perfection. If by legislation unfriendly to the importation of manufactured goods, you compel that community to accept their own manufactures, such as they are, and at such prices as are demanded for them, the inevitable result will be imperfect products at high prices. The aim of producers will be to obtain the highest price for the lowest cost. The effect of such legislative isolation will be the same as the effect of isolation by impassable natural barriers.

No one will deny, that if you would bring the schools, the literature, the science, the art, of any portion of the world to the highest perfection it must be done in direct competition with all that is noblest and most worthy of imitation in the intellectual progress of the world. Herodotus the father of history, and Homer the father of Epic poetry, were the most cosmopolitan men of antiquity. They made themselves acquainted with the knowledge, the wisdom, the civilization of their times. There is every reason to believe, that this is a condition of all progress, of all civilization. Competition is so far from being any man's enemy, that it is a great common force impelling the whole human race toward perfection. The enemy against which some men so plaintively implore their country's protection is purely a creation of their own imagination.

§ 87. We have already incidentally remarked, that *the general principles of the science are all adverse to the monopoly of protection*, and condemn and reject it as an intolerable anomaly. We have already shown that both labor and capital obey laws of natural gravitation, which are irrespective of national boundaries. They tend toward the point of greatest demand as indicated by highest remuneration, whether that point be on one continent or another, or in the remote islands of the ocean. Neither has exchange any natural relation to nationality. It always seeks to buy at the point of greatest cheapness, and to sell at the point of greatest dearness, in whatever latitude or longitude those points may be found. It is confessedly one of the grandest functions of any civilized government, to protect its people in pushing their exchanges to the extreme limits of humanity.

*The true economic theory is that the human race is one family.* The Christian scriptures and our science are in respect to this matter perfectly at one. "All ye are brethren." The wealth of the world is the patrimony of this one family. Our problem as economists is to determine by what laws, and under what conditions, this patrimony can be most increased. The true solution of this problem is, that every man shall employ his labor in producing that which has the greatest value possible to him, exchange that value where it is a maximum, and where the value which he is to receive in return is a minimum. In this way it needs no argument to prove that every man will be richer than in any other, and that as the wealth of a nation can be nothing but the aggregate of the wealth of its individual citizens, every nation will be richest when each of its citizens is richest. That the great laws of human nature which are the natural forces of the science will, when left to their own freedom of action, thus construct the economic system, is just as obvious as that universal gravitation will construct the solar system as it is.

§ 88. To all this we often hear the reply made,—*this is very beautiful in theory, but it is mere theory.* It will not work in the actual world that is. Friction is left out of the account. The real world differs so much from the world of conception as to make the theory quite worthless. We believe this to be the only answer which it is possible to make to the arguments we have advanced. This answer, it should be observed, neither sets aside nor modifies one of those great natural forces on which we have insisted, nor pretends to deny that they must act in the manner we have pointed out. It is admitted then that they exist and must act as we claim. But the assertion is, that there are counteracting forces, by which our results will be essentially modified, so that our conclusions will not stand the test of experiment. The issue has therefore been reduced to the simple inquiry,—what is the friction, what are the counteracting forces which we have failed to allow for? It is therefore incumbent on us carefully to examine all suggestions which seem to point out anything of this character, and allow them their full weight.

## CHAPTER VIII.

### *Free Trade, Objections Considered.*

§ 89. That system of perfect freedom of exchange between different portions of the human family, irrespective of any national lines, which was advocated in a previous chapter is generally called free trade. That term we shall frequently have occasion to use in much that follows. We therefore propose the following,

DEFINITION, *Free Trade is the liberty of every man to buy where he can buy cheapest and sell where he can sell dearest,* without any obstruction being thrown in his way by the interference of government.

The advocate of the most perfect freedom of trade is no enemy to duties imposed purely and simply for the purpose of raising revenue for the legitimate purposes of government. He only protests against imposts which are of the nature of a monopoly,—imposts levied for the purpose of screening certain products from the competition of foreign producers. The general subject of imposts for revenue will be considered in its proper place. It was necessary to say so much here to guard against a common misunderstanding.

Let us then proceed to examine those counteracting forces, which it is claimed set aside the results to which we were conducted in the last chapter, by developing the great natural laws of the science. These laws it is said are purely theoretic. The friction of really existing things it is said renders them useless in practice. What then is the friction?

§ 90. First, *It is said that no nation can prosper without variety of industry,* and that free trade would limit the labor of a nation to the smallest number of industries, and thus be fatal to its prosperity. This argument has been urged, perhaps under every possible aspect, by Henry C. Carey, who is certainly the most popular, and perhaps the ablest advocate of " Protection " in the English language. It therefore deserves to be treated with respect and answered with candor.

That every great and prosperous nation may be expected to exhibit a vast and complicated variety of industry, will be as cheerfully and fully admitted, as any advocate of Protection could desire. *Free Trade is not opposed to variety of industry.* It would not however pursue profitless industry for the mere sake of variety. Accuracy however requires us to say that while the proposition, that a nation cannot prosper without variety of industry, is generally true, its truth is not universal and absolute. For aught we know, it may prove true, that Colorado has mineral wealth so abundant and so permanent, that she may be a prosperous state with a single industry, and that she might be even if she were an independent nation. The natural wealth of a nation may be limited to a single product, and yet that product may be so abundant, and so important to all the rest of the world, that she may rise to great wealth without any variety of industry. As a generalization therefore the proposition fails. It must not be applied in the argument as a universal law. We must look to it that there is not something in the peculiar conditions of the case to render it inapplicable.

In most cases national prosperity will be indicated by great variety of industry. But *which is cause, and which effect?* Do nations attain to great prosperity because they have great variety of industry? Or does their industry expand itself into endless variety, because they are very prosperous? It is very easy to show that in most cases variety of industry is the effect of prosperity, and not primarily its cause.

To the early settlers of that region of vast agricultural fertility, the Upper Mississippi Valley, variety of industry was simply impossible. Manufactures, except the products of the spinning-wheel and the hand-loom, were out of the question. The first settlers had neither machinery nor materials and no capital with which to procure either. Money was worth four or five per cent a month, to be used in purchasing those lands of exhaustless fertility at a dollar and a quarter an acre, and in preparing them for a crop, by subduing the rank growths of nature with which they were covered. Mr. Henry C. Carey himself could hardly claim that manufactures could afford to pay those rates of interest.  The first settlers could do nothing but avail themselves of the exuberant fertility of the soil, and send its produce to the best market to which it would bear to be transported, receiving in return such things as they needed.  Had a protectionist of Mr. Carey's school gone on a mission to those hardy pioneers, to preach to them the gospel of variety of industry, he would have preached to very unappreciative audiences.  To understand how protective duties on foreign manufactures could give them variety of industry, would have been beyond their mental capacity.  They would have been able perhaps to understand that such a duty would render manufactured articles dearer than ever, but surely they had always found them quite dear enough.

Yet prosperity was not impossible to those people.  They did prosper greatly by this single industry, and by the prosperity of their agriculture came in due time the possibility and the necessity of more varied industry.  Accumulated wealth must be valueless, or seek new methods of profitable investment.  Their industry became from year to year more various, because their increasing wealth must find other modes of investment, these new investments would in their turn become the cause of still greater prosperity.  But primarily they were the effect, not the cause of prosperity.

If the Sioux Indians should discover in those barren wilds over which they roam, some tract of fertile land, and determine to abandon the chase and devote themselves to the regular pursuits of civilized life, their industry must at first be purely agricultural.  They must exchange with their white neighbors the products of the soil for the products of mechanical skill which they need.  As they prospered, they would be able to cultivate the mechanic arts among themselves.  This would make their accumulation of wealth more rapid.  The accumulations of successive generations would render variety of industry possible and necessary. To such a people variety of industry is as truly a growth, a necessary growth as the matured oak of the forest is the result of growth from the acorn. Such must be the progress of any people, from the poverty of its beginnings to the wealth of its maturity. Simple industry comes first, then as wealth increases various industry becomes possible and inevitable. To insist on variety of industry as the primary cause of a nation's prosperity, is to manifest a profound ignorance of the laws of national growth. It is in the strictest sense preposterous. It is to insist on the end before the beginning. A greater delusion was never imposed on a credulous people, than to make them believe, that by discouraging the introduction of the products of skill and machinery from abroad, which they need now to comfort their lives and aid their toil, they can secure the production of such commodities at home, under circumstances more favorable than to procure them in exchange for the products of their agriculture, and that they shall thereby become at once a skillful manufacturing people, with all that variety of industry which belongs to nations of old civilizations and vast accumulations of wealth. This argument for protection is certainly fallacious.

§ 91. *Free Trade has no tendency to retard the introduction of every profitable variety of industry.* It can not be too steadily borne in mind, that every man of every nation will increase his wealth most rapidly by buying of him that will sell cheapest, and what is for the interest of every man must be for the interest of a whole world. If therefore any branch of industry can be profitably pursued in the face of all natural competition, free trade will be no hinderance to its introduction; if it can not be profitably pursued, free trade will prevent its introduction only because the products of that branch of industry can be more cheaply imported from abroad than made at home. The mere fact that it can not be profitably manufactured at home is positive proof that men in that community can employ themselves more profitably in producing something else wherewith to purchase that particular product from abroad. Free trade therefore encourages and invites to every kind of enterprise that can be prosecuted with profit, but this is not all which it accomplishes. It saves a community from wasting itself upon unprofitable enterprises. Variety of industry is not a good thing in itself, for a community any more than for an individual. It is only profitable industry that enriches. If for the sake of variety of industry an individual engages in occupations in which he cannot compete with his neighbors, he will be impoverished, not enriched. This is as true of communities as of individuals. No man can commit greater folly than to insist on doing for himself what another stands ready to do for him at less cost. If a blacksmith can earn the making of two coats by shoeing horses while he could make one for himself, it would be nothing but stupidity and folly to leave shoeing horses, to make his own coat, when he had no reason for doing so except that he desired to have a variety of industry. What is folly in an individual is no less folly in a community. The whole truth is, that every man and every people ought to have just so much variety of industry as can be prosecuted profitably. Free trade furnishes the only possible means of determining, whether in given circumstances any branch of industry is profitable or not.

§ 92. Second. *It is affirmed that it is impossible to establish manufactures in a nation where they have not hitherto existed, in presence of the competition of other nations whose manufactures are already in their full maturity.* This objection very strikingly illustrates a certain confusion of thought, which is an unfailing characteristic of argument for protection. It is said the interest of foreign,—say of English manufacturers, is so great in having the American market entirely to themselves, that they will crush out any manufacturing enterprises of our own by a ruinous competition. The confusion of thought appears in mingling with the matter the idea of nationality. Grant that the danger here referred to is real and to any degree imminent, it is just as likely to occur between two different sections of our own country, as between England and the United States. Boundary lines of nations are totally irrelevant to the matter. The manufacturers of the Atlantic States are just as likely to crush out the infant manufactures of the Mississippi valley, as the manufacturers of England are to crush out those of the United States. If for this reason our country needs protection against English competition, the Mississippi valley still more urgently needs protection against the competition of the Eastern and Middle States. If it is impossible to establish American manufactures in face of English competition, it is certainly not easier to establish Western manufactures in face of Eastern competition.

This objection indicates no less confusion of thought in the conception which it implies of the nature of competition. To hear some men talk, one would suppose the whole political power of England herself were to be employed in crushing out an incipient American manufacturing enterprise. By the application of a little analysis, we shall readily see that it is not the combined force of the English nation controlled by one social personality that is to be apprehended. It is the competition of thousands of English manufacturers, with all their mutual rivalries. They will compete with each other just as freely in the markets of New York, Boston and

Philadelphia, as they will in those of London, Liverpool and Glasgow. The question is, whether all these rival interests are likely to be combined in our markets, to crush out an infant manufacturing enterprise by selling below cost. Let us suppose that our woolen manufactures are thought to be threatened with this danger. The case is, that under the regular action of free competition, the manufacturing of woolen can be profitable. In this state of facts that branch of manufactures cannot be crushed out by competition, except by supplying our market with foreign woolens at less than cost. The question then is whether English manufacturers can and will combine together to supply 50,000,000 of people with their products at less than cost. This is an exact statement of the nature of the danger, and enables us to form an exact estimate of its magnitude.

The truth is obvious enough. The only process by which such a destruction of our manufactures could even be attempted, is one by which English manufacturers would bring inevitable ruin on themselves. In this state of the facts, and under free trade, it must be just as easy to found new establishments for the manufacture of woolen on American, as on English soil. The supposed danger is quite imaginary, and the necessity of protecting our infant manufactures is a shallow delusion, which a little tranquil thought would very easily dissipate.

§ 93. Third. *It is said that Free Trade deprives the land of the manures which result from the consumption of its products.*

This is also a point much insisted on by Mr. Carey, and the men of his school. But a careful examination will show that all the truth there is in this objection, is only a verification of Solomon's proverb, "The destruction of the poor is their poverty." That proverb would still be true as ever, if Mr. Carey should succeed in applying his theory of protection to the uttermost. No one acquainted with the subject will deny that, in order to preserve the productive power of the soil unimpaired, it is necessary to restore to it the offal which remains after the consumption of its products. The law of rent is founded in nature. The soil gives generously, but can continue to give, only on condition that when man has served himself of her products, he return to her the unconsumed remnant.

But the possibility of doing this is unavoidably dependent on the various conditions under which land is cultivated, and no artificial legislation can place different countries, or different portions of the same country, in circumstances of equal advantage in this respect. When civilized men first sought a home amid the mighty forests of Ohio and Indiana, they were under an unavoidable necessity of cutting down and reducing to ashes masses of timber which, were it now in existence, would in many instances be worth more than the farms on which it grew. Yet civilization could make no beginning there without that vast and as it now seems sorrowful waste. Even after those forests had been reduced to ashes, the ashes themselves could not be utilized. The manufacturing of potash was not yet established in those wilds so remote from the markets of the world. Even yet the inevitable waste was by no means at an end. The product of those farms could, perhaps for generations, find no market except at distant cities, from which its remnants never could be returned to the land on which it grew. As to fertilizing those farms it could make no difference, whether it found a market in a North American, an English or a South American city.

It has happened thus in all parts of our country by a necessity inherent in the very nature of the case. The products of the farm could for a time find consumers only at a great distance, and could not make the natural return to enrich the soil on which they grew. The tillers of those farms have not only been under a necessity of destroying the magnificent forests which were their spontaneous products, and of allowing the very ashes to which those forests were reduced to lie almost useless on the ground, but of consuming for generations the rich mould accumulated on their farms, by the decay of the luxuriant vegetation of ages, before society could be brought to such a condition of maturity, as rendered practicable the fertilization necessary to restore the productive power of their exhausted land.

It must be admitted that this is rather an inviting theme for pathetic declamation, and if any one has a taste for that style of composition, he may find an abundant supply of it in the writings of Mr. Carey's school of economists. But how it has any real relation to the question under consideration is not very apparent. To establish various industry in the forests of Ohio and Indiana, create a home market for the products of those newly cleared farms, utilize their magnificent forests and provide fertilizers to prevent the waste of the productive power of the soil, was as impossible as to mature harvests while those forests, with a density of foliage which sunbeams seldom penetrated, shaded all the ground. No doubt the wealth of a country is greatly increased by sowing it over thickly with cities and villages and manufacturing machinery. But the evil is quite independent of the nationality with which we trade. It results from the fact that the products of the farm must be consumed at a distance from the spot on which they grew, and not from their being consumed on the other side of a national boundary; and it admits of no effectual remedy so long as it remains true, that the inhabitants of a new settlement can purchase many things from other communities more cheaply than they can make them for themselves. It would be far more convenient for the infant and for its mother, that it should walk rather than creep; but it will still remain true, that creeping is a necessary stage in the process of learning to walk. Lectures delivered to infants and their mothers, on the superiority of walking to creeping, will not be found to be of much practical utility. Mothers will gladly admit the truth of what you say, but babies will still creep before they walk. And so will communities in spite of all the theoretic exhortations of Mr. Carey and his followers.

§ 94. Fourth. *It is asserted that free trade is destructive of national independence.*

We suspect that this objection has more influence in reconciling a great number of minds to our present protective legislation than any or all other arguments. In order to deal with it fairly, we must endeavor justly to conceive what sort of national independence that is which is practicable and desirable. Every man ought to be jealous of his own independence. There is a true independence, the loss of which is the loss of manhood, almost of personality. It is the right and the habit of relying on one's own intellect in the formation of opinions, and of governing his actions by his own free choice. Such an independence is not at all inconsistent with the innumerable dependencies of social life. It is not necessary in order to maintain it, that one should keep himself in such relations to his fellow men, as to be prepared at any time to dispense with the help of all his fellow-beings, and to inaugurate a state of war between himself and the rest of the world, whenever he may think it desirable or necessary. Such a notion of his own independence would unfit any man for the society of men. All true manhood acknowledges all these innumerable social dependencies, as cheerfully as it asserts independence in the only sense in which any wise and good man would be willing to be independent.

*The true conception of national independence* is in principle precisely the same. It is the conception of an independent social personality among the nations, with full right and power and will to exercise all the functions of sovereignty; but still admitting and delighting in all the innumerable social dependencies which bind the human race together in one great brotherhood of nations.

§ 95. It is asserted, *that if we allow ourselves to be dependent on the manufactures of any other nation, we shall be brought into great distress in case of a war with that nation,* for the want of those products for which we have been accustomed to depend on her industry. When this objection is urged, it is forgotten that all such dependence is mutual. If in case of a war with a nation with whose people we have a large trade, we are liable to be distressed by the cutting off of our accustomed supplies, our enemies will also be distressed by the failure of supplies which they have been accustomed to receive from us. If for example we are ever involved in another fratricidal war with England, (and no war between the United States and England can be other than fratricidal,) it is doubtless true, that we shall be put to great inconvenience for the want of what we have been accustomed to purchase from her. But let no one suppose she would be put to no inconvenience for what she is accustomed to receive in return from us. On the contrary she would be very much more distressed than we. We receive from her, for the most part, luxuries, and our manufacturing industry could be rapidly quickened to supply the deficiency. She on the contrary receives from us the raw material of her manufactures, without which her industry must cease, and the daily bread of millions of her people. No fleets and armies could distress England as she would be distressed by bringing the food supply of vast numbers of her people into peril. The mere loss of the United States as a market for her manufactures would annoy and distress her more than all our armaments. So far is it from being true, that our dependence on the manufactures of England would be a disadvantage to us in case of a war, that it would give us an immense advantage in the conflict. If we must have war, let it be with some nation that is dependent on us for a market for the products of her industry, and for the food of her people. He who on this ground objects to free trade with Great Britain is sadly blinded to the real interests of his country.

§ 96. If we take a true view of the nature of national independence, and of the mutual dependence which free trade implies and promotes, we shall never cease to give to the doctrines of free trade our unqualified adhesion. It is the obvious design and will of the Creator, that all the human race should be bound together by ties of mutual helpfulness, and live in perpetual harmony with each other. Nothing tends so powerfully to promote this, as perfect freedom of commercial intercourse. Nations that are bound together by ties of mutual dependence so strong as those which unite England and the United States, especially so strong as they would be if we on our side adopted free trade as heartily and thoroughly as England does on hers, cannot go to war, they must therefore do each other justice, and by so doing preserve the peace. Already in our past history our commercial relations have again and again saved us from engaging in deadly strife. It is devoutly to be wished, that all remaining barriers to perfect freedom of commercial interchange may soon be removed, and that thus the peace of these two great free nations may be secured for all the future.

Every philanthropist looks forward with longing hope to a good time coming, when men shall "beat their swords into plowshares and their spears into pruning-hooks, and learn war no more." One of the most indispensable and hopeful conditions of the realization of such an order of things, is the establishment of perfect freedom of trade among the men of all nations. The selfish national pride which scorns that universal natural dependence of man on man, that mutual helpfulness whereby the products of every soil and climate and civilization shall be exchanged for those of every other, so that all men may enjoy all the bounties of the Creator,— that selfish malignant pride and false conception of national independence, must be banished from the minds of men, and the sentiment of fraternity must succeed.

§ 97. Fifth. It is said that *free trade might be a very good thing, if other nations would agree to it; but that while the rest of the world to a great extent adheres to protection, it is necessary for us to do the same.*

If this is the view taken, it is surely incumbent on us to accept free trade in our relations to any nation that adopts a free trade policy towards ourselves. If this is conceded, then we may at least have free trade with Britain, for her policy towards us is as free as could possibly be asked. The way is then open for perfect freedom of commercial intercourse with England and all her colonies, and our government ought to lose no time in consummating a league of commercial freedom with the whole English-speaking world. The uniting of all the populations of the earth that use the English language, in such a league, would be an event of great and beneficent significancy to all mankind.

But this objection is capable of a much more comprehensive answer. The fact that the commercial policy of any nation is restrictive and exclusive, is no reason at all why we should not buy from the people of that nation anything which we can procure from them more cheaply than we can produce it ourselves, or obtain it elsewhere. The obvious rule of economy—buy where you can buy cheapest—is entitled to cut its way through all national rivalries, jealousies and antipathies. Some nation may, by partial and ruinous laws, exclude from her markets what we have to exchange with her people. Such laws may operate to produce exclusion of commercial intercourse. We may be in such circumstances that we cannot profitably buy of her people unless we can give our own products in exchange. In that case commercial intercourse must be at an end. She has thrown barriers in our way which we cannot surmount. But in such a case, it would be quite unnecessary and useless for us to retaliate, by imposing discriminating duties against the products of her industry. She has herself excluded them from our markets. If my next door neighbor has built a solid stone wall five feet thick and ten feet high, to exclude me from his premises, that wall is perfectly sufficient to prevent any intercourse between us. It would be great stupidity and folly for me to build another similar wall by the side of his, for the purpose of retaliation.

It may however be that the products which she excludes we can exchange elsewhere for something which she will admit, perhaps for gold, which no nation rejects. It may therefore still be true, that in spite of her exclusiveness, we can obtain from her certain needed commodities more cheaply than we can obtain them elsewhere. In that case the impolitic exclusiveness of her legislation is no reason at all why we should not avail ourselves of the advantage of buying of those that will sell cheapest. If therefore her people are disposed to offer in our markets commodities which we need, more cheaply than any one else will sell them, why should we, in mere retaliation for her suicidal exclusiveness, refuse to purchase? To do so is childish and unreasoning folly. If I raise cattle and my neighbor raises horses, it is very childish in me to refuse to buy of him a horse which he offers me at a bargain, because he refuses to buy my cattle when he needs them, and I offer them to him on advantageous terms. Revenge is by many considered very sweet, but it has no commercial value. It is no wiser between nations than between individuals. In either case it is unwise, mean and degrading. If we have not some better reason for retaining our policy of exclusiveness than national retaliation, it were wise to abandon it with as little delay as possible.

§ 98. *It is alleged, that protection is necessary, to encourage the acquisition of skill in manufactures.*

It is inconceivable that such a provision can be necessary, when we remember that wages are higher, as a general rule, in our country than in any country of Europe, and that our country steadily receives a vast emigration from those countries with whose manufacturing skill we have chiefly to compete. There can be no difficulty under these circumstances in attracting to this country by the offer of American wages any number of skilled laborers we may need. The notion that in a case like this it can be necessary to impose on all manufactured goods duties varying from twenty per cent to more than a hundred per cent of their value, for the encouragement of manufacturing skill, is in the last degree absurd, and indicates that he who urges it, draws much more from the resources of his imagination, than of clear practical thought.

*Protection does not encourage but discourages the acquisition of manufacturing skill.* Such skill is the child of free, sharp, practical competition. If American manufacturers are to be as skillful as those of any other nation, they are to become so, by standing face to face with the most perfect manufactures of the world, and competing with them with no shield between. If a protective duty is interposed, it will relieve our manufacturers from the necessity of equalling the best foreign products, and thereby render the acquisition of the highest skill unnecessary to their success. To encourage manufacturing skill by such protection, is like encouraging industry by relieving men from the necessity of labor for the support of themselves and their families—a method which we believe has never been found to be very successful.

## CHAPTER IX.

### *Objections to Protection Considered.*

§ 99. IN the last chapter the objections which have been urged against free trade by its leading opponents were carefully examined. In the present chapter we shall present a few considerations which seem to us quite fatal to the whole scheme of protection. *It is the aim of that system to screen certain branches of industry from the competition of like industries in other countries. The means are entirely inadequate to the end.* No police force which such a nation as ours can employ, can suffice to enforce our present revenue system, along ten thousand miles of sea coast, and three thousand miles of inland boundary. Where (as is to a great extent true under our protective system) the duty sustains a large ratio to the price at which the commodity is customarily sold, the temptation to smuggling is exceedingly strong. It might be anticipated beforehand, that in such a country as ours, it could not be prevented against so strong a motive, and experience demonstrates that it cannot. The difficulty grows largely out of the fact, that the consciences of the people are never with such restrictive laws,—not even the consciences of those who make and advocate them. There are few who would not evade and violate them when they could do so without any risk of incurring the penalty. Such laws can only be enforced by an omnipresent and ever vigilant police force—such a police force as along the whole border of our country is impossible. Consequently the branches of industry to be protected are not shielded from competition as the government has undertaken to shield them, and men who have imported goods under the law, and honestly paid the duties, are greatly injured by the competition of those who obtain foreign goods without paying any duty at all. Those well acquainted with the commercial intercourse between the United States and Canada know the truth of what we affirm.

Such a state of facts *is very injurious to public morals.* All laws which are unsustained by individual conscience are morally injurious. They tend to impair the force of law as a rule of action. There are thousands who will resort to expedients for evading our revenue laws, who would never do a thing which was in itself contrary to their sense of honor and right. To evade the law comes to be regarded as a very venial sin, or no sin at all. No government on earth can afford to forbid what no one would have regarded as wrong had it not been forbidden, and to enforce the prohibition. Such legislation on any subject weakens the hold of the government on the consciences of the people. When the great body of the people in their own individual capacity can be thoroughly convinced, that it is dishonorable to buy a foreign product in preference to a domestic one simply because it is cheaper, the protective system may be enforced without difficulty, and with perfect safety to public morals. But so long as no man sees any dishonor in preferring the foreign to the domestic commodity because of its cheapness, the enforcement of such laws will be often impossible, and always difficult and of evil moral tendency.

§ 100. *The protective system tends to construct the whole economic fabric upon a wrong principle and to give it a wrong direction.* By a code of laws which permeates and pervades all the economic machinery of society, the government treats competition as a public enemy, and provides for shielding from its influence branches of industry in which capital is invested to the amount of hundreds of millions. By this means not only are all those who engaged in the protected branches of industry taught to regard competition as their natural enemy, and to look to the government more and more to shield them from it; but other men, whose trade lies not within the charmed circle, come to regard competition as their enemy also, and become painfully conscious how inconvenient it is to them, and even though they have no prospect of legislative protection, they begin to look anxiously around for some device by which they also may escape annoyance from the common enemy. A nation whose legislation is strongly protective in its character will always be full of innumerable and endlessly varied combinations of producers, whereby they seek to fix their own prices on their products, without the necessity of being controlled by competition.

England has for ages sustained by her legislation and handed down from generation to generation the privileges which distinguish her aristocracy from the mass of her people. Her laws have divided society into two ranks only. But custom has taken the idea from the law, and constructed many other grades as distinct as the one which her laws originated. For many centuries everything in that country has been graded. By a very analogous process, all American trade is at present seeking to secure for itself the privileges enjoyed by the protected industries, and presents the aspect of a general struggle so to constitute all its arrangements as to escape the natural and healthful influence of competition. This is at present among the chief obstacles to the growth of our manufactures, and the expansion of our industry into all that rich variety which our soil and climate admit.

§ 101. *Protection corrupts our national legislation.* Does any one believe that our present tariff of duties is the result of calm enlightened statesmanship, applied with judicial impartiality to all the interests affected by it? Is it the result of any statesmanship at all? He who thinks so, is the victim of a good natured credulity, which is more worthy of the prattling innocency of childhood, than of the sober good sense of mature manhood. It is just such a set of laws as no man living would make, if it were submitted to his judgment to decide what laws are desirable and wise. It is a clumsy patchwork, which has resulted from a compromise between the conflicting demands and confused clamors of all the great branches of our industry that encounter any foreign competition, besieging and begging Congress for more protection — more protection. The question with our legislators is, not whose claims are really strongest and most righteous, but whose clamors are loudest, who can bring most votes to support our party, or if disobliged alienate most votes from it. The bearing of the tariff on the next election has had a great deal more influence than its bearing on the prosperity of our people. That with resources such as ours, and a national debt of more than $2,000,000,000 to provide for, our revenue system should be constructed and controlled by such influences as these, is a humiliation of our country in the eyes of the nations. It is disgraceful to our civilization. To this humiliation however must we submit, till we throw off this nightmare of protection. It must also be added to all this, that in this combination of evil influences, direct bribery of the legislator to procure his vote in favor of the further protection of some particular industry, is we fear no uncommon element.

§ 102. *The protective system is in its own proper nature unsocial.* It tends to reduce the intercourse of nations to a minimum, and proportionally to weaken all the ties of brotherhood which naturally bind the human family together. Such a tendency in such a country as ours is full of danger. Our safety requires that all the forces which tend to national unity be strengthened, and that all divisive forces be as far as possible eliminated. Protection is a divisive force. With the exception of slavery, nothing has ever exposed our national unity to so much peril as the attempt to carry into effect the protective system. Any one who will candidly consider the subject will, we think, acknowledge that our efforts at protective legislation, strangely persisted in, had great influence in producing those violent antipathies which were ultimately developed into the great rebellion.

*Nor are we safe for the future.* If the doctrines of protection are to be accepted as true, there are no two portions of the earth between which there are stronger inducements to apply them, than the New England and Middle States on the one hand, and the great States of the Upper Mississippi Valley on the other. The manufactures of the Northwest are powerfully repressed by the competition of those of the New England and Middle States, and the agriculture of the latter has been greatly depressed, in large districts annihilated, by the competition of that of the Northwest. If protection is the true and proper remedy for such difficulties, then should the Alleghanies be a dividing line of nations. If men become generally convinced that the doctrines of protection are true, and would relieve New England agriculture from its great depression, and speedily give to the Mississippi Valley "variety of industry," the Alleghanies will become a boundary of nations, and no man can predict into how many rival nationalities the territory of the present American Union may ere long be divided.

§ 103. *The protective system as it exists in our country is self-contradictory and self-destructive.* No one will deny that it is possible, that a single branch of industry might be encouraged and stimulated into more rapid growth by the monopoly of protection. Let us suppose that up to a certain time free trade had prevailed, when persons interested in establishing some new industry had found foreign competition inconvenient, and applied to the government for a protective duty. The government grants the request and the revenue law is modified accordingly. The petitioners go away for the present satisfied. Let us suppose that these petitioners were manufacturers of woolen cloth. The woolgrowers are not slow to discover that on the one hand they are obliged to pay more for woolen cloths, while on the other hand they are severely pressed by the competition of foreign grown wool. They apply for protection, and it cannot be refused. This takes away a part of the value of the privilege conceded to the manufacturers of wool, and they are discontented.

The principle of protection is now established, and every industry which encounters any foreign competition will demand and cannot be denied a share in it. The iron men of every grade must be protected, and every dime of protection which is granted to them increases the price of machinery for the manufacture of woolens, and thus damages the woolen interest. The cotton men too must be heard. They have to pay higher wages to their laborers because the cost of living has been increased. Workmen in this climate must have woolen cloth. The cost of machinery is increased and therefore it costs more to manufacture cotton goods. They too must be protected. Soon the woolen interest has lost more by monopolies granted to other industries than it gained by the one originally granted to itself, and it besieges the government more clamorously than ever for more protection, and with a much more powerful argument. It now wants to be protected, not so much against foreign competition, as against the monopolies granted to other industries. These one and all are soon again thronging the lobbies of Congress, demanding more protection. The privilege granted to one industry is destructive of that granted to every other, and no man can tell to-day, whether his particular industry is on the whole benefited or injured by the protection which actually exists, or whether if the whole were at once swept away, his interest would not be actually relieved of an oppressive burden. But all still worship with unfaltering faith at the shrine of exclusiveness, and clamor for more protection, as the panacea for all their ills. The coal interest must have protection, however much that may injure the iron interest, and the iron interest must have protection, however that may affect the woolen and the cotton interests. If protectionists could demonstrate some great law of nature, by which it might be determined with accuracy when and to what amount protection should be granted, the whole thing might be reduced to order and law and reason. But till that can be done, (and it never can be done), it will present a scene of wild confusion, self-contradiction and self-destruction.

It is impossible to escape this conclusion, except by denying *that protection does raise the price of protected products.* Upon such a denial protectionists do often venture. It is a sufficient proof that such denial is futile and absurd, that if the protecting duty does not raise the price of the protected commodities, it can in no manner protect against foreign competition. It can have this effect only by enabling the home producer to demand a higher price for his commodities than he could command in face of the free competition of foreign products. This is the only beneficial influence which it can exert on the home producer. But we are able to produce on this point the sterner evidence of facts. We are furnished the following figures on the authority of a merchant of the highest intelligence, the foreman in the carpet room in one of the largest commercial houses in the city of New York. The following are the items of the cost of a five-frame Brussels carpet per yard, in gold, of English manufacture, in the city of New York, viz.

| | |
|---|---|
| Cost in England | 89 cents. |
| Duty | 64 " |
| Exchange, freight, etc. | 22 " |
| Total cost in New York | $1,75 |

A carpet of American manufacture of the same quality is sold by the New York dealer at the same price with this English made carpet. Does then the protectionist expect us to believe that the American dealer could sell his English carpet at the same price as now, if he were relieved from the necessity of paying that duty of sixty-four cents per yard? Or that the American manufacturer could obtain the same price for his goods as now, if English carpets could be introduced into the market free of duty, or by paying only a revenue duty of ten or fifteen per cent on the cost in England? It requires some courage to assert in view of such figures that a protective duty does not enhance price. It would be easy to procure similar figures in respect to many other products which are highly protected. How long our present protective system is to be adhered to against such facts as these we are quite unable to predict.

§ 104. One point more demands our attention before we dismiss this subject. Mr. Fawcett, after having very clearly demonstrated free trade as the natural law of exchange between men of different nationalities, looks around for some consideration by which to commend charity in our judgment of those who so stoutly resist its introduction into the legislation of the nations. In this line of thought he comes to the conclusion, that though free trade is certainly for the greatest good of the whole, yet there are certain classes that are benefited by an exclusive system. We can not accept this conclusion. It may indeed be true that when the exclusive system has been long established, and trade has adjusted itself to it, there may be classes who would suffer by a return to the natural and healthful system of free trade. It is seldom possible to right a great wrong without hurting somebody. When the wrong was introduced many were most seriously and unnecessarily injured. During its existence, it is quite probable that persons may have so identified themselves with it, that their interests will suffer when it is removed. It is generally much better that such persons should suffer, than that a great wrong should not be righted. *But we deny that any class can be permanently injured by substituting free trade for the monopoly of protection.* It would at first view seem, that the repeal of the English Corn Laws must have reduced the price of agricultural products, and therefore been injurious to land-owners. And it is true that free trade has kept the price of wheat from rising while the population of the country has been immensely increased. But though the price of wheat has not advanced with that increase of population, rents have advanced. A smaller portion of the bread of the English people is grown on their own soil, but a much greater breadth of land is demanded for other products which cannot be brought from a distance, and which pay a higher rent than wheat can afford. The agricultural interest of England has not been injured by the repeal of the Corn Laws. Consequent upon that great measure of British statesmanship, England has experienced an addition of one-fifth to her population, a vast enlargement in every department of her trade, and a vast accession to her wealth unprecedented in any other portion of her history. In that increased prosperity her agriculture has shared. Facts prove that the selfish exclusiveness by which she sought to foster her agriculture was as unwise and suicidal as it was selfish and exclusive. Such must be the effect of free trade in every case. Every one's true interest lies, not in compelling his neighbor to receive from him what he could buy elsewhere more cheaply, but in producing that for the production of which he possesses greater advantages than any other producer. The highest prosperity of a nation and of every body in it, of the world and all that dwell therein, requires that every man should be diligently seeking to produce more cheaply than any one else can, something which is desired by the greatest possible number of consumers. In this direction free trade turns universal effort. Protection turns the effort of every man into the direction of compelling as many as possible to purchase his products whether for their interests or not. The former tends to universal honest thrift, the latter to equally universal dishonest sham. No fair-minded man, after carefully examining this subject in all its bearings will doubt, that the abandonment, speedy and entire, of that system of legislation called protection, and the adoption of free trade in all our relations with the rest of the world, would procure for our country as great an increase of prosperity in every department of our industry, as England has experienced as the result of adopting a similar policy.

# PART III.

## DISTRIBUTION.

### CHAPTER I.

*Preliminary Principles.*

§ 106. THERE seems at first thought to be room for a doubt, whether the two parts of our science which we have distinguished as Exchange and Distribution are really separated from each other by any clearly definable boundary. The one law of competition is alike universal and equally controlling in them both. It will be shown as we proceed that we can no more escape from it in dealing with the questions which Distribution presents, than with the questions of simple Exchange. A little reflection will however convince us, that they are separated by a distinct natural boundary, which ought not to be lost sight of. In treating of Exchange, we have been considering the nature of value, the laws which regulate the exchange of one commodity for another, and the instrument by which exchanges are facilitated. The discussion of these subjects is complete in itself, and may be pursued to exhaustion, without involving any of the applications of the law of competition which remain yet to be considered. The question for how much a given commodity will be exchanged in the market may be decided without involving any consideration of the methods by which its equivalent when received is to be divided among all the interests which were concerned in producing it. The former of these questions belongs to Exchange, the latter to Distribution. There are very few commodities which are the exclusive product of a single laborer. Even if some products seem at first thought to be so, a little consideration will generally show us that they are not. The laborer who seems to be alone concerned in it used tools, and those tools were produced by labor previously exerted. He was fed and clothed while he was engaged in the work. That also implied preëxerted labor. The material on which he wrought had value when it came to his hand. When we purchase the product from the laborer who made it ready for our use, we must compensate him, not only for his immediate labor bestowed upon it, but for all this preexerted labor. Nor is even this all. He has paid and we must repay him for the rent of the land on which grew his food and the material of his clothing consumed while employed in that labor, and for the use of the capital and for the oversight and labor concerned in its production. We cannot buy a pin or a button into the production of which all these things and many more have not entered. It may be that so small an article as a pin may have laid under contribution not only many trades and industries, but the remote continents and islands of the earth. All must be adjusted, each must have its share. To determine on what principles and by what laws this division is accomplished is the aim of this part of our science.

DEFINITION. *Distribution is that part of Economics which explains the laws which prevail in assigning to each of the parties concerned in production their respective shares in the result.*

Great confusion and error in dealing with this class of subjects are constantly occasioned by not bearing in mind, that *the questions with which we have to do are not ethical, but purely economic.* The laws which determine the several results are not moral, but natural laws, as far removed from the control of human wills as cohesion or electricity. The question is not how ought the proceeds of production to be shared? but what are the natural laws which do and will determine the share of each? just as in physical astronomy we inquire, not how the planets ought to move but how they do move in obedience to an irresistible force impressed upon them. Economic questions are precisely analogous. We never can deal successfully with them unless we bear this in mind. The condition of the public mind on this class of questions is to a great extent morbid, and demands a remedial treatment. We shall confer incalculable benefits on society, if we can succeed in convincing men, that natural laws control this class of questions, and not the caprices of human pride, selfishness and tyranny.

§ 107. The principles already laid down are so preeminently important in this division of the subject, that we deem a little recapitulation desirable if not absolutely necessary. *In no part of our science is the law of competition more prevalent and more potent.* It is our business to show how that law would divide, and when uncounteracted does divide the products of labor; and to point out those artificial devices by which this law is evaded, and temporarily, sometimes even for long periods, rendered inoperative. We have shown how this is accomplished in relation to exchanges, and pointed out the disaterous consequences which result from it. If like violations of fundamental law exist also in this branch of our subject, it is equally our province to point them out, and indicate the remedy. Such attempts whenever made can result in nothing but confusion and disaster.

Let it also be borne in mind, that in our view *all living human beings are to be regarded as laborers.* All attempts to divide human beings into two classes—laborers and not laborers—must fail and result in confusion of thought. The capitalist is a laborer, not less than he that plows the field, or works a steam engine. The artist, the poet, the student, the mother, are all laborers. Infants in their cradles are laborers in prospect, and must be reared to take the place of others that are soon to pass away. The old and the decrepid are laborers that have done their work, and their support is a necessary charge on the world's industry.

In the same manner all the accumulated results of labor are useful only to assist and sustain the labor that is now living. The attempt to divide wealth into that which is used to aid and sustain labor, and that which is used to gratify desire, can result in nothing but confusion. *What is it to support labor?* Is it to give to a human being, considered as a mere working machine, just so much food and clothing and shelter as are absolutely necessary to keep the structure of bones and sinews and muscles in working order? Does it not mean more than that? To give him the means of living a social, an esthetic, a moral, a religious, a human life? The life of a civilized, developed man? Are not then all products which are employed in enabling human beings thus to live, the true and proper sustentation of labor? If not how are we ever to draw the line between what is and what is not used for the support of labor? How are we ever to determine what portion of the expenditure of a man or of a community is applied to the support of productive labor, and what portion of it is to be set down to the gratification of desire? Is it not the simple truth that the gratification of desire is the one only object of all labor, and that it is therefore in the nature of the case, the only possible reward of labor? No man ever did or ever can draw a definite line between that which is employed to gratify desire, and that which is the reward of labor. The distinction is not definite and therefore not scientific.

Let us *illustrate this* by an example. Let us suppose that a man of great wealth sets aside one million dollars to build and decorate a palatial residence. This fund is no less employed in paying wages and furnishing helps to labor than before. The stone quarriers and stone hewers, the masons, the carpenters, the house decorators, the artists in painting and statuary will feel the stimulus of every dime of this capital just as before. Even after his palace is completed, he may rent it, and then it will be a part of his capital, as truly as though he had spent it in building a mill. Or he may use it for his own residence, and then its annual income will be a part of the wages of his own labor. Even that which he expends in clothing and decorating his person and the persons of his wife and children must equally be employed in supporting labor, as truly as in the case of any other outlay. It is true that when it has been expended it will be capital no longer, but the same is true of the wages he has paid to the humblest laborer. It is true therefore that what this man expends for the gratification of desire is as truly employed in sustaining and helping labor, as any other portion of his wealth. He may even be an epicure and a gourmand, but his cook is as truly a laborer as his carpenter, and his cook-stove is as truly fixed capital as any of his steam engines.

§ 108. This general account of the various interests to be provided for in Distribution seems at first view so complicated as to be incapable of being reduced to any

general system.  This however is merely in appearance.
We must here recur to our general classification.  *All
wealth is composed of two elements only*, Labor and Capital.  These only are concerned in all Production.  Our problem is therefore reduced to this simple form—to show how the products of production are divided between the Labor and Capital concerned in any process.  A twofold division of the subject is therefore clearly indicated, viz.

*I. The share which falls to the laborer.*
*II. The share which falls to the capitalist.*

We are aware that something must yet be said in justification of this classification, but we prefer to consider that subject in connection with land and rent, and therefore postpone the matter for the present.

---

## CHAPTER II.

### *Wages Determined by Competition.*

§ 109. DEFINITION. *That share of the result of any productive process which falls to the laborer is called wages.*

The aspect under which this subject presents itself in those nations that have attained to the most advanced civilization is not the most favorable to an understanding of it, in its elementary principles.  In the first rude beginnings of society, every man is a laborer without capital.  He must provide what is necessary to the support of life, while he invents and fabricates his first simple tool.  When he has made that tool, he is its owner. He has become both a laborer and a capitalist.  If he exchanges his products, he will demand compensation both for his labor and his capital, in the price he will demand for his commodities, and so far as he can under the law of competition, he will obtain both wages and profit. He cannot arbitrarily and by his own will determine either the one or the other. Even in these rude beginnings of the economic system, competition will assert its stern supremacy as a law of nature. As soon as the results of his labor, assisted by such tools as he can invent and fabricate, are more than sufficient to furnish necessaries, he can decide by his own will how much he will expend in the gratification of other desires than that of gain, and how much he will invest in improved tools to render his labor more productive. He is *both a laborer and capitalist,* and he can judge for himself what wages he will demand for that labor which he expends in the management of his capital.

*The greater the extent to which this condition of things can be perpetuated in the most advanced stages of civilization, the better* it is for the individual and for society. It is always true that the laborer who works with his own tools and upon his own capital, will for that reason be more industrious, more skillful and more frugal. The products resulting from such a natural combination of labor and capital will be more abundant and more excellent, because the laborer is constantly stimulated by the consideration, that all which he produces is his own, to be disposed of according to his own will. The best economic system for every country and for the world is that in which, to the utmost possible extent, labor and capital are united in the same person. All political and social systems which tend to collect capital into few hands, and to reduce the many to the condition of laborers without capital, are impediments to the increase of the wealth and happiness of mankind.

§ 110. It is however inevitable that, to a greater or

less extent in the progress of society, the laborer will be destitute of capital, and the capitalist will find the necessity of employing more labor than his own hands can perform, in order to put all his capital to use. *Hence the relation of employer and employed becomes inevitable.* As soon as this relation originates, the question of wages necessarily arises, and we are forced to discover and apply the natural laws on which its adjustment depends. This question has been growing in importance and in difficulty for generations. At present it is very obvious, that capitalists who employ laborers and laborers who work with other men's capital are engaged in a conflict with each other of which it is difficult to foresee the end. Violent passions and bitter antipathies have sprung up in the progress of this conflict, which unless the strife is terminated by a satisfactory adjustment, threaten anarchy and revolution. Only one mode of adjustment is in the nature of the case possible. The natural laws which prevail in this department must be ascertained and expounded to the satisfaction of both parties. Such an understanding of these laws does not at the present time exist in either of the parties. If there is a science of wages, this is the time when it ought to be expounded.

*It is wrong to speak of this conflict, as we are accustomed to do, as a conflict between capital and labor.* In this country at least it is still true, that a very large portion of the labor is performed by men who own capital, and in all countries capitalists are laborers. The conflict is not between labor and capital, but *between laborers who have no capital, and capitalists who have need of other labor than their own,* to utilize their capital. To avoid therefore any confusion of thought which might find its way into our discussion of this part of the subject, we shall use the word employer for the capitalist who hires laborers, and the word employé for the laborer who is hired to work upon capital which belongs to another. This will locate the conflict precisely where it is, between employers and employés.

On the side of the employé it is assumed, that his wages are determined by the arbitrary, selfish and tyrannical will of his employer, and that this is the reason why his portion is so scanty and inadequate to the comfortable support of himself and his family. He is apt also to forget that the foundation of that fortune out of which comes the capital that furnishes him the employment he has, was very probably laid in frugal self-denial quite as severe as that which he is obliged to practice. In such circumstances it is quite impossible that the two should meet each other on terms of friendship and confidence. The needle-woman for example, wearing away her life "stitch by stitch," in her miserable garret, believes that she is the victim of her employer's grasping greed of gain, that the starvation allowance which she receives is dealt out to her by his arbitrary and tyrannical will. Nor is she alone in this opinion. Thousands who in a most commendable spirit of philanthropy compassionate her sorrowful lot, unite with her in this severe condemnation of the greed of her employer. Our literature is full of such denunciation. The inquiry is therefore one of great urgency,—Is there a law of wages? If so, what is it? And what are the causes of the terrible suffering we often meet in the case of persons who are compelled to live on the wages of their labor? These are grave questions, and if our science can answer them, the world will acknowledge it as a benefactor.

§ III. *Wages are not controlled by the arbitrary will of the employer.* The facts are not consistent with this supposition. It is true that some classes of laborers are in a condition as miserable as they could be, if it were in the power of the most selfish of employers to dole out just such compensation as they pleased. But these cases of extreme suffering are exceptional, not normal. It will be shown also in the progress of this discussion that these exceptional cases are due to a violation of the natural laws which belong to the case, that there is a law of wages which, had it been allowed to have free course, would have prevented the mischief. There is abundant proof in the history of humanity, that if the arbitrary will of the employers could dictate wages, all employés would be in a condition the most abject. This is by no means the fact. It is true indeed that the agricultural laborers of England are in a very distressed condition, but those of many other countries are in a condition of comfort and thrift. The condition of agricultural laborers in this country is so easy and advantageous, that many of them become rich land owners and capitalists. The condition of employés generally, though in many cases not satisfactory, is by no means consistent with the supposition that wages are determined by the arbitrary will of employers.

§ 112. *There is positive proof that wages are determined, even in such extreme cases as that of the needle-women alluded to above, by the law of competition, and that neither employers nor employed can escape from that law.*

Let us still further examine that case. There is a feeling rather than a conviction in many minds *that the law of competition is stern, harsh and cruel, and ought not to be applied to such a case as this.* If they should say what they think, they would address the employers of such women in some such language as the following. What if the market price has fallen to the starvation rates which you are paying these women? You ought to be ashamed to accept their services on such terms. What if this is all their work will bring in the market? Why not do them simple justice by paying what their work is really worth irrespective of competition? This is very plausible, and seems to a great number of people entirely conclusive. Let us apply it to the case.

How then shall we ascertain what is the real value of their work? This is a question from which we cannot escape. No man can do justice till he knows what it is. Discarding competition therefore as inapplicable to the case, how shall we find the real value of any work? Let us suppose that a report of the distresses of the needle-women in and around some great city has reached the ears of their employers, and deeply moved their compassionate feelings. A meeting of employers in that trade is immediately called, to consider what can be done for the relief of all this suffering. They are honorable men and wish to do justly and mercifully. They are quite convinced that the wages of these poor women are not sufficient to sustain life, and they have no heart to starve helpless women for gain. They agree at once, that as competition has brought down wages to this ruinous point, they will not apply it to the case any more, but pay the women what their work is worth irrespective of the market price. All unite in applauding this resolution. Justice, philanthropy, can ask no more.

How then shall these noble men *ascertain what the work is really worth? But one method is possible in the very nature of the case.* It must be ascertained how much time will be occupied in making any garment, say a shirt. That question being settled, it must next be ascertained what it would cost a woman to live in comfort during that time, and lay aside a little for days when she will be unable to work. How much must she pay for food, clothing, fuel, rent, and all other necessaries and such comforts as contribute to length of life and efficiency as a laborer? Every one says this is right. How then is the question to be answered? By the price current of course. We have no other means of answering it, and every one knows that the price current is purely a product of competition. Thus while intending to emancipate themselves from the demon of competition, these men find that they are still in his grasp, and cannot proceed a step towards the accomplishment of their humane intention, except by following his lead. The attempt to escape from the law of competition in the economic world, is just as hopeless as the attempt to escape from gravitation in the material world. Its control is absolute, universal and unrelenting over every economic question.

§ 113. But it may be said, that though these employers cannot escape from competition, they can emancipate the poor needle-women from it, and fix their compensation without reference to it.

This attempt will succeed no better than the other. These employers are honest, earnest men, determined to do justice, and follow up the inquiry till they reach the result, that in order that seamstresses may live by their work, the prices paid must be doubled. A new price-list is therefore made out on that basis, and made public. A joyful announcement is that to the starving needle-women. But no sooner is this great rise in the prices made known, than the number of applicants for work in that line is increased in a far greater ratio than the advance in the price of the work. There are probably three or four—it would not be strange if there were ten women who would be glad to make shirts at a dollar apiece to every one that would make them at fifty cents apiece. These starving women have not escaped the crushing effect of competition, the direction from which it comes only is changed, it is more destructive than ever. Before it was a ruinous competition in price. Now it is a still more ruinous competition for any work at all.

Yesterday one was ruined by work at starvation prices. To-day she has no work at all, being quite driven from the market by the application of a crowd of well-to-do women, whose condition is not necessitous, and who would not think of working at such prices as had been fixed by competition.

*The evil is still further augmented by a new competition which is sure to spring up in another quarter.* The additional cost of manufacturing must be added to the price at which the garment is offered to the customer. This must diminish the demand for the goods. Many women who have been accustomed to buy ready-made clothing for their families will now find the difference between the cost of the material and the cost of the ready-made garment to be so great, that they will make it themselves. The employers will therefore sell fewer garments, and have much less work for the needle-women to do. The employers, instead of benefiting their suffering employés by their well meant effort to protect them from competition, have rendered their condition much worse than before. They have tried to relieve them from the crushing effect of competition on price. They have raised up an army of new and powerful competitors for the work, and greatly diminished the amount of work to be done.

Two inferences from this case are inevitable. First, *That employers cannot benefit employés by arbitrarily raising wages above the point at which competition would fix them.* Second, *That every such effort arbitrarily to raise wages must inflict serious injury on all those who are dependent on the occupation in question for a living.* Of this it would be easy to furnish innumerable illustrations. The one we have given above must suffice. It will be asked then —can nothing be done for such crushed and suffering employés as these distressed needle-women? We answer, their employers as employers, can do nothing for them.

Arbitrarily raising their wages will injure, not benefit them. Their employers have the same opportunity that all other persons have of relieving their sufferings by a generous Christian charity. There are other aspects however of this and like cases, which, though of great interest, are not relevant to our present point of inquiry. They will be considered in another place.

§ 114. *Wages are not therefore determined by the arbitrary will of employers.* The notion that they are so is a mischievous delusion. In a fair case, where competition has had free course, employers cannot raise them above the point determined by competition. Every attempt to do so will prove equally disastrous to employés and employers. The sooner both parties know that they are bound by a law of nature from which they are alike powerless to escape, the wiser and happier they will be, and the more agreeable and comfortable their relations to each other.

It should also be borne in mind, that the competition which determines wages (the amount of capital being given, and on that supposition we have proceeded in all this chapter) *is the competition of labor with labor, and not of labor with capital.* It not only is not the arbitrary will of the employer that determines wages, but, so far as there is any will in the case, it is the will of the employé. Wages settle at a certain minimum point because, in the conflict of competition employés select that point as their minimum. Circumstances are found to be such that those most anxious for employment prefer to make their stand at that point and risk being unemployed rather than bid lower on the one hand, and on the other they judge it to be better to accept what is offered than to incur the risk of failing of employment if they stand out for more. This is the only will power that is concerned in fixing the minimum of wages. The employer has a precisely similar will power in determining the maximum. As there is a point at which those most desirous of employment, will bid no lower, so there is a point at which those most anxious to obtain laborers will bid no higher. Between these extremes each party uses his own judgment as to what his interests require, and when an employer finds one who will consent to work for such wages as in the circumstances he judges it best to offer, a contract will be made. In no case can one will determine the question. A contract is always the coincidence of two wills. Competition is the force by which the coincidence of two opposing wills is brought about.

Precisely here we must meet *the question of combination to resist competition.* Why may not employés combine their wills into the will of one social personality, and by refusing to work except at such wages as that combined will prescribes, fix their own rate of compensation as high as they please? On the other hand why may not employers combine and determine wages at as low a point as they please? It is true beyond a question that if the capitalist has more capital than he can use with his own hands, the surplus will be quite useless unless he can employ laborers. On the other hand it is equally obvious that laborers without capital must be employed by some one who has capital. Why then may not either party by combination determine wages by a social will? This brings us face to face with one of the gravest questions of modern civilization. Our next chapter will be devoted to the consideration of it.

## CHAPTER III.

### *Wages as Affected by Combination.*

**§ 115.** *Two classes of combinations require our attention*—combinations of those desirous of obtaining employment entered into for the purpose of raising wages—and combinations of employers to reduce wages.

Before entering however upon the examination of particular combinations, it is proper to remark, *that there are general considerations which reveal plainly enough the impracticability of all attempts to control wages in this manner.* The interests of the several persons or parties that enter into such a combination never can be the same. It may be better for one laborer to accept one rate of wages rather than run the risk of failing to get employment. That rate may be to many others quite ruinous. If combination fixes on the higher rate, the man whose interests require him to accept the lower rate will feel that the combination works to his injury, and wish to escape from it. Others will be conscious that without the combination they could obtain higher wages than the combination demands. They will therefore be reluctant to enter into the combination, and impatient at being bound by it. The same difficulties will stand in the way of combinations among employers. This is the reason why such combinations are seldom of long continuance. They have within themselves natural antagonisms, which constantly tend to disruption. Individuals not artificial combinations are the natural units of the economic system. Individuality will assert itself.

The statement of the case made at the conclusion of the last chapter shows clearly enough the impracticability of all such attempts. If on the one hand employés can by combination and refusing to work except on their own terms, compel employers to accede to those terms, to save their capital from being useless, on the other hand it is equally in the power of capitalists by combination among themselves to compel their employés to accede to their terms, or submit to starvation. Combination on one side is very likely to provoke it on the other, and nothing can be expected from it but a dead lock, which will render capital and labor equally useless. Such a dead lock is too serious in its consequences to continue long, and will be likely to end in a willingness of both parties to submit the case to the natural working of competition.

§ 116. Combinations of labor against competition assume the form either of strikes or trades-unions.

*A strike is an agreement entered into by employés, to demand certain prescribed terms, and to cease work until those terms are acceded to by their employers.*

It is admitted that under certain conditions such an agreement may temporarily succeed in obtaining the wages demanded. If the occupation in which the strike occurs is one in which a degree of skill is requisite, such as can only be acquired by some instruction and practice, and if the combination can be made to embrace all the persons possessing that skill, that are within the reach of the employers, it is evident that the demands of the combination must be acceded to or work will cease. If the wages demanded are so high as to leave employers no prospect of any profit in continuing the work, it will stop, till either the employés recede from their demands, or other laborers can either acquire the skill, or be imported from abroad. In one or the other of these ways, the dead lock will in time be brought to an end, and the employés will fail of their object, after having inflicted much loss on their employers and brought on themselves a great deal of suffering.

*If the wages demanded are not so high as to leave employers no margin of profit,* if it would still be better for them to accede to the demand than to stop work, they will be likely, for the time being, to do so. But it will hereafter be shown, that every mode of employing capital has its natural rate of profit, and that capital cannot be retained in any mode of investment, where that rate of profit cannot be realized. If therefore the wages demanded in the case supposed are such as to reduce the rate of profit on capital employed in that industry below this natural standard, capital will be withdrawn from it and otherwise invested, the trade will languish, fewer laborers will be employed or demanded, and those already employed in it will be compelled either to withdraw from it or recede from their demands. Thus wages will decline to the natural standard as determined by competition, and the strike will be ineffectual. It will be proved that a law of nature is too strong for human will-power, though strengthened by combination.

There may be still another case. It may be that when the strike took place *wages had been reduced by a combination of employers to a rate which was really below the point which would have been fixed by free competition.* In this case the employers will not be able to obtain workmen to take the place of the strikers, either by importing them from abroad or by training new ones. If therefore the employés are able to hold out for a time, their employers will accede to their demands, if they are not above the rates which would have been determined by competition. If their demands are above that rate, they will not be acceded to, except temporarily, till an adjustment can be made by capital withdrawing from the trade, and thus diminishing the demand for labor in it.

In none of these cases therefore can a combination of employés succeed, except in the single one in which it coöperates with competition instead of resisting it. The result of this whole discussion shows therefore conclusively, that employés are quite powerless to protect themselves against the results of free competition by any combination among themselves.

§ 117. *Trades unions are combinations of laborers of another form* and aiming at other objects besides the protection of their members against competition. So far as they are fraternal associations of artisans of the same trade, for the purpose of promoting friendly relations of sympathy and helpfulness, they lie entirely outside of the sphere of our science, and we have nothing to say of them here. They are however permanent organizations with established rules and regulations, and often propose not only to regulate the wages of their members, *but to dictate to employers the methods in which their affairs must be conducted in many other particulars.* Especially they often attempt to confine the trade to a limited number of artisans, by refusing to work for any employer who receives more than a prescribed number of apprentices in proportion to the number of journeymen in his employ. Such organizations are ramified over whole nations, and it is said that some of them are not even confined by national lines. It is obvious that if such an organization can succeed in attracting to itself and bringing under the control of its regulations all who have the skill of the trade, and preventing the accession of new members except in such limited numbers as its rules prescribe, certain very important results must follow, which all good citizens would do well to consider.

If a trades-union has the direct control of all artisans who are qualified to exercise their trade in a given country, the trade cannot be carried on except in accordance with its regulations. Employers in that trade must pay the prescribed rate of wages, or obtain no workmen. If after paying such wages as the union prescribes, the trade is not remunerative, owners must reimburse themselves by exacting higher prices from the public for their products. These products the community must have, and must therefore pay the price demanded by the only men who have the skill to produce them. This is of course the assumption of an unlimited power of taxation of all other trades, and of the whole community. By limiting the number that can be instructed in the skill of the trade, they exclude many young men who desire to enter it, from sharing its profits, and compel them unnaturally to swell the stream of competition in other trades and occupations. In short they establish their trade as a perpetual monopoly.

§ 118. Let us now inquire *how such a scheme is likely to fare in the economic system of this modern world.* It is evident that if one trade may build itself up into such a monopoly, so may any other. If the principle is admissible and practicable in one case, why not in another? Soon every trade may be a monopoly. Each may be a permanent society making its own regulations, prescribing its own wages, and limiting its own numbers as narrowly as it pleases, each virtually dictating the price at which its commodities shall be sold, each thus exacting from every other, and each exacted upon by every other, and each losing vastly more by the exactions of all the rest, than it can possibly gain by its own. In such an order of things society would entirely lose its fraternal character, and be composed of many rival fraternities, each hostile to every other. This results from the very nature of a monopoly, whether created by legislative enactment or by voluntary association. Nothing is adjusted by natural competition, every thing by hostile exaction. Meanwhile a large portion of the community are incapable from the nature of their occupations of organizing any monopoly at all, and are exposed to the exactions of all, without any possibility of self-defense or retaliation.

We have seen the tendency of "Protection" to organize every protected branch of industry into such a monopoly hostile to every other and to society at large. The only difference between that case and this is, that is a monopoly created and sustained by legislation; this is an attempt to establish a monopoly without the aid of government. In principle and aim the two cases are exactly alike. Their common object is to protect their industry from the beneficent natural law of competition. It is, we think, obvious enough, that if such a system of ideas can be carried out in practice, either in the one case or the other, the civilized nations of modern christendom are threatened with very serious disaster. Can the attempt succeed?

§ 119. *The ultimate and general success of such schemes in an age of freedom and intelligence is impossible.* Such ideas have prevailed and been put in practice in the past ages of European civilization, to an extent of which the men of the present time have very little conception. Till a comparatively recent period, even in England, every trade was a monopoly sanctioned and encouraged by the government. But the time of such legislation has gone by forever, or at least till the Dark Ages return upon the world again.

In the present conditions of society, it is *impossible for such an association to attract to itself all the workmen who possess the skill of the trade.* Many will have the good sense to prefer the chances of success under freedom and natural competition. This is true as a matter of fact. Such workmen will be favored and encouraged by employers, and find their own advantage in their independent position. The trades-unions will not therefore be able to obtain the monopoly of the trades. They will equally fail in their efforts to limit the number who can acquire the skill of the respective trades. Artisans who are not attached to any union will freely instruct young men wishing to acquire the skill of any trade, and their numbers will be indefinitely multiplied. For the same reasons which were given in connection with the strikes, they will not be able to resist competition in determining the wages of their own labor. They can permanently succeed under the same conditions and only under the same conditions as strikes, that is when there is an abnormal condition of things in which wages are lower than the rate at which competition will fix them, so that competition itself will co-operate with their efforts to raise the rate.

§ 120. *There is another insuperable obstacle to the success of any combination to raise wages above the standard of competition.* Grant that by such combinations they may take the question of wages into their own hands, and appropriate to themselves just so much of the gains of production as they choose, the consequence will be, that capital will cease to be accumulated, because it will cease to be of any benefit to its owner. If capitalists discover that nothing can be gained by accumulating, that laborers really own all that is accumulated, they will not save for the barren purpose of calling it their own. Laborers will soon discover that they have killed the hen that laid the golden eggs, that by refusing to capital its proper share of the gains of production, they have annihilated that by which their labor was supported and assisted. Our country is at the present moment abounding in sorrowful proofs of the truth of this assertion. A very few years ago, at a time when wages were higher than at any former periods of our history, the daily papers were filled with reports of the strikes of employés in almost all the leading branches of trade, clamorously demanding more wages and often with additional details of violence offered to laborers who still chose to work, and of the reckless destruction of the property of their employers. At this time our doors are almost besieged by tramps, telling the pitiful story of being out of employment, and begging for a piece of bread to save them from imminent starvation. Who has told us or can tell us how much of the present destitution is due to the fact, that by the strikes of those years of extravagance, employers were induced, by the pressure of present seeming necessity, to pay wages which they could not afford, and as a consequence have now no capital with which to pay any wages or employ any laborers? As from day to day we are feeding these poor wretches, we are much reminded of those years of the arrogant extravagance of laborers. One extreme follows another. Laborers about to engage in a strike should think of the fable of the hen that laid golden eggs.

§ 121. *It remains to inquire whether employers can, by combination, reduce wages below the standard of competition.* This part of the subject may be disposed of in very few words. It is never more than a very small portion of the capital of the world or even of a single country that can be brought into any such combination. Let us take as an illustration the great coal monopolies of Pennsylvania. Those great companies can and do combine for certain purposes which are injurious enough to the general welfare. But they have little prospect of success in any effort they may make to reduce wages below the market rate. The demand for labor in the United States is so great, that that portion of it which is represented by these companies is, in comparison with the whole, quite insignificant. The coal fields of the whole country are so extensive, that those of Pennsylvania are relatively too small to exert any appreciable influence on the demand for labor. If the miners employed by those companies do not emigrate to other fields, rather than work for wages that are below the market, the fault must be in their own stupidity and folly. In a great free country like this the laborer who remains under any such attempted oppression has small claim on public sympathy.

*It is always necessary to the success of any combination of capital, that it should have the reputation of paying fair wages to its employ's.* Otherwise its interests will greatly suffer from the difficulty of obtaining a sufficient supply of competent laborers. Of this our great competing lines of railways afford a striking illustration. For certain purposes they manifest a disposition to combine for the purpose of resisting competition on the most gigantic scale. But they have little power to reduce the wages of their employés below the standard of competition. Not one of them would dare to let the impression go abroad, that their employés are less liberally rewarded than those employed in other branches of industry.

All the conclusions of this chapter might be confirmed by *an appeal to facts*. Multitudes still cling to the belief that the law of competition can be resisted by combination of human wills. New combinations are formed from time to time and some of them obtain a temporary success. But it is only temporary, they soon fall to pieces, and the stream of wages settles back into the well-worn channels of competition. Were the history faithfully written of all the efforts of this sort which have disturbed the quiet of the economic world within the last fifty years, we think it would convince any candid mind of the impracticability of ever adjusting matters between employers and their employés by any such methods. The conflict never can be terminated, except by an appeal to some established and recognized natural law. We admit that in peculiar circumstances that law has sometimes produced results which are far from satisfactory. But it will be shown in the progress of this treatise, that those results are not due to competition pure and simple, but to vicious social or political arrangements which have turned aside competition from its natural and legitimate course.

§ 122. In all that has been said in this chapter of combinations against competition, it has been presumed that, in the efforts of either party to dictate terms to the other, *peaceable means only will be used.* As in this conflict physical force is always on the side of the employés, they only are for the most part under any temptation to resort to unlawful means. If they not only refuse to work except on terms of their own dictating, but resort to violence, to hinder other laborers coming in and accepting employment in their places, and in destroying the property of their employers, the thing will then have passed out of the sphere of science, and we must look upon it as we do upon any other insurrection against the supremacy of the laws, and the peace of society. The government should suppress any such outbreak of violence with the utmost promptness and rigor. It is the foremost duty which the government owes to the economic interests of the people. That any man is at liberty to judge for himself what wages he will demand, or whether he will work at all, all admit, and the government will protect every one in the exercise of that right. But the employer owns his capital, as truly as the employé owns his labor, and will judge for himself what wages it is expedient for him to pay, and whether in given circumstances he will run his machinery or allow it to stand idle. If one laborer will not accede to his terms, he may employ another that will. If this matter is to be carried through by force on either side, there is nothing for the community but revolution, anarchy, the annihilation of capital, the cessation of productive industry, and the extreme distress of all classes. It must however be borne in mind that if one party resorts to violence the other party must appeal to that force which the government knows how to wield for protection.

---

## CHAPTER IV.

### *Variation of the Rate of Wages.*

§ 123. IN the two preceding chapters we have shown *that competition is always a controlling force in determining wages*, and that it cannot be permanently resisted by any possible combination of human will-power, whether on the side of employers or of the employed. But competition is not a blind force. It acts through rational minds and free wills. It does not therefore come to the same result in all cases, but its determinations are as various as the circumstances and conditions in view of which it is called to act. The rate of wages fixed by competition is not the same in different places at the same time, or in the same place at different times. The wages of different persons vary widely from each other, as well as the wages of different occupations.

It is our object in this chapter to point out *the leading causes of these variations of the rate of wages*, and to show that they all result from the law of competition applied to a great variety of circumstances and conditions.

§ 124. The first cause of variation which we shall

mention *is the changing ratio between the number of laborers without capital seeking employment, and the amount of capital dependent for its productiveness on hired labor.* It is common to state this case in another form, to say that the wages of labor are dependent on the ratio of the number of laborers to the amount of capital. This is not accurate. All that capital which is kept employed by the personal labor of those that own it, and all the laborers who work with their own capital are to be left out of the account as having no influence on the rate of wages. If all capital were employed by the labor of its owners, and all laborers used their own capital, there could be no wages, however great the amount of labor and capital might be. Bearing this limitation in mind, it is plain that the rate of wages is a function of two variables—labor and capital.

The amount of labor remaining the same, *any increase in the amount of capital employing labor must necessarily increase the demand for laborers.* A man who has only capital enough to aid and sustain his own labor can hire no laborers unless he is willing to be idle himself. He who has enough for two laborers will wish to employ one, and so often as he adds to his capital a sufficient amount to fit out another laborer, he will demand another. This holds universally. Other things being equal, the more capital any one has the more laborers he will demand. The same will be true of all capitalists who own more capital than they can employ with their own hands. It is true that some modes of employing labor require a much greater amount of capital to each laborer than others. In the statements just made we must be understood to mean by the amount of capital necessary to fit out a laborer, the average amount to each laborer, taking all the different modes of employing labor into the account. With this understanding of the language just used, it is strictly true that the demand for labor varies directly as the amount of capital dependent for being utilized on hired labor. Wages will therefore vary in the same ratio. The greater the amount of such capital in the market, the more will its owners bid against each other for laborers, and the higher the point to which wages will be raised. If in a free and prosperous community wages are very high, it is an indication that the amount of capital seeking to employ laborers is very great in proportion to the number of laborers that can be employed. The rapid increase of the wealth of employers by legitimate production implies a corresponding increase in the wages of those whom they employ.

On the other hand, by an exactly similar mode of reasoning it would be made apparent that, the amount of capital dependent for its utilization on hiring labor remaining constant, *if the number of laborers without capital is increased, wages will decline.* The demand for employment will outrun the supply, laborers will bid against each other under the apprehension of being unemployed, and employers will obtain the labor they need at lower rates. If this state of things continues for a course of years or for generations, the condition of the laborer will become worse and worse, and pauperism and starvation will be unavoidable. Many writers on the subject have come to the sorrowful conclusion, that this is the inevitable fate of the laborer in countries of dense population. We hope to show in another part of this treatise, that if economic laws are observed, such apprehensions are as groundless as they are gloomy.

§ 125. If both the amount of capital seeking to hire laborers, and the number of laborers seeking employment are variable, *then the wages of labor will depend on the ratio which these variables sustain to each other.* If the capital increases more rapidly than the number of laborers, wages will be constantly advancing; but if the number of laborers seeking employment increases more rapidly than the capital, wages must with equal constancy decline. In this law we find an explanation of the exceedingly low wages paid in India and some other countries of very dense population. Population has increased because the cost of the necessaries of life is in that climate very small. On the other hand the government of the country has been arbitrary and despotic, and the rights of property have never been protected. The present condition of the country presents all the phenomena of an exceedingly dense population with vast numbers of men who depend on employment for their daily bread, yet little capital has been accumulated.

The dependence of wages on the ratio of the number of laborers seeking employment to the amount of capital dependent for its utilization on hired labor is one of the most important principles of our science. It shows conclusively, *that the impression so commonly entertained, that employers and employés are natural enemies to each other, is entirely without foundation.* If employers prosper by legitimate production, their demand for laborers will be increased, and the law of wages is such as to insure to laborers a share in that prosperity. The employer will have demand for more laborers, and will be compelled to offer them more favorable terms in order to obtain them, and, for long periods and in the general course of trade, employers can escape from this necessity by no combinations. On the other hand, if the employer fails to receive his profits he will have no increased demand for labor, he will soon find no motive to continue the processes of production, he will seek out more profitable methods of employing his capital, and the laborers he has employed will be out of employment. It is always in some degree difficult for the employé to appreciate his relation to the capital that employs him. His employer is a wealthy man, and enjoys those comforts and elegancies of life which wealth can purchase. His employés are often in straightened circumstances, and from necessity lead frugal lives, denying themselves many of the comforts which their employer enjoys. They are apt to forget, that the foundation of that very fortune which furnishes them employment, was probably laid in the practice of just such frugal self-government as that in which they are living; that if their employer or some ancestor of his had not practiced just such self-government, the capital which now helps and sustains their labor would never have had any existence. Capital and labor, employers and employés are not natural enemies, with interests antagonistic to each other, but fellow laborers for a common end. So this relation will be regarded by both parties, whenever the principles of our science are generally understood and accepted.

§ 126. Another cause which creates variation of the rate of wages *is the use of labor-saving machinery*. It is obvious this must be one of the elements of the problem. No one introduces a machine or even a simple tool into any industrial process, except for the purpose of accomplishing the end aimed at by a diminished amount of labor. An instrument that will not accomplish this is not labor-saving, and will therefore never be used at all. The first effect therefore in all cases of introducing labor-saving machinery must be, that a given end is attained with a less outlay of labor. Our first thought might be, that this settles the whole question, and that the use of labor-saving machinery must diminish the demand for labor and reduce the rate of wages. But this will be found to be a very superficial and deceptive view of the subject. No one indeed will deny that machinery enables a man to attain a given end with less labor; and could the inventor of the machine keep his own secret and confine the use of it to himself alone, he might be able to sell his products without any reduction of price, and in such increased quantity as to supply the whole demand, and drive all other labor and capital from the trade. In that case he might greatly diminish the demand for labor in that trade without increasing it in any other trade.

But such a secret cannot be kept, and the inventor, well aware of that fact, will be easily induced by the grant of a patent right, to communicate his secret to the public. As soon as this is done, competition in the trade will speedily approximate its profits to the general level, and the result will be a reduction of the price of the commodity whose cost is affected by the machine, nearly in proportion to the diminished amount of labor necessary to produce it. Such a reduction in the price of the commodity will produce a vast increase of the demand, resulting from the fact that great multitudes now use it, who at the former price were quite unable to afford it. In the course of the past century many commodities which at the beginning of the period were confined to the palaces of the rich, have found their way to the humble dwellings of the sons of toil. By this process, in the case of most really valuable labor-saving machines, the increased demand for the commodity has very far more than balanced the saving of labor in its production, *and in the ultimate result immensely increased the demand for labor in that very department.* Perhaps no better illustration can be found than the art of printing. To say nothing of printing itself, the demand for labor in manufacturing printing paper exceeds beyond all comparison the whole demand for labor in the book trade which could have existed, if the art of printing had not been invented. The history of labor-saving invention furnishes many other examples of the same tendency, which are equally pertinent and equally striking A careful examination of the facts of history would undoubtedly justify the conclusion, that the use of labor-saving machinery has immensely increased the demand for labor, in the very departments of industry where it has been most employed. We have tried in vain to call to mind a single instance of a successful machine which has come into general use without producing this effect. We once thought the sewing-machine would prove an exception to the general rule. But whoever calls to mind the elaborate workmanship of ladies' apparel, which has come into use along with the sewing-machine, and we think as a consequence of it, will be convinced that it is no exception to the rule.

Exceptions there may be in particular establishments, or within very narrow limits. Mr. Fawcett furnishes a few particular cases of the sort. But none of them have any tendency to invalidate the general principle. No principle of the science is, we think, established on a firmer basis. Considering the influence of machinery in increasing the demand for labor, it is in that view alone one of the laborer's best friends.

§ 127. A certain class of writers in this country, more distinguished by an amiable philanthropy, than by any clear philosophic insight, have taken a very different view of this matter. Seeing that all labor-saving machinery does diminish the amount of living human labor necessary to the accomplishment of a given result, they indulge the expectation that labor-saving invention will be carried to such an extent, as to dispense with the necessity of a large portion of the human effort which has hitherto been necessary for the supply of human want. Hence they indulge in a dream of a coming millennium of human labor, in which no part of the human race will be under a necessity of putting forth more effort than would be really necessary for the preservation of health and the full vigor of the human constitution. In that good time which they dream is coming, they anticipate that the chief occupation of all persons will be the cultivation of the intellect, and the enjoyment of the pleasures of high art. The sentence pronounced on our first ancestor,—" by the sweat of thy face shalt thou eat thy bread"—they think is to be repealed in that happy age of labor-saving invention.

Such persons have certainly mistaken the results which the improvement of machinery is to produce in the future of this world. It has always shown a tendency *to increase rather than diminish the demand for human labor.* In a former part of this treatise it has been shown, that in order that men may feel the full stimulus to labor which is provided in the constitution of man, it is necessary that all portions of society should enjoy not only the necessaries of bare existence, but such comforts and conveniences as constitute a truly civilized life. It is by means of labor-saving invention, if at all, that this result is to be achieved. It is by this means that the civilizing influences of society are to be so quickened and extended, as to reach men of every grade and condition. In order to the attainment of this result, men are not to lead aimless and purposeless lives in the enjoyment of the pleasures of the appetite and the tastes, but lives of activity and energy, in so multiplying the comforts and beauties of life that all may share them. The age of machinery is not to dispense with human toil, but to render the success of human effort possible, we would fondly hope actual, in providing for universal well-being. The destiny of the race is not by labor to dispense with the necessity of labor, but by labor to attain the appropriate end of all labor, a civilized humanity.

8*

§ 128. *The principles just explained do not seem to be applicable to any great extent to agricultural machinery.* It was shown in a former part of this treatise that agricultural machinery has not thus far proved to be, to any considerable extent, labor-saving. Reasons were also assigned for believing, that the same must for the most part be true in all the future. Should the opinions there expressed stand the test of future experience, as they certainly do of the past, machinery never can have much influence on the demand for labor in that department. Even if machinery should yet be invented to reduce the amount of human labor requisite for conducting agricultural processes in the same ratio in which it has been reduced in manufactures, it would still remain true, that the influence exerted on the price of agricultural products would be very much less than it has been in the case of manufactured goods. The price of agricultural products must always depend very largely either on the rent of land, or the cost of transportation. These elements of cost would both remain, however much the labor requisite might be diminished by machinery. If then such inventions are ever made, it will be a case in which labor-saving invention diminishes on the one hand the demand for labor, and on the other hand brings little compensation in the cheapness of the product. We have given our reasons for believing that it is very improbable any such thing can ever occur. Even if it does occur, the truth will still remain unimpaired, that the tendency of labor-saving invention on the whole is, not to diminish, but greatly to increase the demand for labor. The conclusions of the two previous sections will not therefore be invalidated.

§ 129. Another cause which produces variation of the rate of wages *is the cost of living.* It is customary to say, the cost of food, or the cost of the necessaries of life. We object to this as inaccurate. It implies the assumption that the rate of wages is to press downward, till finally at the maturity of the process, a bare existence is all that is to be left to the laborer. This is not the necessary nor is it to be the ultimate effect of competition. Neither is this an accurate statement of the case. It is not mere increased costliness of food or of the necessaries of life that raises wages. It is the cost of living. We are aware that there are large classes of laborers in many countries, whose wages are so low as to place their whole lives on the very verge of starvation. But it is yet to be shown in a subsequent chapter, that this is not the result of any natural law, but of a violation of natural law.

*Neither is it true that wages do in fact depend only on the cost of necessaries.* It has previously been noticed that the minimum of wages is always determined by the fact that those most anxious for employment prefer to run the risk of being unemployed, rather than make a lower bid. In determining the point at which such a stand is to be made, any man who has before his mind a standard of living in some degree of comfort would take into the account not only what it would cost him and those dependent on him to escape starvation, but what it would cost him to live according to his conception of life. If he finds that in a given position no wages are offered which will enable him to support such a mode of life, he will change his position, he will seek some new employment, he will emigrate if need be, in order to find some position in which he can earn a living. In the present condition of the world, and with present facilities of locomotion, no laboring population will quietly remain where they must work at starvation prices, *unless they have been reduced to utter despondency by generations of experience in hopeless poverty.* Such a population may from sheer ignorance, stupidity and despondency, accept as a remuneration for their labor the naked boon of continued existence; no other will. We shall show hereafter that such a *compensation is not in the sense of our science, wages*. It is not the result of competition. The economic conditions of such a life differ very little from those of slavery. It is noticeable in respect to all those populations in whatever country that live in this abject condition, that they have very little voice in determining their own wages. Their employers have it all their own way, and when they find that the wages which their laborers receive are not adequate to save them from starvation, the employers themselves yield to necessity and pay higher wages.

It is therefore true that in all cases in which wages are really determined by competition, *it is the cost of living and not the cost of mere necessaries* that influences the rate of wages. If it is not possible by equitable legislation and a sound and healthy intellectual and moral training of a people, to secure such conditions of society that all wages will be thus determined, the outlook toward the future of the civilized world is gloomy enough. We shall have occasion to return to this subject in a subsequent chapter.

## CHAPTER V.

*Causes of the Variation of Wages for Particular Persons and Classes.*

§ 130. THE last chapter was devoted to the consideration of the general causes which are liable to produce variations of wages. The wages however received by one person or one class of persons are found to differ very greatly from those of another. It is desirable before we dismiss the subject of wages, to point out some of the leading causes.

One of the most important of these causes *is the diversity of men's natural gifts.* There are some products of human effort which are held in the highest esteem by all civilized men, the power to produce which is possessed by very few human beings, and consequently the products themselves are always rare. The men possessing those rare endowments are able to demand wages that are limited only by the desire which men have for these peculiar products, and the wealth of the community. Most of the works of genius are to a greater or less extent embraced in this class, and are liable in favorable circumstances to command prices which seem almost fabulous.

To the same class are to be referred *the extraordinary profits sometimes realized by men of great eminence in the professions.* It is because their abilities are so rare as to place them quite above the reach of competition. They have the glorious gift of genius of which they have a natural and god-given monopoly. Their services in cases involving vast amounts of property, or the life and health of persons possessing great estates, are esteemed so valuable, that men will pay almost any price for them, rather than not obtain the advantage of them. We are economists, not moralists, and therefore have nothing to say of the moral responsibility of such men. They enjoy a precious gift of the Creator, and if they use it wisely, it is a glorious life they live.

§ 131. *Wages are higher in proportion to the expense of time and money that must be expended in acquiring the skill requisite* for performing services of which they are the reward. Much labor requires no peculiar education at all. But there are occupations the labors of which cannot be successfully performed without an expensive education for the business. Such labor must be more highly compensated than that which requires no such preparatory outlay. If any community refuses to pay such superior compensation, if one can get no remuneration for the capital expended in acquiring such an education, no one will be at the expense of acquiring it, and the community will soon have to live without educated labor. That which will bring nothing in exchange will, we have seen, soon cease to be produced.

The degree of that compensation will depend directly *on the perfection and rarity of the skill acquired and brought into use.* If for example the medical profession should fail to give evidence of any decided superiority in the treatment of disease, over the quack, or a mere nurse, people would be willing to pay very little for professional skill. But the physician who acquires a wide reputation for eminent skill in administering remedies for the maladies to which men are liable, will find an enlightened public willing to give him a liberal reward for his services. The principle holds here as everywhere else, that the greater any man's superiority in any kind of labor to the rest of the community, the higher the wages he can demand for his labor, and the more other men can afford to give him. The skilled laborer has therefore the greatest possible inducement to bring his skill to the highest perfection, and what is for his interest is equally for the interest of the whole community. Men are often envious of one who acquires a reputation for skill, by which he is able to command very large compensation for his services. This is illiberal and inconsiderate. The only reason why one can command such compensation is, that men find that his services are still cheap, even at the price he demands for them.

§ 132. Another cause of wide variation in the rate of wages *is found in the amount of confidence reposed.*

Services are often demanded in positions in which not only eminent professional or mechanical skill is requisite, but wisdom, sagacity, soundness of judgment in estimating men's characters, and a power of controlling their passions and directing their wills, and above all unquestionable moral integrity are not only important but even indispensable. Just in proportion as such qualities are regarded as desirable in any position, and as the union of them all is rarely found in one person, the man who possesses such a combination of traits will command higher wages than other men. The world is not so bad in any civilized country, that eminent wisdom and high moral integrity are without value in the market.

It is however true that many positions in which such qualities are esteemed indispensable *confer so much dignity and honor on those who occupy them, and give such advantages of social position*, that men are willing to accept them at a lower rate of compensation than they could command in less honored situations. For example, men of the highest legal attainments and personal reputation will often consent to occupy a position on the judge's bench for a salary much smaller than the income they might expect to receive at the bar. This consideration explains the comparatively low salaries received by some men of great eminence. The reverence and affectionate homage of mankind is more desirable to an honorable and generous mind than money.

§ 133. There are *numerous causes affecting in many subtle ways the wages of different persons and classes*, which it is neither possible or desirable to particularize. One of them is the uncertainty of success in any occupation. Men will encounter that uncertainty only because they see the prospect of proportionally higher wages in case of success. The wages of those who do succeed must be high enough to compensate for the lost labor of those who fail. Constancy or inconstancy of employment influences wages. If employment is irregular or uncertain men must be paid for the time they are obliged to spend in waiting for work. The ease or difficulty of the labor, the pleasantness or disagreeableness of the occupation, have a good deal of influence on wages. Even the disgracefulness of an occupation is sometimes the reason why it commands large pay. Men must be well paid for doing dirty work. We think in the present state of public opinion in this country, no one would engage in the liquor traffic, who did not expect to realize large gains.

§ 134. *There are certain occupations which are of such a character that large classes of persons are disposed to engage in them, whose constitutions, tastes, habits and education disqualify them for most other avocations.* Of course competition in these occupations is very strong, and wages are proportionally low. If one-half of the human race were without eyesight, and there were a few occupations in which blind men could succeed, the competition for these employments would be exceedingly strong. They would become exclusively employments for the blind, for wages would sink to so low a point, that a comfortable living could not be obtained from them. This is in principle precisely the case of the suffering needle-women alluded to in a former chapter. It is in place here to resume, as we promised to do, the consideration of their case, and we shall find it a very instructive one. The causes that produce the starvation prices at which seamstresses are often compelled to work, do not at once meet the eye of the public. There are large classes of persons in every civilized community, who never enter into that general competition by which wages are determined. *The competing unit is to a great extent, not the individual, but the family.* The male head of the family is responsible for the support of all its members, and buffets the wild waves of competition for them all by his single personal power and will. The women of such families enjoy a sheltered existence, protected from many of the storms that beat on all the out-door world. Yet there are large and increasing numbers of women who are not thus protected, and are obliged to engage single-handed in the rude struggle for existence which we call competition. They naturally seek those occupations which do least violence to female tastes and habits, and are most suitable to the delicacy of female fingers. The needle is apt to be a favorite resort, and their competition is very largely thrown upon the employment of the seamstress. The consequence is inevitable, ruinously low wages.

But the evil stops not here. In those peaceful homes where so many women are passing their tranquil lives, there are many who are painfully conscious of the lack of sufficient employment. They would rather earn something in almost any agreeable employment, than live in idleness and earn nothing. It is not necessary for them to do anything for their own support, their living is secure. But they would like to be a little independent in their spending money. They are therefore glad to take in sewing, even at the lowest prices, to employ their unemployed hours, and therefore enter into direct competition with all other women that earn money with their needles. *Women whose life depends on the needle find their wages depressed by the competition of those who are not working for a living at all,* and to whose comfort in life it is of no real importance, whether they receive high wages or low. It is surely no occasion of wonder, that, in a struggle so unequal, starvation comes to the woman who must not only live by her needle, but perhaps support children, or even a husband disabled by disease, or still worse by vice.

In such circumstances as these, it is quite useless and childish to call employers by hard names, or denounce the law of competition. Employers are no more deserving of censure than any one who buys and wears their cheap made clothing. We have shown that they are just as much held in the grasp of an inexorable law as the needle-women themselves. Nor is there any occasion to denounce that law. It has in this very case performed its appropriate function faithfully and beneficently. It has afforded the clearest possible proof, that these women are seeking a living where it cannot be found, and that they ought at once to abandon the needle, and seek some other mode of employment.

§ 135. This case clearly reveals the fact, *that there may be in civilized society obscure and subtle forces, that exert great influence on wages, which at first thought would hardly be suspected of sustaining any relation to the subject.* It is not any natural necessity which concentrates so great a force of female competition upon this one occupation. There are modes of employment for which many perhaps most of the needle-women are well fitted, that are not at all crowded, and in which they would receive wages sufficient to support them in comfort and happiness. Such an employment is domestic service. But thousands are repelled from this and other avocations which are quite open to them, by fear of the loss of social position. Multitudes of women would rather live from day to day at their needles on the very verge of starvation, than engage in an occupation imagined to be less socially respectable with every assurance of comfort and plenty. It is surely desirable that all classes of society should be educated out of a prejudice so silly and mischievous.

We cannot forbear remarking in this place, *that this is one of the points at which our science necessarily touches that of ethics.* The great multiplication of this class of women among us is largely due to the unsatisfactory condition of domestic life. Large numbers of young men of the finest promise are quite unfitted for domestic life by self-indulgent vicious habits, and therefore never marry. It requires no great skill in arithmetic to prove, that, as the numbers of the two sexes are almost precisely equal except as inequality is produced by emigration or other accidental and transient causes, if large numbers of men live in celibacy, an equal number of women are sure to fail of obtaining their natural protection and support in domestic life. The number of women compelled to engage single-handed in the struggle for existence is thereby greatly increased. This is becoming an enormous evil in American society. Many writers on economics lay a great deal of stress on the imprudent marriages of the poor. We are not disposed to enter into any controversy with them on that subject, but, in a true view of the matter, our science has more and stronger words to say against that vicious celibacy, by which thousands utterly fail to discharge their duty as the natural supporters and protectors of women. American society, American economy is suffering a great deal more from vicious celibacy than from imprudent marriages.

§ 136. *The aid of our science will be invoked in vain by those who at the present time are clamoring for the abolition of that protectorate of women,* which was alluded to in a previous section. It is one of the wise provisions of the human constitution, by which man willingly bears the severer and ruder toils and struggles of life, in order that woman may be sheltered in the tranquil seclusion of home, and perform in greatest perfection her great function of rearing up in long succession the generations of men, that are to bear forward civilization towards its highest perfection; that when the parents pass away, the children may be prepared to take their places, stronger in all that constitutes the highest humanity, than those who have gone before them. Division of labor is true economy, the more perfect the division the more perfect the economy. The progress of civilization will not dispense with this most primitive and most necessary of all divisions of labor, but will cultivate both parties in it up to the highest possible adaptation to their respective functions.

§ 137. There is at the present time an uneasy feeling in many minds, growing out of the suspicion, *that there is some misadjustment of the economic system, whereby women are deprived of their natural share of the products of industry.* It is one of the numerous cases in which restless spirits seek to relieve themselves by denouncing and censuring somebody, without being at the trouble first candidly to inquire, whether anybody is censurable, or if anybody, who and for what. It is claimed that when women do the same work as men and do it as well, they ought to receive the same pay. The very form of this proposition shows, that the person who affirms it is looking at the ethical and not at the economical view of the subject. "Ought" belongs not to economics. It is our business as economists to inquire what is the natural law which determines woman's wages. It will not take long to discover, that it is the same law of competition that determines all other wages. We have demonstrated the universality of this law. Is there then some arbitrary and artificial adjustment of the economic machinery of the world, by which the law of competition has been made to bear unfairly on women? This is claimed, perhaps in some cases justly. It may be that law in a few instances, and custom in more, may have shut out women from competing for wages, in modes of employment in which they might have had a fair prospect of success. Whatever obstacles of this sort may have existed, we are not disposed to defend them, and they are certainly assailed by forces which must sweep them away. If women have not had a fair chance, they are sure to have it soon. But a thoughtful person, whether man or woman, will surely not fail to see, that the organization of the sexes, their constitution both of body and mind is such, that women will always enter the arena of competition for the prizes which labor wins, under great, unavoidable, natural disadvantages, and that consequently in the labor markets of the world, there will be one rate for men and another for women. It is with this great stubborn natural fact, that we as economists are compelled to deal. He who demands that in this struggle female muscles and sinews, female force and endurance shall command, or if he prefers to say so, ought to command as high wages as those of the other sex, has engaged in a desperate struggle with the laws of nature, and we must leave him to manage his case as well as he can. To us it seems quite desperate. We would really advise him to give it over at once, for we think he is sure to be vanquished at last. It really does seem to us, that from the very organization of the sexes man's labor will always rate higher in the market than woman's, and that eloquent denunciations will really accomplish very little towards making it otherwise.

At the same time it would be very difficult to show, *that, at least in all ordinary cases, women do not receive the same wages as men, when they do the same work and do it as well.* For example, if one wants to employ two teachers in the same school, one male and one female, he will certainly offer much higher wages for the former than for the latter. The reason why he will, is that he knows that by the law of competition he can obtain the services of a woman at much lower wages than he must pay for a man. But why does he employ the man at all? Why not two female teachers instead of one man and one woman? Evidently because he expects service from one of them, which a woman cannot so well perform. He does not offer the woman lower wages than the man, with the expectation that she will perform the same service, but with the distinct intention, that the man shall do that which will not be expected of the woman. Since he wants a man's work, he sees the necessity of offering a man's wages.

§ 138. Is it asked why not place male and female teachers at once on the same basis of pay? We answer a law of nature forbids it, renders it impossible, just as was demonstrated in a previous chapter in respect to the wages of needle-women. To offer man's wages for the place that was to be occupied by a female teacher would be a grievous injury to all women well-qualified for the place, who would gladly perform the service desired for wages determined by competition. Teaching is one of those occupations upon which the competition of women, obstructed and shut out by natural disadvantages from many other modes of employment, will be concentrated in great force. Wages will therefore be inevitably depressed. Eloquent men, and perhaps still more eloquent women may declaim against it, and produce any amount of commotion in the popular mind, but they cannot help it. It is a law of nature they are resisting, and no eloquence can prevail against it. If a woman is wanted for a teacher of children and youth, competition will make her wages low. If you want something done in the school-room which you suppose a woman cannot so well do, and therefore think it necessary to employ a man, then you must pay him as much as he could obtain in other employments, where equal skill and talent are required.

In dealing with this question of woman's wages, it is a grievous wrong to woman to forget, that in her high and God-appointed function, the best and noblest services she ever performs for the world, are high above all commercial valuation, and are performed in such relations to domestic society, that her own proper reward is secured to her, without entering the arena of competition for wages. Those who forget this are not the true friends, of women.

§ 139. We have dwelt the longer on this subject of woman's wages, partly because the public mind is morbidly excited on the subject, and greatly needs to see it in the clear light of scientific analysis, and also because it forcibly illustrates some of the most important principles of the general subject of wages. The suggestions which have been made in the two previous sections are capable of a very wide application. The principal function of competition undoubtedly is to determine price. But that is not its only function. *It is in most cases the safest guide one can have as to the occupation which he should pursue.* There are many persons whose life is in a great measure a failure, because they will not follow its indications. When one has found that in any given employment he cannot obtain for his services a living compensation, he ought to regard it as a clear indication that he has mistaken his calling, and to seek some other method of serving his generation. This remark is applicable to many men who have attempted professional life, but cannot succeed in it. One should assume that he was not made in vain, and therefore if he cannot succeed in one thing he should try another.

*We would even apply this principle to those who have undertaken the sacred function of the Christian ministry.* We apply it here however under a very grave limitation. Men do not always value most that which is most precious and most needful to them. There are cases in which the noblest thing a man can do is, to spend his life in rendering services to mankind which they do not appreciate and will not reward. If a Christian minister finds that he does succeed in rendering such service to mankind, by promoting their moral and spiritual interests, let him never abandon his high function on account of the scantiness of his pecuniary reward. But if on the other hand he finds that his labors in the ministry fail to yield him a support for himself and those dependent on him, and yet sees no satisfactory evidence, that his labors are successful as a preacher of righteousness and an advocate of the highest moral and spiritual truth, he is quite at liberty to serve God and his generation in some other occupation.

## CHAPTER VI.

### *Ownership of Land.*

§ 140. HAVING considered the various phenomena of wages, it would seem appropriate that we next proceed to the examination of the remaining branch of Distribution, the share of the gains of production which falls to capital. But a preliminary question will first demand our attention. The received method of treating the subject recognizes three parties between whom the proceeds of production are to be divided, viz., land-owners, laborers and capitalists. *We have recognized but two parties viz., laborers and capitalists*, and have proposed to regard land as fixed capital and rent as the profit of it. Before we proceed further we must assign our reasons in justification of this division of the subject. For this purpose it will be necessary to examine a question not generally regarded as belonging to the science,—*the nature and foundation of property in land.* It seems to us that the want of a correct understanding of this subject has led to an erroneous theory of rent, and rendered men's minds tolerant of violations of fundamental economic law in regard to the tenure of land, which would otherwise seem unendurable. The discussion of this question is also necessary in order to justify the position taken by us in the preliminary chapter of this treatise, that no ownership of any material thing can be acquired, except by human labor bestowed upon it, whereby it is rendered capable of being serviceable to man. We shall therefore devote this chapter to a consideration of the ownership of land.

§ 141. Undoubtedly the first aspect of this question, is, that in the arrangements of nature, land, like the water of oceans, lakes and rivers, or the atmosphere which envelopes us all, is the free gift of the Creator to all men alike, and can be the property of no one. There are perhaps not a few who so regard it at the present time, and nourish in their souls an ever glowing sense of injustice at what they regard as the unjustifiable monopoly of the private ownership of land. It becomes therefore necessary for us clearly to point *out the foundation of the private ownership of land* in some incontrovertible natural law, or submit to a most radical economic revolution. There is not a question which the economist is under a more imperative necessity of examining. If the private ownership of land is not the clear and inevitable result of natural law, it cannot be permanently sustained as a law of society arbitrarily established and enforced. In this as in all other sciences, the laws of nature and all their legitimate consequences will remain forever, all else will be swept away.

In the first chapter of this treatise, it was enunciated as the fundamental law of the science, that every man owns himself and all which he produces by the exertion of his powers. It was also stated as a consequence of this law, that when any man expends his labor upon a material substance which he has received as the gift of God, no human labor having been previously exerted upon it, by expending his labor upon it, he becomes the owner of the material thing which by his labor he has made capable of gratifying human desire. If for example one finds a tree in some primeval forest to which no one has established any previous claim, cuts it down, and fabricates it into articles of beauty or utility, his labor expended on it makes him the owner of the wood, in order that he may enjoy the benefit of the labor he has expended on it.

§ 142. A more attentive comparison of air, water and land will show, *that the last of the three is distinguished from the other two by a most remarkable difference.* The two first mentioned require no modification by human effort to fit them for man's use. The condition of the air cannot be rendered more fit for human lungs than it is. It always envelopes us ready for our use. Nothing which man can do will improve either its quantity or its quality. All we can do in respect to it, is to see to it that we do not shut ourselves out from its free circulation in its own primitive perfection. Man cannot improve the atmosphere by any efforts of his, and therefore he cannot own it.

The same is true of water as it exists in oceans, lakes and rivers. No man can make the clear water of Lake Michigan his own. If water can only be obtained by digging a well at much expense of human labor, he who digs the well owns the water. This has been held to be true ever since the days of Abraham and Lot. It is recognized even among the wild wanderers of the desert. The water of the Mississippi cannot be owned, though he that has placed it in barrels, and carried it to families living at a distance from the river may obtain compensation for it.

But land differs widely in this respect both from air and water. Of itself in its natural state it supplies no want of man. It can only be made to afford human sustenance by being subdued and cultivated. In its natural state it is as useless as the tree growing in the primeval forest. It supports game, and that is the property of any one that can capture it. By capturing it, the huntsman acquires the ownership of it but not of the land on which it grazed, and over which it ran. Untilled land produces wild fruits, and he who gathers them, owns them, but not the soil on which they grow. If land could only minister to human well-being by its spontaneous productions, it could no more be subjected to ownership, than the oceans or the great lakes.

*Portions of the ocean are subjected to national ownership by the outlay of labor and capital* by which they are rendered capable of being navigated in safety. That portion of the ocean adjacent to the land, where buoys are established, light-houses built and sustained, and channels leading into harbors are improved, is recognized as belonging to the government that makes these outlays of labor and capital upon it. The principle for which we contend is recognized even in respect to water, wherever it is possible to apply it. For the most part however man's labor can make no modification of the ocean by which he could appropriate it.

§ 143. But he that subdues the land, destroys the forests that shade it, or any other spontaneous vegetation that hinders the growth of food for man, and tills and sows it, *acquires the ownership of it,* just as of any other natural substance, which by his labor he renders subservient to human uses. Two men are rambling together among the fastnesses of the Rocky Mountains. One of them discovers a tree of rare fitness for the manufacture of articles of beauty, and by his labor bestowed on it he makes it his. The other discovers, in those regions of almost universal barrenness, a tract of land capable of abundant productiveness. He removes from it the wild, luxurious but useless growths of nature, draws water from the mountain stream that rushes along its border, and thus provides for its perpetual irrigation, encloses it against the incursions of animals, and plows and sows it. This man owns the land by the same natural title by which the other owns the tree which he cut from the original forest. No man can show any distinction in principle between these two titles. In both cases alike we recognize the only ownership which man can acquire of anything which God has made. Man enters on all land by the same process. Land on which no human labor has been bestowed yields nothing to human well-being. All its availability for this purpose is dependent on conditions which human labor alone furnishes.

It may perhaps be said, that in the case just supposed the man that first plowed and planted the land *would be entitled to gather the harvest which he has sown, but no more.* This is certainly untenable. The labor which he has expended upon it has no exclusive reference to that one harvest, but is a permanent preparation for every future crop, and he will be the same absolute owner of it at the end of the year as at the beginning. A single crop will by no means compensate him for his labor. He has conferred on it the capability of being a permanent instrument of human well-being, and that capability by the law of nature he owns. He will stand in the same relationship to it at the end of any number of years, as when he planted the first crop. If he continues to keep that land in a state of fitness for cultivation, the time will never come, when he or the person to whom he has transmitted his title, will not be by nature's law the one only owner of it.

§ 144. It will then be asked *what is the origin of that ownership of new lands which the first settler buys from the government?* How is the government the owner? The common idea is perhaps, that the savage tribes that roamed over North America when the Europeans came to it, were the owners of the soil, and that our present government owns it by having purchased this title by treaty. We cannot regard this view of the matter as at all tenable. We cannot admit, in the first place, *that these savages ever did own the soil.* They never did that which alone creates ownership. They never made any modification of the land by labor expended on it, which fitted it to be an instrument of production. They roamed over it like the herds of buffalo, and lived on its spontaneous products, just as the wild beast did. But by so doing neither the buffalo nor the savage acquired ownership, the latter no more than the former. He that gathers blackberries or shoots deer on a piece of ground does not become the owner of it. No one owns a tree of the forest because on a single year, or for many successive years, he gathered the nuts that grew on it. The European settlers of North America took possession of no capabilities of production, which the labor of those savage tribes had created. As those savages retired before them, they had exactly the same labor to perform which they would have had if there had never been any human inhabitants of the continent before them. In this respect the case was exactly the same, that it would have been if wild beasts only and not men had retired before them. What they took possession of everywhere was the work of the Creator, and not the work of man. The assumption that these savage tribes were the owners of the soil is therefore without any foundation at all, and the influence which it has exerted on the literature of Christendom, and on our policy toward the Indian, is exceedingly to be deplored.

§ 145. *Nor again are these tribes independent nations.* Nationality implies a defined national domain, laws, institutions, a stable government, able to give substantial guarantees for the fulfillment of its part of any treaty stipulations. Every treaty we have ever made with the Indian has been at two points radically void. On the one hand the Indian was not the owner of that which both parties made believe he sold to us: he had no title and could therefore give none. On the other hand, we stipulated to do that which the nature of the case made it certain we could not do. We guaranteed to the Indian the perpetual possession of the hunting grounds to which he retired. It is devoutly to be hoped our government will never make any more such promises to the Indian, except on condition of his becoming a civilized tiller of the soil. Without that condition the whole power of our government cannot fulfill such a promise. There is a higher law than any human government can enact, that predestines the soil of North America, not to be hunting grounds for any horde of savages, but to yield all its resources of whatsoever kind to the ends of civilized humanity. Assign to any Indian tribe any spot you please, if the Indian uses it as a mere hunting ground, you cannot make him the owner of it. God does not give ownership of this earth in that way, and you can not. While it is held only for such a barbarous use, civilization in its progress over the continent will discover its resources which no savage can ever develop, and will demand and obtain its own; and no treaty which any government can make can doom those resources to perpetual uselessness, that a horde of savages may perpetuate their barbarous life. The law by which civilized man is to increase and replenish the earth will always prove to be superior to any claim which savages can set up to their hunting grounds, and any treaty which a great civilized nation may make with a savage tribe in disregard of that law is a solemn farce, the pretense of making which is a crime, not the yielding to an inevitable natural necessity of permitting it to be broken.

§ 146. If we are asked *what we will do with the Indian*, that is a question which does not belong to our science, we must turn it over to the Christian moralist and statesman. All we are concerned with at present is, to set aside, and disabuse men's minds of the notion that our title to our lands originated in purchase from savage tribes, who never did that which our science must regard as creating the only possible ownership. One word however we must say of the treatment of the Indian, to protect ourselves from misconception. The European occupants of North America should have always treated the Indians as men, to be protected in all their rights, to be restrained by any necessary exertion of force from doing wrong, and to be encouraged by all practicable means, to forsake their savage life, and adopt the habits and accept the blessings of civilization. Give the Indian every thing to encourage him in his efforts to live a civilized life, nothing to aid him in perpetuating his barbarism. Our policy toward the Indian has so long been constructed on a false assumption, that it may be no easy matter at this late day to return to sound principles in our treatment of him. We trust however that it is not quite impossible.

§ 147. From this inevitable digression, we return to the question, what is the origin of that title which the settler buys from the government? We answer it is the title to these lands which the government has acquired, by *surveying them into convenient parcels*, and marking them out by metes and bounds, whereby every man can identify the farm he has purchased, and be saved from all disputes with his neighbors about boundaries, by *extending over them the jurisdiction of a civilized government,* thus rendering life and property in a great measure secure from the very origin of the settlements, and by affording to the inhabitants of the remotest frontier, *protection from the incursions of savages.* These helps provided by the government for the bold pioneers of civilization are very cheaply purchased, by paying the price which the government exacts for the fee simple of the lands. Previous to the entry of the government on these lands, by making such provisions as these for the benefit of the future settler, they were, like the rivers that water them and the atmosphere that overlies them, without an owner. By entering on them and making these necessary provisions for civilized colonization, the government became the owner, and conveys its ownership to the individual purchaser.

As to the question, *by what title the United States claim the right to enter on certain lands, and acquire the ownership of them* in the manner described above, rather than England or any other foreign power, it does not belong to us to discuss it. That question does not relate to the ownership of the soil, but only to the right of political jurisdiction, and depends on certain arbitrary understandings entered into by the civilized nations of the world, rather than on any clearly defined natural law It belongs therefore to the writers on international law and not to us.

§ 148. It may perhaps be objected to this view of the nature of ownership, *that the labor originally expended in bringing land into cultivation is greatly overpaid by perpetual ownership.* It must be admitted that, in some cases, it does seem to receive a very high compensation. In view however of all the facts this is, even in these cases, more apparent than real. When the land possesses great natural productive power, and the labor required to subdue it is comparatively small, the outlay necessary to constitute ownership is largely rewarded by the value of the permanent possession. But it should be borne in mind, that this outlay is often made, when the interest on money is not less than five per cent per month, and consequently one hundred dollars is equivalent to one thousand dollars in ordinary circumstances. Besides it should not be forgotten that the beginnings of civilized cultivation often involve exposure to many hardships and perils, for which it is very reasonable that the first settler should receive compensation.

*Nor is it by any means generally true that the labor expended in acquiring the ownership of new land is very largely rewarded.* We suspect it would be difficult to find a well-informed man who believes, that the present market value of the lands of the United States at all exceeds the actual cost of subduing them, and bringing them into their present state of cultivation, or in other words, that the present rental of the whole country exceeds interest at current rates on the cost of improvements. It is probably impossible ever to obtain any answer to the question we here raise, which would be even proximately accurate. But there is certainly a great deal of cultivated land in this country, the annual rental of which would fall very greatly below current interest on the cost of improvements made on it. If there is also a good deal of land the rental of which would exceed the interest on the cost of improvements, that affects not the question before us. Land is by no means the only example of a material substance of which ownership has been acquired by labor expended on it, the value of which greatly exceeds the value of the labor so expended. A gold hunter opens a mine and finds gold in paying quantities. In virtue of the labor of opening it, he owns it with all the riches which it contains, no matter how vast the sum. If by a fortunate effort of ingenuity one invents a machine for which the world will willingly pay him millions, he is entitled to those millions, and may refuse to disclose his secret, except for value received. A man may be equally fortunate in laying claim to a piece of land by bestowing labor upon it. Many have been thus fortunate, but this by no means sets aside the principle, that the ownership of any material thing which the Creator has made, is obtained only by labor bestowed upon it, whereby it becomes capable of supplying human want. It is nothing different from what occurs in relation to all other material possessions, where the principle is confessedly applicable.

§ 149. *There is one other objection to this doctrine* which to some persons may seem weighty. It must be owned that land has one seeming peculiarity, distinguishing it from most other kinds of property. It is very likely to be enhanced in value by the progress of population, wealth and civilization, without the expenditure of any additional labor in its improvement. That there is such a general tendency cannot be denied. Yet the facts are after all by no means uniform. With the steady growth of some of the New England states in all the elements of civilization, within the last fifty years, a large portion of their land has greatly declined in price, instead of advancing, as this general statement would imply. The investments made fifty years ago in improving it have proved as bad as those in some other parts of the country have been good. When a man lays out his labor on a piece of land, and takes the land as his reward, he does not know that the community around it will advance in civilization. It may decline. In that case his investment will be a loss and not a gain. He expends his labor at a risk. If things turn in his favor, he will gain, if against him he will lose. In this respect this case does not in any degree differ from any other outlay of labor. In this as in all other things, no man is certain when he expends his labor, that he shall gain that which he seeks by the outlay.

There is always a presumption however, that he who by an expenditure of labor acquires the ownership of a good piece of land, will obtain a possession which, by the growing prosperity of the community, will on the whole increase in value. It will hereafter be shown, in treating of the rent of land, that this probability is allowed for in every contract for rent. No man receives as high interest on his landed capital, as on capital invested in other ways. He willingly consents to receive a part of his interest in the presumed regular enhancement of the price of his land by the progress of society. It is an advantage which he does not get for nothing, but constantly pays for it.

We come therefore to the conclusion that, in relation to our science, land is simply and only a gift of God to man, which in its natural condition is without value, but which is rendered by the expenditure of human labor on it, the most powerful and important instrument of supplying human want. It is as truly and simply fixed capital, as a water-wheel or steam engine. So we have classified it in this treatise, and so we shall continue to regard it, in considering the share of the gains of industry, which natural law will allot to capital.

# CHAPTER VII.

*Interest.*

§ 150. THE share of the capitalist in the gains of production must next be considered. These, according to the nature of the investment from which they are derived are called either *Interest*, *Rent* or *Profit*. Of these Interest is the least complicated and will therefore be first considered.

DEFINITION, *Interest is compensation for the use of capital which is entirely entrusted to another, to be repaid to its owner at a specified time, and with such consideration for its use as may be agreed on.*

In some cases *compensation for the use of capital* is all which is included in interest. The security for the repayment of the sum loaned according to the conditions, is regarded as perfect, and therefore no consideration is paid for any risk. Loans to stable and regular governments, for example like those of England and the United States, are regarded as being of this character. Loans secured by mortgage of real estate may be made as secure as anything human can be. But in a great number of loans from one individual to another, a greater or less degree of *risk* is encountered, and the capitalist receives compensation both for the use of his capital while in the control of the borrower, and for the risk which he encounters that it may not be repaid to him according to the contract. The lender will demand a higher rate of interest in some cases than in others, according to his estimate of the risk incurred. This is the reason why some governments are able to borrow money at the very lowest rates, while others can scarcely borrow it at all, and if at all, only at very exorbitant interest. The same is true of individual borrowers. It will be the lot of the man who is ill able to pay any interest at all, that he will pay a much higher rate than the man whose means of payment are most abundant. It is not because the lender desires to oppress the poor, but because he must have insurance for the risk he runs.

§ 151. *The principle on which the payment of interest is founded* is very obvious. A man may possess capital which he cannot himself use. He may be incapacitated by the infirmities of age or disease so to manage it as to derive profit from it. He may follow an avocation in life in which he cannot invest his gains so as to derive advantage from them. If he can get nothing for the use of his capital, he will not incur the risk of entrusting it to the hands of another, but will lay it away as safely as he can for future use. The only motive therefore which can induce him to part with it is, that he may receive a fair compensation for its use, and for any risk which may attend the transaction. He will seek a borrower, and he will find some one of good credit, who will be willing to pay him the market rate of interest. For there are always those who have power and skill to labor, but no capital with which to procure necessary tools and materials.

The *same competition* which controls all other values will no less assert its supremacy in determining the rate of interest, and that rate which competition has established for loans involving only ordinary risk will be demanded by the lender and willingly paid by the borrower.

It is not easy to see what excuse *the legislator can plead for interfering in this matter.* And yet in all the past history of the world he has shown a strange but universal propensity to do so. In most countries of the world a reason might have been given for it, which can have no validity in this country at the present time. In numerous instances both ancient and modern, governments have not only undertaken to compel the fulfillment of contracts, but have enforced the payment of debts by the imprisonment of the debtor, and even by selling him into slavery. If governments resort to such measures for the collection of debts, it is quite reasonable that they should so construct the law as not to favor the increase of indebtedness, or even to discountenance the lending of money on any terms. Perhaps this is one of the reasons why usury laws have been so persistently adhered to. But if this is so, a more humane treatment of the debtor should be accompanied by their abolition. When as at the present time in this country, the law not only exempts from seizure for debt the person of the debtor, but also a considerable amount of his property, in the form of necessary household goods and tools of his occupation, that reason for legislative interference between the borrower and the lender can no longer have any weight.

It must however be conceded, that the propriety and wisdom of the usury laws of other ages, and perhaps of other countries in our own age, cannot be safely judged by our standards. It may be clear, that laws regulating the rate of interest are incongruous with the general freedom of our system, and a violation of economic law ; but it will not hence follow that in countries where all the economic forces are in a great measure counteracted and held in abeyance, such laws may not be necessary for protecting the debtor against the cruel exactions of the creditor. No one familiar with the Latin classics can fail to see, that under Roman laws there was such a necessity.

The law of ownership means that the owner will decide by his own free will on what terms he will part with his capital, and it equally means that the borrower will decide on what terms he will consent to take it. Till these two wills are brought to coincide in the matter, there may be force, but there can be no loan; and when they are at one by free competition, it is impossible to give any good reason why any other personality should interfere in the case. There can be no such interference without a direct violation of ownership. We say nothing of the morality of such interference, but we do say that it is a violation of that original law of ownership which is the foundation of our whole science. It is moreover a futile and useless interference, an attempt to control by statute law that which a law of nature has already decided, and placed quite beyond the sphere of human legislation. It is within the domain of natural law, and therefore statute law will in vain attempt to meddle with it. The law may forbid the capitalist to demand or accept more than a given rate of interest, but it cannot compel him to lend at that rate. If he can use his capital more profitably in other ways than by lending it at that rate, he will not lend it. It may forbid the borrower being compelled to pay more than a given rate, but it cannot enable him to obtain money at that rate. It may forbid two human wills consenting together at any other point than that determined by the law, but it cannot make them consent at that point. It may throw obstacles in the way of borrowing and lending capital, and thus do great injury to both parties. But it cannot make them borrow and lend on any other terms than those they mutually agree upon. While men retain within themselves an intuitive perception of the nature and inalienable character of ownership, laws forbidding men to contract to lend and borrow money on such terms as seem to them fit, will be essentially nugatory, and provoke unceasing efforts at evasion, and men will be ingenious enough to render those evasions successful. While the general spirit of trade is as at present, these predictions will be everywhere verified by fact. The law will moreover fail to find any support in the conscience of the community. There will be a feeling in the hearts of men, that the law violates the property rights both of the borrower and of the lender, and efforts at evasion will either not be regarded as wrong at all, or be judged very leniently, as sins of so venial a character as not to merit any severe condemnation. We ask all thoughtful men who are practically acquainted with this matter, to judge for themselves, whether the above picture is not a true exhibition of the facts as well as of the theory of the case. If this is so, more words are unnecessary. The sooner our legislators withhold their hands from all interference in this matter, the better it will be both for trade and morals.

§ 152. When borrower and lender are left free of any legislative interference, there is probably no case in the whole economic system in respect to which *competition acts more freely* than in determining the rate of interest. There are seldom or never any attempts to control it by combinations, either of lenders or borrowers. The rates actually paid in different countries at the same time, and in the same country at different times, vary between very wide extremes. In some countries, in transactions supposed to involve no risk, it is as low as two per cent per annum. In some cases, as for example in the new states of our own country, it is sometimes as high as fifty or even sixty per cent per annum. It is perhaps generally supposed that in these last cases rates of interest seemingly so exorbitant can be occasioned only by the great risk which the capitalist incurs. But so far as our observation has extended, this is by no means a fact. These rates are often due largely to the exceedingly low rates at which the government offers the perpetual ownership of some of the most fertile lands in the world, and the scarcity on the frontier of the money with which only the purchase can be made. Most men who emigrate to the frontier wilds carry little with them except their power to labor. For the small sum of money necessary to procure for them the perpetual ownership of a farm of a sufficient size, and indispensable tools, implements and domestic animals, they can afford to pay almost any rate of interest that may be demanded. In many cases they hope, not without reason, to repay the loan out of the first two or three crops from the land. They are therefore willing to give to the money-lender a liberal share of the very large profits they are likely to receive, rather than not obtain the small sum of money which is quite indispensable to their success. Indeed one has only to study the conditions under which the borrowing and lending of money is transacted in a prosperous frontier settlement, to become quite convinced of the inexpediency and inherent absurdity of laws regulating the rate of interest. If in such circumstances usury laws could succeed in limiting the lending of money to a prescribed medium rate of interest, that success would be the greatest possible injury both to borrower and lender. The borrower would be unable to obtain money when it would be a very great benefit to him to get it, even at a much higher rate of interest than that demanded, and the lender, unable to obtain his share of the gains of the transaction by lending his money, would himself purchase the land of the government, and sell it out to the actual settler on terms much less favorable to him, than to have lent him the money at the high rate of interest proposed.

§ 153. It can hardly be interesting or profitable to trace out the nearly *innumerable causes which produce variations of the rate of interest* between these widely remote extremes. Through all the fluctuations which they occasion, they are as true to the one law of competition, as the tides of the ocean are to the law of gravitation. Sometimes doubtless risk is the chief element of variation, as is apparent in the rates of the government loans of England and Holland on the one hand, and those of Turkey and Egypt on the other. Sometimes high rates of interest are occasioned, as in Australia and in our own new states, by the large profits that can be realized from the possession of capital, and the great scarcity of money in a community of recent emigrants. Men who have plenty of money have no motive to emigrate to the wilderness, and are not easily persuaded to send their capital where they are not willing to go in person.

Any *occurrence which raises men's hopes of gain to be realized from the investment of capital* in active trade, will make them more anxious to obtain it, and willing to offer a higher rate of interest for it. Any thing which diminishes the profits of trade and depresses men's hopes will render them less desirous of borrowing money, less disposed to compete with each other for the possession of it, and therefore reduce the rate of interest. The phrase " value of money " has two very different meanings. In one use of it, it means the value of the precious metals as compared with the value of other commodities. In this sense it has been shown that the value of money is less liable to fluctuation than any other commodity, and that therefore it is better fitted than any thing else to be the medium of exchange, and the standard of all value. In the other use of it the meaning of the phrase is the rate of interest which money will command in the market. In this use of the term few things are more fluctuating in value than money, and therefore few things are more suitable to be left to the influence of free competition.

*The tenure of land in fee simple, and the existence of perfect freedom of exchange in respect to it,* have a most salutary influence on the interest market. They tend greatly to secure it against violent fluctuations, and dangerous extremes, and enable all that very large portion of the community that under such a system own land, at all times to borrow money at the lowest current rate, without paying for extraordinary risk. For this reason all those provisions of the law which, under the intention of protecting the debtor, make the foreclosure of mortgages difficult, expensive, or subject to long delays, are on the whole injurious to borrowers, rather than beneficial. The more direct and speedy the remedy of the creditor is, in case of the failure of the debtor to pay according to contract, the lower the rate of interest at which he will be willing to lend money. It is probable that this is one of the causes why the rate of interest is so high in British India. It is not merely on account of the scarcity of capital, but also partly because, owing to the absence of the tenure of land in fee simple, few are able to give any satisfactory security for money borrowed. This is a curious illustration of the tendency of the tenure of land to exert an influence on all the economies of a community. Free trade in land tends to freedom in every thing else.

§ 154. It may seem to some that the fact that the rate of interest may differ very considerably in two neighboring countries at the same time, as is the fact in respect to England and Holland, *is inconsistent with what we have said of the cosmopolitan character of capital.* Why, it may be asked, should a Hollander lend his money at home at two per cent, when he can obtain for it in the English funds three and a quarter per cent? The answer is, that this is not by any means a national affair. The same thing is just as likely to occur in respect to different parts of the same country, as between different nationalities. There have been times when the current rate of interest in Illinois was fifty per cent, while in Massachusetts it was six per cent. And yet the lender in Illinois certainly incurred no extraordinary risk. The explanation of the phenomenon is found, not in any relation of capital to nationality, but in the fact that a capitalist always prefers to have his capital near him, under his own eye, and under social conditions with which he is familiar. Especially he prefers to invest it under laws which he understands, and with the administration of which he is well acquainted. In such circumstances he would rather accept less interest, than make an investment in circumstances which he regards as less desirable. It is an additional consideration applying to foreign investments, that in case of a war between his own country and that in which the investment is made, payment would be suspended during the war. This of course would be regarded as a very great objection to a foreign investment, unless the peace of the two countries was regarded as in a great degree assured. Undoubtedly the danger of the occurrence of war between the different nations of the earth is a very great obstacle to the free circulation of capital. The nations of the world can never enjoy the full benefit of the universal human relations of capital, except on condition of maintaining universal peace.

§ 155. *The rate of interest always declines with the gradual progress of a community in wealth and general civilization.* This is abundantly established by reference to the past history of civilization. The fact is doubtless partly owing to diminished risk. With the healthy progress of society trade becomes more regular, systematic and sure in its results, governments become more stable and just, and are more skillfully administered for the protection of all the rights of property. But this is certainly not a complete account of the matter. It seems to be a great law of human progress, that of all the elements that enter into the economic system of the world, capital is that which increases most rapidly. If a savage enters on the attempt to become a civilized man, with nothing but his bow and arrows to begin with, he must first accumulate a surplus over self-support, to buy a rifle. With that greatly improved instrument, he will be able to accumulate much more rapidly than before. In a short time he will not only be the owner of a rifle, but he will have besides an accumulated surplus by which he will be able to procure the means of rendering his labor still more efficient, and his accumulation still more rapid. The same principle seems to hold for every successive step of his progress. Each new invention, each new natural force that is made the helper of his labor, not only compensates for the outlay of capital it has cost, but greatly multiplies his surplus for still further and more important investments. In this whole matter, the Scripture is constantly fulfilled: "To every one that hath shall be given." With each new triumph of man over the powers of nature, other and greater triumphs become possible, which before were quite impossible, and we can set no limits to the possibilities of the future except the limits within which gravitation and inertia confine us.

*But capital obeys the same law of supply and demand which prevails everywhere in the economic world.* If one element increases more rapidly than any other, it will inevitably decline in price. This one consideration fully explains the certain and steady decline of the rate of interest in all countries of growing wealth and civilization. It is the prodigality of nature's provision for all man's prospective wants, and for his highest possible development.

§ 156. Some of the most important consequences of

this law we are not prepared to examine at the present stage of our inquiries. There is however one important relation of the law, which it is proper to point out in this place. This sure decline of the rate of interest suggests the thought, that it must at length reach a point beyond which the gain to be derived from capital would become so small, that there would be no sufficient inducement for any further effort at accumulation, and that consequently *capital would cease to increase, and the rate of interest would become stationary.* We are not disposed to deny that at some distant future point of human progress, there may occur a maturity of civilization over this whole earth, such as would produce a stationary condition both of capital and interest. But a little consideration will convince us, that that point is yet so remote in the distant future, that the prospect of its being reached should awaken neither hope nor fear. There may be for aught we know a limit to the solar system, beyond which inevitable disaster awaits it. But the danger is too deep in the dark unknown future, to awaken any present apprehension. The danger of any such disaster in the economic world can hardly be more imminent.

In considering this matter that *cosmopolitan nature of capital* which we have already demonstrated, should not be forgotten. In order that this minimum possible rate of interest should be reached, the demand of the whole world for capital must be far more perfectly supplied than it is at present supplied in such countries as England and Holland, where the rate of interest is lowest. At an interest of three and a quarter per cent in one of these countries, and two per cent in the other, in transactions involving no risk, the accumulation of capital is still prosecuted with great zeal and energy. How much lower point it may reach without causing a cessation of accumulation we have no experiment by which it can be determined. But the experiments with which we are here furnished are quite sufficient to prove, that the increase of capital cannot be arrested till the demands of the whole human family are far better supplied than the demands of either of those countries are at the present time. On the supposition of a long future of peace over the whole earth, and of such reforms in the governments of the world as will render property as secure everywhere, as it now is in those two favored countries, this worldwide demand for capital could not be so completely supplied except in some exceedingly distant future age.

§ 157. There is another consideration which tends to postpone the day at which such a stationary condition of the economic forces of the world can occur to a still more distant future. As the interest on capital is diminished, *the demand for it must be increased in a very rapid ratio.* The case is closely analogous to the increased demand for labor which, we have shown, results from the use of labor-saving machinery. The first effect is that labor is dispensed with, and the demand for labor diminished. But the immediately succeeding effect is, that millions are to be supplied with the cheapened product, where before only thousands could enjoy it, and this increased demand far more than compensates for the diminished amount of labor requisite to produce a given quantity. The aggregate result is, as we have seen, an almost unlimited increase of the demand for labor.

So is it in the case under consideration. A vast increase of capital would be necessary to supply all which would be demanded, for example in the United States, at the present rate of interest. But if the rate of interest should decline, as it surely will, by the regular process of increasing wealth and prosperity, to two or three per cent, who can compute the vastness of the demand for the use of it which would come with those low rates of interest? How many and how vast would the enterprises be, which would then become practicable and easy, which at the present rates of interest are not to be even for a moment thought of? Who can compute the amount of capital which would be absorbed in enterprises which in the present state of things would be quite chimerical, and yet in the state of things supposed would be easily rendered actual? The same would be true over the whole world. In such a state of things enterprises would everywhere be undertaken and carried through, which in our times are never thought of. It would expose one to ridicule barely to suggest many an undertaking, which in such circumstances would be far more easily accomplished than the Suez Canal or a continuous line of railway across the continent of North America in our own times.

At those low rates of interest the possible uses of capital would become so numerous and the amount necessary to satisfy them so great, that *a very great increase of the capital of the whole world would hardly have an appreciable influence on the general rate of interest.* Ever so great an increase of capital in one country would be like a flood in a single river, causing it perhaps to overflow all its banks, but having no sensible influence on the level of the ocean. The capital of the world is oceanic, as truly as its medium of exchange. When the rate of interest for the whole world shall have been brought down by general prosperity to two per cent, the additional increase of capital necessary to reduce it to one and a half would run far up toward the infinite. Those who are alarmed at the prospect of a coming stationary period are certainly troubled with groundless apprehensions.

§ 158. It may be suggested in reply to the conclusions of the previous section, that they are founded *on suppositions not likely to be realized,* that the world is not likely to have a long future of universal peace, that the governments of the world are not likely to be so reformed as to make rights of property as secure everywhere, as they now are in the most civilized countries. Then surely we may dismiss all our apprehensions about the occurrence of a stationary condition of economic forces. Without the fulfillment of those conditions, it never can come. Meanwhile it is certain the condition of the world is becoming from generation to generation more favorable to great economic enterprises, and inviting openings are presenting themselves for the investment of capital in many and remote lands. If some countries are becoming gorged with capital, and do not present at any particular time satisfactory modes of investment, the world is before the capitalist, and the capital which will not yield him interest in his own country will not fail to find a remunerating demand elsewhere.

Nor is there any reason to suppose that *the resources of labor-saving invention are yet exhausted.* When we consider the demands for more capital which have been created by the inventions of the last century, we have surely little cause to apprehend any lack of demand in coming ages. Who is able to compute the time requisite to accumulate a sufficient amount of capital to give to the whole world the full benefit of the inventions of the last century? When will the world be rich enough to procure for itself the advantages of the railway system for all its peoples, as they are now enjoyed by a few of the more civilized nations of the world? There can be no reason to fear that the emigration of capital from countries where it is superabundant, and the use of it in multiplying labor-saving machinery to supply the wants of the world, will not so sustain the rate of interest for a long time to come, that there need be no apprehension that it will touch a lower point than it has already reached in a few favored countries.

---

## CHAPTER VIII.

### *Rent.*

§ 159. THE word rent is used with a good deal of latitude of signification. It is not only applied to land and all permanent improvements of it, but to many other of the more permanent forms of fixed capital. The peculiarities however which make it necessary to give it a separate consideration in this treatise pertain only to land and the various permanent structures reared upon it—to land in actual use for the various purposes for which it is employed in the processes of production and exchange. In our definition we shall confine the word within these limits, taking no account of various other forms of property to which it may be loosely applied.

DEFINITION. *Rent is the compensation received for the use of capital invested in land.*

As no human possession can be more secure from liability to loss than capital invested in land at its market value, the compensation received for it will be *for use only*, without any consideration of risk. It cannot therefore be higher than interest at the lowest rate, on the present value of the land. The nature of the case would lead us to expect that it would be even lower than the rate of interest, in cases in which the security is supposed to be absolute. A presumption always exists, that the *value of the land will be steadily enhanced with the progress of society*. For this reason a landholder will always be willing to receive a lower rate of interest for his capital invested in land, because that capital itself is presumed to be increasing in value. In addition to this in some countries, as for example in England, the land owner enjoys considerable advantages of respectability, dignity and social position, for himself and his family, which all men value, and for the sake of enjoying which, he is willing to invest his capital at a lower rate of interest than he would expect from other investments.

It is also true that the national passion for owning land which so permeates all English thought, custom and literature, is not entirely extinct even yet in any of the peoples that are off-shoots of England, that still use the English language, and read English books. Perhaps even more than this is true. Perhaps *a desire to own land has its seat in human nature itself.* Perhaps it is natural for man as man, to feel a peculiar sense of dignity, independence and personal importance, when treading on his own soil, and sitting beneath his own roof. We suspect that men universally have a pleasure in the ownership of land, which renders them willing to invest capital in land with the expectation of receiving from it less value in return, than they would demand from most other modes of investment.

§ 160. One question relating to rent has received a great deal of attention from economists, and occasioned much diversity of opinion. That question respects *the cause of the increase of the rent of land which always attends an increase of population and wealth*, unless that increase is accompanied by the introduction of agricultural products from more remote sources of supply. The theory of the subject now generally received by the leading representatives of English economic thought is that published in 1817 *by David Ricardo, in his Principles of Political Economy and Taxation.* It has been generally regarded since that time by writers of the English school, as a complete solution of the question. It may be succinctly stated thus: *The rent of any piece of land at any time will be precisely equal to the difference between the net value of its products and the net value of the product of the poorest land, whose products barely pay the expense of cultivation, without any rent.* The reasoning by which it is sustained is something like the following. In the first settlement of a country, there can be no rent, for there will be more land of the best quality than can be cultivated, and therefore any one can have as much land as he pleases without rent. When all the land of best quality has been brought into cultivation, and by reason of the increased population proves inadequate to furnish the necessary supply of agricultural products, then poorer lands will be brought into use. At the same time lands of the best quality will begin to pay rent, because one would be willing to pay for the choice between land of the first and second quality the difference of the productiveness of the two. When the supply of the second class is exhausted, land of third class fertility will be entered on, the second class will bear rent, and the first class still higher rent, and so on, the first class rising higher and higher as the increasing demand for agricultural products forces cultivation downward to poorer and still poorer lands. The answer which this theory gives to the question under consideration is, that the cause of the increase of price of agricultural products is the necessity of deriving them from poorer lands, and therefore at an increased cost of production.

§ 161. With that *first settlement of a country*, in which Ricardo's theory assumes that a certain state of facts must have existed, we were ourselves familiarly acquainted for many years, and are all able to bear witness of our own personal knowledge. The case furnishes a striking illustration how ill men succeed in determining on theoretic grounds, what facts must have been in a given case, while they are quite ignorant as to what they really were. What actually occurs in such circumstances contradicts what the theory assumes at every point. The notion of a state of things in which cultivated lands will bear no rent, is as fabulous as the centaur or the mermaid. Of two tracts of land adjoining each other, one would be under cultivation, the other not. Both would be of equal and unsurpassed fertility. The tract under cultivation would pay a rent of one third of the crop. The zero point from which rent is to be reckoned has no existence in fact. The reason is obvious; any piece of land that bears cultivation will pay a rent equal to the interest on the capital invested in it, making allowance of course for those considerations which reduce the rate of interest on capital invested in lands below the general average. These new lands under cultivation will pay a rent equal to the capital invested in them at this rate of interest. The Creator does not give us land in a state of readiness for the plowman and the seed-sower. It must be subdued, rank and useless natural growths must be removed at the expense of no small amount of labor, the whole must be surrounded by an enclosure, and furnished with strictly necessary buildings. The prairie lands of the upper Mississippi valley probably presented, in their natural state, as few obstacles to cultivation as any which have been subdued by man. Yet even they could not be fitted for cultivation for a less sum than six dollars to ten dollars per acre, including of course the payment made to the government for the land itself. This investment must be made in many instances, when the interest of money is as high as fifty or even sixty per cent per annum. Men who are without capital would be glad of the opportunity of paying one third of the crop for the use of the land in a state of readiness for seed-sowing, through equally good lands adjoining them were unused.

§ 162. Neither is the theory more successful in indicating *the successive steps by which lands of different degrees of fertility are brought into cultivation.* A great many other considerations besides natural fertility influence the choice of first settlers. The land is nearly all covered with a deposit of rich mould, resulting from the vegetable decay of ages, and will produce a few luxuriant harvests before its permanent quality becomes apparent. A forest of timber or a spring or a stream of water will often have far more influence on the choice, than the permanent qualities of the land. Mr. Henry C. Carey rejects Ricardo's theory of rent, but in his statement of facts, he is hardly more fortunate than Mr. Ricardo's theoretic assumptions. He represents that cultivation almost invariably begins on the comparatively barren hill sides, and makes its way slowly and gradually down to the rich alluvion of the valleys, where the most fertile lands are found. He can hardly have been an accurate observer of farming in new settlements, or he would not have made such statements. The circumstance which affects the choice of the new settler more than any other seems to be, the cost of preparing the land for cultivation. It may happen that the very best land may also be that which requires a very small outlay to subdue it. Or it may happen that the choice falls on a well-drained hillside, which can be very easily subdued, and will bear a few good crops, but will not be permanently fertile. It frequently happens also that some of the richest lands are encumbered with such natural obstacles to cultivation, that the rent they will yield will not pay the cost of subduing them, till the community is already far advanced in wealth and population. Some of the best lands on earth are lying quite uncultivated, awaiting the time when rents shall have advanced to such a point as to justify the outlay of capital necessary to subdue them. All the facts of the case entirely justify and sustain our reasonings and conclusions respecting the ownership of land. It is to be regarded as fixed capital, and rent is compensation for its use.

§ 163. *Ricardo's theory of rent radically fails by substituting cause for effect and effect for cause.* The real cause for the increasing price of agricultural products, as wealth and population increase, is the constantly growing demand for them. Their price would rise and equally rise, if there were no poorer lands that could be cultivated, or if the supply of them must be perpetually derived from the same unchanging sources. Increasing demand always occasions increased price. If the amount of capital needing to employ laborers is large, and the number of laborers that can be employed is small, capitalists will bid against each other under the apprehension of failing to get the laborers they need, and raise the price of labor. So as the number of mouths to be fed is multiplied while the supply of food remains stationary, men will be apprehensive of failing to obtain a supply, bid against each other and raise the price without any consideration whatever of the sources from which the supply comes. The sources of supply and the cost of production may remain absolutely unchanged, yet if the demand is increasing, while the supply is stationary, men will become apprehensive, and their apprehensions will have an effect on the price. This is the one cause of the rise of rents with increasing wealth and population. *It is exactly analogous to the rise of the rent of land to be used for purposes of trade in the heart of a great city.* With the growth of the population and trade of the city, the demand for those lands for certain uses which cannot be supplied by any other lands, constantly increases, and the price rises accordingly, and this increase of price will be limited only by the number and wealth of those that want it.

§ 164. On precisely the *same principle the rent of land used for agricultural purposes is raised, by the increase of wealth and population.* The increased rate of rent does not depend on population alone but, as in the case of land used for purposes of trade, on wealth also. If the people were all too poor to pay any more for agricultural products than they had been paying, they could bear no increased price, it would produce starvation. If the amount of capital in any country is small in proportion to its population, rent will be low however densely it may be peopled. But if population and wealth increase, an advance in the rent is inevitable. Increased demand for agricultural products will compel increased rent. Poorer lands, if any exist not hitherto cultivated, will be likely to be brought into cultivation. Entering on those poorer lands will however be the effect of the increased price of agricultural products, and not the cause of it. Lands will be brought into cultivation perhaps, which had lain neglected for ages, because agricultural products are so dear and rents so high, that these lands will now make a good return for the capital expended in reducing them to cultivation. Rent is not high because these lands are cultivated to produce food, as Ricardo's theory would have it, but these lands are under cultivation because the demand for agricultural products is so great that they will yield a rent which will satisfactorily remunerate the capitalist for subduing them. Rents would have been even higher than they are, if there had been no poorer lands to be brought into cultivation, and no long neglected lands which could be rendered fit for tillage by large outlays of capital.

§ 165. Many writers have made much of "*the law of*

*diminishing returns*" in connection with rent. We have hitherto said nothing on that subject, because we think the principle so obvious as hardly to require statement, much less argument. It seems to us that any farmer of ordinary intelligence knows, that, up to a certain point, the more he lays out in the judicious improvement and cultivation of a piece of land, the larger returns he will get, in proportion to the outlay; but 'that beyond that point, though the product will perhaps still be increased by additional outlay, it will not be increased in proportion to the cost. The more he expends, the less his percentage of profit will be. This is the law of diminishing returns. It is also true, that as rent rises, it becomes profitable to expend more in the cultivation. This is because the increased demand for agricultural produce enhances the price, and thereby compensates for the diminished quantity that is procured by a given outlay. In a given state of the market, five laborers will obtain from a given farm produce to the value of one thousand dollars. In the same state of the market, the produce of ten laborers would only be worth fifteen hundred dollars. But if by increased demand agricultural products have risen in price, so that what before sold for fifteen hundred dollars, would now command two thousand dollars, it will be as profitable to employ the labor of ten men, as it was before to employ but five. That is, the advanced price of agricultural products makes it profitable to employ a greater number of laborers for a given amount of product. The same holds of rent. According to Ricardo's theory agricultural products are dearer and rent higher because it costs more to produce a given amount. No, say we, they are dearer only, because there is a larger demand for them, and because they are dearer, it is profitable to produce them at a greater outlay of both rent and labor. They are not dearer because an additional supply is produced at greater cost, for they would be much dearer than they are, if no additional supply could be produced. The greater cost of the additional supply has no tendency whatever, either to raise the price of agricultural products, or to increase the rent. Both these phenomena are caused only by increased demand for agricultural products, and instead of being intensified they are mitigated by the additional supply, though at increased cost.

§ 165a. The most important consequence deduced from Ricardo's theory of rent, is the doctrine that "*rent is not an element of the cost of obtaining agricultural produce.*" Mr. Fawcett asserts this paradox, and quotes Mr. Buckle as saying, that this proposition "can be grasped only by a comprehensive thinker." It really seems to us that an intellect not very comprehensive is quite competent to perceive that it is not true. In proof of this doctrine the supposition is made, that by an act of the government all rents were made free. Such an act of wholesale spoliation it is claimed would make agricultural products no cheaper than before. It is true that if the same population remained with the same wealth wherewith to purchase, the same demand would exist as before. But these conditions would not be fulfilled. The hundreds of thousands whose capital is invested in lands, and the still greater number of thousands dependent on them for their employment and their bread, would be deprived of their living and reduced to starvation, because they had nothing with which to purchase food. Their necessities would therefore be withdrawn from the demand, and the price would fall. There is just as much propriety in making the supposition, that by an act of the government the wages of agricultural labor were abolished, and laborers compelled to till the soil without compensation. If this could be accomplished and agricultural laborers still live, it would equally be true that agricultural products would be rendered no cheaper by this gigantic act of spoliation. The same demand would remain to be supplied, and the price would remain unchanged. Will these gentlemen therefore allow us to make the inference, that the labor employed in the cultivation of the land or rather the wages which it receives "is not an element of the cost of obtaining agricultural produce?" It is quite true that if the holders of agricultural products could bring them into the market, without having incurred any expense either for rent or wages, other things remaining unchanged, they would be able to obtain the same prices for them as now. But such a supposition is fundamentally contradictory to the very nature of ownership. They are the owners of what they offer in the market, because they have paid both rent and wages, and he who purchases of them must of necessity repay not only wages but rent also.

§ 166. Mr. Fawcett speaks of the supposed act of government making all rents free *as the "abolition of rent."* Such an act of tyranny would not be the abolition of rent. It would be simply taking the rent from the owner of the land and giving it to the farmer that for the time being tilled it. Suppose a neighbor of that farmer, perceiving that great gains could be realized by cultivating land without paying any rent for it, should apply to the fortunate incumbent for the use of half his farm. The prompt reply would be, you may have it if, as a private transaction between you and me, you will pay me a fair rent for it. The farmer understands very well that the tyranny of the government has despoiled the owner of the land for his benefit. Why call such a transaction the abolition of rent?

*No government can abolish rent any more than wages.* We have shown that land becomes private property only because of the labor bestowed upon it to render it an instrument of human well-being. It is capital. That capital has descended to the present owner. Food can no more be produced without the use of the capital invested in the land than without the labor that tills it. Nor is this all. A farm is in an important respect analogous to the human body. As the body constantly tends to decay, and can be kept in vigor only by constant repair, so a farm constantly tends to revert to that natural state from which it was redeemed by labor and capital, and more labor and capital must constantly be employed to preserve it in a state of vigorous productiveness. The tenant farmer has no interest in preserving the permanent productiveness of the farm, and will make no outlay which will not conduce to the abundance of the harvest immediately expected. Buildings will go to decay, and all other permanent improvements will be neglected and deteriorated. The original outlay necessary to bring a farm into cultivation must in the course of a half century be renewed two or three times, and at greatly increased cost. New and better dwellings and out-buildings must be provided, drainage must be resorted to, more permanent enclosures must be constructed, and generally the farm must not only be saved from decay but brought up to such a degree of cultivation, as the present state of agriculture demands. A temporary tenant has no motive to provide for any of these things. Ownership and rent only furnish the requisite motive. Lands that have no owner will rapidly revert to their natural condition, and cease to produce food for man and beast. Rent is therefore as necessary and inevitable an element in the cost of the products of the soil, as the labor that annually tills it. The man who brings the produce of the farm to market, must equally demand compensation for rent and wages, and the amount he will be able to obtain will depend on the population and wealth of the community relative to the supply of his products.

§ 167. There is *another proof* equally strong that rent is an "element in the cost of obtaining agricultural produce." It is an admitted fact, that England has within a comparatively few years added nearly one-fifth to her population, and yet during that period the price of agricultural products has scarcely advanced at all. It is also admitted, that the reason why the price of food has remained nearly stationary is to be found in the fact, that large supplies have been imported from other countries. These supplies have been largely obtained from our own country. Why is it then that agricultural products from the interior of North America, transported a thousand miles by land, and three thousand by water, are yet offered in the London market at prices so low, as to prevent any advance in the price of food resulting from so great an increase of population? It is not because these supplies are derived from richer land. The produce of wheat per acre in England is probably greater than in the United States. It is not because they are the produce of cheaper labor. The wages of agricultural labor in the United States are probably more than twice as great as in England. It is because those supplies are derived from lands whose rent is scarce one-fifth what is paid for lands of like productiveness in England. The one cheap element in the cost of procuring American agricultural produce is rent. Every Englishman who in these days eats comparatively cheap bread, should gratefully remember the low rent of the United States. When land rents in the region around Chicago shall approximate, as at no very distant day they will, the rents of land around London, Englishmen must either eat very dear bread, or derive supplies from other fertile regions not yet invaded by accumulated wealth and dense population. Rent is an element in the cost of obtaining agricultural produce.

§ 168. It is also noticeable that Mr. Fawcett himself *does not after all derive the doctrine to which we object from Ricardo's theory of rent*, but from the consideration that if all rents were free, the same demand for food would still remain, and therefore prices be unchanged. This is admitting precisely what we contend for, that the fundamental element in the case is the demand which results from a given condition of wealth and population. We trust therefore that it is apparent to all readers, that Ricardo's theory of rent is not sustained by the facts which occur in the origin and progress of land culture, that it depends for all its plausibility on the fallacy of assuming that to be a cause which is only an effect, and that the chief consequence which men have sought to deduce from it, and for the sake of which the theory itself has been for the most part defended, contradicts fundamental natural law and is quite erroneous, and that it is not even deducible from the theory itself. We cannot refrain from expressing our wonder, that this theory and the paradoxical inference which men have sought to deduce from it, can have for fifty years maintained their position as fundamental laws of the science. We can only explain the fact by the consideration, that the general belief of the doctrine that rent is not an element in the cost of agricultural produce is fitted to afford powerful support to those land monopolies which have been very prevalent in European history, and one of which still prevails in respect to the tenure of almost all the lands in Britain. Of this subject however we shall speak hereafter.

§ 169. It is also noticeable that *the same fallacy is resorted to in explaining the price of minerals when the rela-*

*tion of demand to supply is changed.* If for example the demand for iron should at any time increase beyond what existing mines could supply, or if demand remaining the same the supply afforded by existing mines should diminish, the price would rise. It is claimed that the reason of this rise in price is to be found in the fact that less productive mines must be wrought, requiring a greater amount of labor and capital to obtain a given amount of metal. This is incorrect. The price has risen only because the demand relative to the supply has increased. The price of the metal would have been still more increased if there had been no other mines that could be resorted to. Less productive mines are wrought because the increased price of the metal makes it profitable to work mines which at former prices could have been worked only at a loss. The working of a less productive mine is therefore effect and not cause. The principle will hold in all similar cases. Ricardo's theory of rent will be found to involve the same fallacy wherever it is applied.

It is quite correct however in certain cases to speak of the cost of production as having been increased, or of the cost of living as having been advanced by the necessity of deriving supplies from more costly sources. If by the utter failure of the coal supply of England, she were compelled to obtain all which she uses from the coal mines of North America, the costliness of her manufactures would truly be said to be caused by the necessity of deriving supplies from more costly sources. But if, the coal supply of England remaining unimpaired, the demand for coal should in any way be so much increased and the price of it so much raised, that it could be carried from North American mines, and sold in England at a profit, it would surely not be sound philosophy to ascribe the enhanced price of coal in England to the necessity of transporting it across the Atlantic. The price would have been much more enhanced, if there had been no American coal to transport.

---

## CHAPTER IX.

### *Profit.*

§ 170. ANOTHER form which the gains of the capitalist assume is profit. It is next to be considered.

DEFINITION. *Profit is the compensation which the capitalist receives from employing his capital in any process of production or exchange.*

It differs from interest in embracing a greater number of elements. Interest is compensation for the use of capital, and such ordinary risk as one must for the most part incur when he entrusts it to another. Profit embraces interest on the capital employed, and in addition to it compensation for the *peculiar risk* which is incidental to the modes in which capital is employed, and for the labor, skill and pains-taking of the capitalist in superintending and directing the process. The interest element in profit of course varies with the variations of the rate of interest. A capitalist will expect, in addition to compensation for the risks of trade, and his own personal services, such a rate of interest as his capital would command in the market. He will of course not take into the account the minor almost daily fluctuations of the rate of interest which are liable to occur, but the more permanent changes in the interest market will be taken into the account in determining what rate of profit will be satisfactory. Any capitalist would be willing to engage in any business with a prospect of much less profit when the current rate of interest was five per cent than when it was ten per cent.

Of course profit *must closely sympathize with interest* in that steady decline of the rate which, as has been shown, is always occasioned by the increasing wealth and civilization of a community. As society becomes more mature, it will not only become easier for laborers possessing skill, industry and integrity, to borrow what they need in aid of their labor, but all commodities into the production of which capital enters will be produced at lower prices, or at least brought more within the reach of all classes of the community, in consequence of the abundance of capital and the smallness of the rate of profit. As already admitted for reasons shown, agricultural products are not subject to this law.

§ 171. In this as in all other departments of our science *competition is the supreme law.* It is frequently asserted that competition will reduce the rate of profit in all the different modes of employing capital to a common standard. This cannot be admitted. It would be true if all the other elements that come into consideration in choosing the mode in which one's capital is to be employed were equal. But they are far from being equal. Some modes of employing capital necessarily involve great risk, others very little. If capital is to be employed in manufacturing gunpowder or in purchasing a steamboat to run upon our Western rivers, it will be exposed to great risk, and no man will make such an investment without a prospect of profits large enough to insure him against this risk. Other modes of employing capital are very numerous in which no such extraordinary risk is incurred. Men can afford to engage in such branches of trade at a much lower rate of profit, and competition will therefore settle the rate of profit in them at a much lower point. Before engaging in any branch of business, prudent men will insist on a prospective rate of profit, which will fully insure them against all its foreseen risks.

Some modes of employing capital compel the capitalist to engage in occupations which *are disagreeable, or are not held in much respect and honor* by the community. Few capitalists will desire such investments, and consequently those who are willing so to invest their capital will encounter very little competition, and therefore obtain compensation for the undesirableness of the occupation itself in other respects by a high rate of profit. It is to be deeply regretted that not a few capitalists are found who are willing to accept high profit as a compensation for violated conscience, and are therefore willing to invest their capital in producing that which is destructive of the prosperity, the happiness and the virtue of those from the indulgence of whose appetites their profits are derived.

Other employments of capital *are agreeable and regarded by the community as conferring dignity and respectability* on those who successfully engage in them. They are apt to acquire a high social position for themselves and their families. Men are often willing to invest their capital in such employments for very little profit above bare interest and risk. They regard their personal services as in a great degree compensated by the dignity, respectability and desirable mode of life which they enjoy. Of course there is great competition for such investments, and the rate of profit is very low.

§ 172. These considerations are quite sufficient to show that so far is it from being true that competition reduces the rate of profit in different modes of employing capital to a common standard, it must necessarily result in producing very wide diversities in this respect. One law does however prevail through every department of trade. Every mode of investing capital does find its own level. *It does establish a rate of profit which is natural and proper for itself.* Competition will clearly determine how much weight all the advantages and disadvantages of any investment have in men's minds, and what rate of profit will be accepted in each particular investment. Whenever in any case profits are found to exceed that natural rate, capital will have a tendency to leave other modes of employment and flow towards that in which the excess exists, and will continue to flow, not till all profits are equalized, but till each mode of investment has its own proper rate of profit, after all advantages and disadvantages have been duly considered. There is not equality but a constant tendency to equilibrium of rates of profit.

This law is not however so stringent as not to leave room for wide diversities of the rate of profit in different establishments employed in the same trade. *Personal characteristics* may exert very great influence. Superior sagacity, wisdom and skill in management may obtain ample compensation by raising the profit far above the general average, and this sort of superiority can only be reached by the competition of other men possessing equally eminent qualities in the management of affairs. No free competition can deprive any man of the full benefit of his own wisdom and skill.

In an order of things in which competition is not interfered with by any impolitic legislation, it will determine with unerring accuracy *what branches of industry may be most profitably pursued in any place at a given time.* If any commodity is offered in the market at a cheaper rate than that at which it can be manufactured there and then, it is proof conclusive that the capital of that community cannot be profitably employed in manufacturing it. The reason why it cannot is, that it is already employed in producing something else which yields a higher profit. Any legislation which so obstructs the introduction of that commodity into the market, as so to raise its price that capital can be profitably employed in producing it, is simply compelling the people to pay more for that commodity than its real value, and creating artificial motives to induce capitalists to withdraw from more profitable investments and engage in those that are less profitable. It is taxing the community to pay capitalists for wasting their capital.

§ 173. All this goes on the supposition that the investment of capital is left to be determined by perfectly free competition. In speaking of wages, we were at considerable pains to ascertain to what extent the influence of competition may be modified by combinations to resist it. It is equally important here to inquire to what extent the same natural force may be *modified or counteracted by combinations of capital*. It is alleged that where a vast fortune is owned by one person and therefore managed by a single intellect and a single will, such a capitalist may and often does obtain the control of the entire supply of some commodity for perhaps a whole nation, and thus become able to exempt it entirely from the influence of competition, and set his own arbitrary price upon it. It is also asserted that where this cannot be done by a single capitalist, it can be by a combination of capitalists whose interests are common. It is plain that the best possible protection of the community against such oppressive combinations is the widest freedom of trade. If an exclusive commercial system falsely called "protection of domestic industry" confines the supply of some commodity to a small number of easily accessible sources, as for example to a single country, a monopoly of that commodity in one or a few hands is rendered easy, and the community may be expected to suffer from such exactions, and a community determined to maintain such legislation should utter no complaints of being oppressed by combinations of capital. "Protection" of the producers of a commodity thus monopolized is protection of a combination of grasping capitalists united in a league to practice gigantic exactions upon a community, whose exclusive legislation has rendered it powerless to resist them. It is a strange state of things and not very agreeable to contemplate, when a duty nearly prohibitory on the one hand discountenances the introduction of the coal of British America into the seaports of the New England and Middle States, while on the other hand a combination of the Pennsylvania coal companies is assisted by that "Protection," for months and years in succession, to exact from ten millions of the American people such prices for their coal as their arbitrary will dictates, screened from foreign competition in order that they may succeed in strangling all competition at home. Such an anomaly our people have endured and patiently tolerated under the paralysing influence of the nightmare of "Protection." Under such laws combinations of capital in particular lines of industry to dictate arbitrary prices to all the rest of the community will always be easy and of frequent occurrence. The only protection of the community against the coal monopolies is free trade in coal, and if the community has not intelligence and spirit enough to demand the application of that remedy, it richly deserves to suffer all the exactions which those monopolies can impose. But if our ports are open to the trade of all the world, subject to no other imposts than those that are strictly necessary for purposes of revenue only, such combinations can very seldom be successful, and will be rendered too hazardous to be often attempted.

It must however be admitted that there are a few cases in which the supply of some important commodity is by the nature of the case *so much confined to a very few hands*, as to render the success of such a combination possible, and in the present condition of the public mind in this country, not improbable. Petroleum is an example of this. Our great parallel lines of railway between the interior and the Atlantic coast furnish another example. In either of these cases it is difficult to see what means the people have of protecting themselves against exactions, which at first view seem limitless. Are they limitless?

§ 174. The competition that naturally exists in the case is *between capital in one particular mode of investment and all other capital.* Those interested in the one mode of investment are seeking by combination arbitrarily to dictate prices to all the rest of the world. Such an attempt is in the long run very likely to prove self-destructive. The petroleum trade will suffice for an illustration. Within a few months a combination of holders has nearly doubled the price of that commodity to the consumer. The consequence must eventually be a greatly diminished demand. All other modes of artificial illumination will be resorted to more freely than before. Less artificial light will be used on account of increasing economy, and the area over which petroleum will bear to be transported will be diminished. Discovery and invention will also be stimulated to search after other methods of illumination, and other sources of supply. More recently it is announced that the combination is falling to pieces by the Canadian confederates refusing to abide by the terms of it. Would it not be wise for our government to aid those American capitalists who are struggling hard to maintain so praiseworthy a combination, by imposing a prohibitory duty on petroleum produced elsewhere than in our own country? This would at least be a consistent carrying out of our policy in respect to coal. Who stands ready to prove his consistent statesmanship, by introducing a bill for that purpose in Congress?

§ 175. The *great railway combination referred to above* is one of still greater interest and importance. These lines of road seem to possess the power of combining to establish the rates of transportation both for freight and passengers at any point they may agree upon. Thus a small number of railway magnates seem to possess a power of taxation, which if not unlimited is at least of very indefinite extent. It is true they have sometimes a good deal of difficulty in agreeing together what that fixed point shall be, and while they disagree, the community enjoys a season of temporary relief. But for the most part they are agreed, and the public has only to pay the prices which they impose. The excitement of the public mind on this question has been intense, though often we think, neither intelligent nor wise. The doctrine has been widely inculcated that the public has peculiar rights in the case, growing out of the fact that railways are held and worked under acts of incorporation granted by the legislature, and not by individual capitalists. But is it not evident that their rights and privileges are neither more nor less than individual capitalists would possess in like circumstances? The evil lies in the ease with which they can control an immense capital by the power of a single will. But this does not result at all from the fact that they are corporate and not natural persons, but from the greatness of the enterprises and the vast amount of capital necessary for their construction and working. It cannot be denied that these great corporations do often for months and even years in succession so combine as to a great extent to set the law of competition at defiance. When, on the occasion of ascertaining that the crop of Indian corn in the great interior for a certain year was much larger than usual, the "representatives of the great competing lines" spent a social evening together at Fifth Avenue Hotel, and closed the pleasant interview by adding ten cents to the freight of a bushel of Indian corn from the Mississippi to the Atlantic coast, the public were confounded, the economists were made acquainted with a new law of price, but neither the public nor the economists saw any way of evading the tax so unceremoniously imposed. No one has yet succeeded in showing how these corporations can be made amenable to the law of competition.

Not only do such combinations set aside competition in determining the price of transportation, but cases certainly have not been wanting, in which a great railway company has been able *to exert such an influence on the Legislature, as to prevent the chartering of any parallel line to compete with it*, and thus to prolong the monopoly indefinitely for the future.

§ 176. This last mentioned evil could be easily remedied. Instead of granting a special charter to each railway company, *all should be constructed under the provisions of a general railway law*. Any capitalists might then, by simply complying with the provisions of the law, construct a railway wherever they might think it would yield a profit, and all capital invested in railways would be constantly liable to encounter new competition. Such liability would be a great protection to the interests of the public. The remedy is to be sought, as in a great many other instances, in allowing the largest freedom for the investment of capital.

This however affords no security against *combination of parallel lines*. If we are correctly informed a recent decision of the supreme court of the United States sanctions the principle, that the Legislature may prescribe by law a maximum rate of transportation. Such a law wisely drawn would probably afford the public considerable protection. But that decision of the supreme court does not reach far toward the root of the evil. Fixing prices by law is not much more in harmony with sound principles of economy, than dictating them by the will of one of the parties. All economic arrangements must be elastic. Prices cannot be uniform. They refuse to be regulated by any cast iron rule. Rates of transportation which would be exorbitant at one time, or in one set of circumstances, would be ruinously low in other cases. Man has not yet discovered any other method by which prices can be equitably adjusted except that of competition. If railways reject that method it is difficult to see how it is possible to make the law supply its place.

§ 177. The public ought to find *protection in the sagacity, integrity and wisdom of the men who manage our great lines of railway*. Nothing can be more evident, than that the prosperity of these great companies will always depend on the prosperity of the great interior, especially on its agricultural prosperity. In an enlightened view of things, the real interests of the railways will be best promoted, by enabling the farmers of the interior to transport the products of their farms to the markets of the world at the lowest rate which will afford a reasonable compensation to the carriers. That will stimulate production to the greatest possible activity; and insure to the railways a constantly increasing amount of traffic, the profits of which under the law of competition will rapidly increase for a long time to come. It is evident that the agricultural productions of that vast interior region and especially the growth of maize can be indefinitely increased, with scarcely any increase of the cost. It would be about as easy to double the agricultural products of that portion of our country, as to double the quantity of woolen and cotton cloths produced in England. Increase of demand is the only lacking condition of an almost indefinite increase of the agricultural products of the Mississippi Valley. If the great railway companies study their own real interests, they will encourage and foster and not oppress that greatest of American industries. In such a case a selfish and grasping policy would be unwise and suicidal. In speaking of the combinations of laborers to raise wages above the natural rate, we had occasion to point out the danger of arresting the natural increase of capital and palsying the hand that feeds. The same danger exists however on the other side. It is admitted that capitalists are apt to be sagacious, but it must also be admitted that they are often too greedy of immediate gain to be truly wise. Whoever will devise a method of establishing a rate of transportation on these great lines of railway on the basis of open and equal competition, will doubtless confer a great benefit on all the parties concerned. Surely while these great companies set so stupendous an example of combination to resist competition, no one should be surprised that their employés combine for higher wages, and that every where strikes are of very frequent occurrence. Such examples in high places are very likely to be followed.

§ 178. We cannot however refuse to admit, that this railway problem is in some of its aspects *complicated and difficult*. The occurrence of an exceptionally large harvest in the interior of the country presents some questions of real difficulty, which are not always considered. On the one hand should the railways attempt to transport all which should be offered, at rates of moderate profit to the stockholders, it would probably be many months before the necessary amount of "rolling stock" could be procured to meet the demand. The prompt filling of all orders would be impossible. On the other hand if the railway companies should make haste to procure the necessary equipment, as soon as that emergency was over, their "rolling stock" would greatly exceed their needs, and a large amount of unused capital would be on their hands.

It should also be borne in mind, that if it were possible to send promptly to the great markets all which would be offered at moderate freight rates, *the supply in those markets would be so greatly in excess of demand*, as to reduce the price to a point ruinously below the cost of production, and thus prove very injurious to the farmers themselves. If competition could be brought to bear in determining freight rates, it is certain those rates would be greatly raised in such a case. The case may not differ much from the practice of the Bank of England, to raise the rate of discount, when pressed with more applications for discount than it can safely grant. It accommodates those who pay highest. At low rates of freight it is certain the roads can not carry all which in such circumstances would be offered. To raise the freight rates is the only method of reducing the amount of work demanded, within the limits of possible performance. It should also be noticed that this mode of procedure comes fairly within the limits of the law of competition. The arbitrariness of the proceeding may be more apparent than real. It may be only saying, we cannot accommodate all, we will serve those who will pay best. An honorable private gentleman in any profession might feel himself quite at liberty to say the same. To one who stands at a little distance and surveys this contest, wisdom and justice would seem to unite in requiring, that these great companies should at all times provide such an equipment as experience has shown can be kept on hand with profit, to fix the medium price of transportation at rates of fair profit, and to raise the rates when the traffic exceeds the capabilities of the line, and reduce them again when the extraordinary demand ceases. If the public could know, that the great competing lines are conducted on this principle, all reasonable men would be satisfied that competition has all the influence it can have in such a case. If to this it is replied that the line which should be conducted in this way would be ruined by the competition of parallel lines, it is perhaps a sufficient answer to say, that since it is plain the railway companies do not trust one another, it is perhaps not strange that the public does not implicitly trust them.

We must leave this subject with the conviction, that in the present circumstances of society, the public *has no very satisfactory assurance, that there are not some cases in which capitalists devoted to particular industries can, by combinations for the purpose, protect themselves from free and open competition* for periods, and perhaps for long periods, and thus exact upon the public according to their own arbitrary wills. If this is so, these cases must be taken from the court of economics—it cannot deal with them—and referred to that of ethics. If such cases really exist, the question will fairly meet us, to what extent honorable men can avail themselves of such opportunities of arbitrary exaction.

§ 179. It cannot be denied that some inevitable evils are connected with the aggregation of large masses of capital under a single management. But there *are advantages also* which civilization can not dispense with. Without such aggregations, those vast enterprises which form the most striking characteristic of our times would be impossible. In many other cases in which they are not absolutely indispensable, they greatly increase the productive power of capital. Large establishments are, from the very fact that they are large, often much more profitable than small ones. It costs nearly as much to superintend a small operation as a great one. Motive power can often be much more economically used in a large establishment. There are many other expenses which do not by any means increase in proportion to the size of the establishment. In many branches of industry these advantages are so great, that if the demand were not greater than the large establishments could supply, competition would drive the small establishments out of the trade. But the forming of large combinations of capital is not always easy. The demand for the commodity produced must therefore be still partially supplied from smaller establishments. The larger will, however, other things being equal, enjoy larger profits.

## CHAPTER X.

### *Underlying Conditions of Free Competition.*

§ 180. IN the whole progress of this treatise thus far, we have been following the law of competition in its application to all the various phenomena of labor and capital. It seems desirable, before proceeding to the remaining questions to be discussed, to point out and insist on three underlying conditions of the sound and healthful working of competition. These three conditions are,

1. *Perfect freedom of exchange in all circumstances.*
2. *Such a degree of intelligence in both parties to any*

*transaction, as will place them on a footing of substantial equality.*

3. *Moral integrity.*

By insisting on perfect freedom of exchange, we do not object to the right of society *to protect itself against any trade which is destructive of health and morals.* Against all such trades it is the duty of the government to protect the community as truly as against the contagion of small-pox. But in respect to all articles not injurious to society, and possessing exchangeable value, freedom of exchange is a fundamental law of humanity. Many of us fail to see how profoundly fundamental it is. Its import may be thus generalized. It is a first law of society that he who offers a higher value for anything than any one else offers for it, or sets upon it, is the natural owner of it, and in the view of a sound economy should meet no obstacles in becoming the actual owner of it. In our previous discussion we have vindicated such freedom of exchange in respect to the commodities of commerce, and in respect to all transactions between employers and employés. But there is one application of the principle which it seems quite necessary to insist on, before we proceed further, for to talk of free competition without the fulfillment of this condition, is in many cases to delude ourselves with words which can have no meaning. *We refer to the application of freedom of exchange to the tenure of land.*

181. The ownership of land which is acquired by labor bestowed on it is absolute and entire. It includes not only the right to hold and use and enjoy, but the right to exchange it for anything which the owner regards as more desirable. *A law which renders the land inalienable is a direct violation of this natural ownership.* It may be that the present owner of a farm derives his title to it by inheritance from an ancestry that never

possessed such absolute ownership. Their title may have originated from the grant of a conqueror who held it only by the law of force. But it is now impossible to repair that act of violence, by restoring the title to the natural heirs of those from whom it was wrested. The real owners are the present holders. The present value of the land is due to the capital and labor which they and those from whom they inherit have bestowed upon it, and the law should recognize the absoluteness of their title, by removing all obstacles to the freedom of exchange. The present owner may *have no taste for agricultural pursuits*, and no talent for prosecuting them successfully. Land is not therefore the instrument which he needs to aid the work of his life, and will therefore never in his hands be brought up to its full productive power, and never render to humanity the service of which it is capable. He will pursue perhaps the line of life for which he is qualified by his taste and his talents under a great disadvantage, because the instrument which he possesses is not that which he needs.

Near by him is one who has *both taste and talent for an agricultural life*, but he has no land. That farm is the very instrument which he needs to aid the labor which he is best fitted to do. He is able and willing to give for it a sum of money which seems to the owner of the farm much more desirable than the farm, because with it he can obtain the instruments and helps that will aid him in the work of his life. If now he owns the land in fee simple and no unnecessary obstacles obstruct the transfer, he will exchange it for the money, and both parties will thereby be greatly benefited. But if he holds it by an inalienable tenure, or the transfer is encumbered by many difficulties and expenses, the farm will probably remain comparatively unproductive, his own labor must be done under a life-long disadvantage, and his neighbor must shift as well as he can without the land he needs. It requires no argument to show, that the exemption of that land from the freedom of exchange is hurtful to every person interested in the ownership of it, and to the whole community. Nature's beneficent system is interfered with, one of her fundamental laws is violated.

§ 182. Let us not leave this topic till we have some correct conception how widely this mischief spreads itself, in a community in which land is generally exempted from the freedom of exchange, and how deeply it penetrates. We need not look far into the history of nations, to assure ourselves that it is *the highest ambition of the agricultural laborer everywhere, to own the land which he tills.* To accomplish this he will impose on himself unremitting toil, and submit to a life of the severest self-denial and frugality. The ownership in fee simple of the land on which he labors is his natural savings-bank. Let the possession of land be subjected, like that of all other property to perfect freedom of exchange, and burdened with no exorbitant expense for conveyance; and the ever active desire of the laborer for the land he tills will, through the innumerable incidents to which the life of every community is subject, find its opportunity. A case like that already supposed will occur. Or the owner of land will become involved in debt, and his lands will be sold in payment. Or he will leave his farm to many heirs, and it will be sold to facilitate partition. Or by some other one of innumerable possible incidents the same thing will be accomplished, and nature's intentions will become effect. Ownership will pass to him that most desires and most needs it. The tiller of the soil will become its lord.

But if the land is owned in great estates by a title which forbids any present owner to alienate it, *the laborer has no hope.* He never can be any thing but a landless drudge. The ownership of the soil he tills is not "warranted and defended," but forbidden "to him and his heirs forever." He and his fellow laborers sink more and more deeply into the condition of a degraded class of "hewers of wood and drawers of water" for the favored proprietors of the soil of their common country. A hereditary class have a monopoly or rather the exclusive possession in perpetuity of the only property which can be of any real importance to the agricultural laborer. A class of men, who with their ancestors who have gone before them, have given to the lands of the country all the real value which they possess, not only do not own those lands, but are virtually by law forbidden to own them. They spend their lives in a long succession of generations without the stimulus of hope. They may save, but they have little inducement to do so, for the savings bank is their only place of deposit, and the interest it pays is so small that it makes scarcely an appreciable addition to their income. They have no interest in trying to make their labor more efficient, for they will themselves derive no advantage from its increased efficiency. The buoyant forces are all taken out of their lives. It is sorrowful to read the philanthropic words of enlightened and humane Englishmen, deploring the condition of the English agricultural laborer, and in real earnestness inquiring what can be done for him. Should these words ever meet the eye of such men as Mr. Fawcett and Mr. Joseph Kay, they may perhaps attach little importance to opinions coming from the far off interior of North America. But for all that we know whereof we affirm, and must speak that we do know. Nothing can they do for this wretched class of their countrymen, and we claim the privilege of saying, our countrymen too,—nothing effectual, till they can procure the abolition of this hateful land monopoly, and thus give to every Englishman that fair chance which nature intended for him of owning that which he more desires and more needs than any one else.

§ 183. There has been and there still will be much effort to set all this aside, by proving that after all *large farming is more profitable than small farming.* Doubtless it can be easily proved, that the owner of a large farm enjoys some advantages over the small farmer. It is easier for him to avail himself of those agricultural machines which require a pretty large outlay of capital. But *it cannot be shown that small farmers cannot combine together* to secure those advantages, just so far as they are found really to reduce the cost of perfect cultivation. American experience shows that they can and will do any thing of the sort which their interest requires. Great landed proprietors need give themselves no philanthropic solicitude, lest the land should not be well cultivated if it should pass out of their hands. It has already been noticed, that agricultural machinery is not to any very great extent and probably never can be labor-saving. It is also far more important to the economy of a large farm than it can be to that of a small one. However that may be, no advantages which any intelligent man can expect from the use of agricultural machinery can make any compensation at all for degrading millions who should be self-active, self-impelling, self-superintending men, into mere machines, to be impelled and guided by the will and intelligence of an overseer. They say one overseer can superintend a hundred laborers as easily as fifty. But each one of those fifty or one hundred laborers will accomplish more as his own overseer, tilling his own land, and will produce better results than any overseer can obtain from him when reduced to the position of a mere working machine. Such is the precise difference between the agricultural laborer that never treads a foot of his own soil, or knows the luxury of sleeping under his own roof, and the man that owns the soil he tills, lies down at night in his own cot, and superintends and urges on his own labor.

§ 184. It may perhaps be urged as an objection to this view of the subject, *that English tillage under their system of large proprietorship is more thorough and complete than American tillage* under our free system. No American who has had the opportunity of making the comparison will deny this assertion. English tillage is more thorough and perfect, but it does not hence follow that, in our circumstances, it would be better. The English farmer and the American farmer are employed upon problems of quite different conditions. The problem of the English farmer is, to obtain the greatest profit from land of very dear rent, with very cheap labor. The American problem is, to obtain the greatest profit from land of very cheap rent, with very dear labor. Any sensible man would employ more labor at fifty cents a day on land whose rent was twenty dollars a year, or even twenty-five dollars, than he would if his labor cost a dollar a day and his rent only five dollars a year. Precisely this difference exists in the two cases, and fully accounts for the different degrees of thoroughness of the cultivation. The perfection of English tillage does not result from the tenure of the land, but from very high rents and very cheap labor. Any English traveler in the United States may easily satisfy himself, that in all instances in which the price of our lands approximates the English standard, the thoroughness of our tillage improves in much the same ratio.

We must not lose sight of another fact, which shows conclusively, that on the whole large farming under a great permanent proprietorship, is not more profitable than the small farming of freehold estates cultivated by the owner. Any man that owns a large farm can, provided no unnecessary difficulty or expensiveness obstructs the transfer, *sell it in small parcels, each suited to the wants of a small proprietor, who is to till it with his own labor, for much more than it can be worth under one management,* and the tillage of hired laborers; and the small proprietors who may buy it at these high rates will be far more prosperous, and live in a far higher style of comfort, than the laborers that tilled it under the single management and ownership.

§ 185. We are liable to be asked why, if this is so, English lands *are continually being aggregated into large farms*, and the holdings rapidly becoming less numerous. The answer is obvious. English law from the time of the Conquest, backed up by English custom founded on the law, and if possible more imperative than the law itself, attaches an unnatural dignity, personal importance and social position to the owner of land. These advantages excite in every man of wealth an artificial eagerness to be a landholder, and make him willing to pay more for it than, considered merely as a source of income, it is worth. Primogeniture greatly increases and intensifies this passion for land. The law sustains primogeniture by giving the landed estate of all intestates to the oldest son. Custom follows out the same idea, and extends it where the law does not carry it. To will one's landed estate to his oldest son comes to seem right, it is custom, it is respectable, it is English; to divide it equally among his children smacks of agrarianism, it is an approach toward—something not quite English. Law and custom combine to aggregate landed property into the smallest number of holdings, and to throw the labor of tillage as far as possible upon laborers to whom the ownership of land has become impossible. All the attractions of rank, so powerful to English minds, attach themselves to land, and raise its price far above its worth as a source of income. There can be no equal competition between the land owner and the laborer in circumstances such as these. The laborer has been degraded by being subjected to these unfavorable influences for successive generations, and can conceive of nothing as possible to him but the hard lot in which he lives. He has no home of his own to be rendered tidy and neat and beautiful by female care and taste; his wife and daughters and sisters having no home function, often sustain at his side the labor of the field, and swell the superabundant supply of labor which keeps down its wages to the very verge of starvation. This sad picture might be verified in every particular, by citing English authorities of the very highest respectability. If English philanthropy will do anything for the agricultural laborer with permanent effect, she must direct her efforts to the total and perpetual abolition of her land monopoly.

If we are told that we Americans know little of the *difficulty of accomplishing so fundamental a revolution*, both in the political and social life of England, we reply that is very probable. Yet we do know enough of the serious difficulties of the case, to discern very clearly why English philanthropists, statesmen and Christians are very averse to looking this question full in the face in all its painful aspects. We once had a question involving still more alarming difficulties. We were compelled to meet it. With nearly three hundred years of experience of the beneficent workings of free trade in land, we are competent judges of the necessity of abolishing a land monopoly, however difficult it may be. We are willing to hear lectures from the other side of the Atlantic, on the monopoly of protection; we need them, some of us are grateful for them. Many of us are grateful for the support and encouragement we received from Englishmen in our conflict with slavery. But we are soundly qualified to give lectures on land monopoly. Of these two monopolies, both of them sadly out of place in the last quarter of the nineteenth century, the land monopoly is beyond comparison the more fundamental, and the more subversive of all sound economic principles.

§ 186. A second underlying condition of free competition stated in the first section of this chapter is—*such a degree of intelligence in both parties to any transaction, as will place them on a footing of substantial equality*.

Every transaction of exchange which is conducted by competition *assumes such equality*. No honorable man will negotiate an exchange with another party, knowing that he is ignorant of the value of his own property, and of that which is offered him in exchange, or if he does exchange with him, it will not be on the principle of competition. He will take upon himself the entire responsibility of making sure that the ignorant man suffers no loss in the transaction. A farmer cannot enter into competition with his domestic animals. According to his own knowledge he must give them what they need, and they can only have what he gives.

On precisely the same principle, individual men and classes of men may be so far degraded below the ordinary standard of intelligence, *as to be disqualified to transact many of the common affairs of life by competition*. There are classes of laborers who are in this very condition in respect to all contracts for wages. They might perhaps obtain higher wages from other employers than they are receiving. But they do not know it, and have too little mental activity to raise the question. It may be that higher wages are paid for such labor as they are accustomed to perform in other districts not far away, and to them not difficult of access. But they do not know it, and are too spiritless to raise the inquiry. We are told the difference between the wages of agricultural laborers in the counties of Wiltshire and Yorkshire, England, is five shillings a week, or considerably more than one-fifth of the entire wages which the Wiltshire laborer receives. Why does not competition equalize the wages paid in these two counties? For the most part the answer is the ignorance and stupidity of the Wiltshire laborer. The laborer might emigrate to some other country of cheap land, abundant food and high wages, lands too of liberty and security of life and property. But such laborers know not that there are any such lands, or that emigration is to them possible. In short it is a thing of most frequent occurrence, that in highly civilized countries large classes of men settle down into such conditions of ignorance and semi-brutality, that competition can do nothing for them. The pretense of competition is a mere sham, and will result only in stripping the ignorant man of his all, to enrich his sagacious and quick-witted competitor. While these classes continue in this degraded condition, our science can do nothing for them. It cannot reach them. It may point out as we are trying to do the causes of their unfortunate condition, and put in a plea for the removal of them.

§ 187. *It is for this reason only that public provision for education claims the attention of the economist.* We rejoice to say that there is in this country almost a unanimity of opinion, that the government ought to provide against the existence of any such degraded and ignorant classes in the bosom of society. The only point of difference which exists among us in respect to this matter relates to the manner in which provision shall be made for the supply of this want. There are those who think that the sovereignty over society should be divided, that one portion of it should be committed to the secular or civil power, and another very important portion of it to a spiritual power called the church, and that the education of the people should never be undertaken by the former, but entrusted entirely to the latter.  The civil power may raise money by taxation for the support of schools, but it must entrust the management of them entirely to the ghostly power of the church.  It would be a novel arrangement indeed, that the civil power expressing the common voice of a free people should annually raise many millions of money to be entrusted to the management of a distinct sovereignty, sustaining no responsibility to the people that contribute it, and perhaps owing allegiance to a foreign prince.  But we have nothing to say in this place of this matter.  It belongs to morals and not to economics.

Neither shall we attempt to define with any accuracy *the limits of that system of education* which should be provided for all the people at the expense of the state. Public education comes within the sphere of economics only from the necessity of qualifying all the people for entering into that competition, which we have seen is the controlling force throughout the economic world.  It is obvious that a system of public instruction must, in order to accomplish that end, afford to every citizen the means of acquiring a sound acquaintance with our noble mother tongue as spoken, written and printed, and thus come into communication through common and public discourse, personal correspondence and periodicals and books, with the existing actual world, and with the civilization of our own age and of all ages.  He should also be supplied with a knowledge of numbers, as requisite for all the ordinary purposes of computation and accounts. The great outline facts of geography, history and science will be everywhere open to the easy acquisition of any one who possesses such a knowledge of a civilized mother tongue, and of the science of numbers. We do not affirm that the state ought not to provide for all the people a much more extensive education than this. But we do say on the one hand, that no one can be fairly qualified to meet the competitions of life without having received an education substantially fulfilling these conditions. On the other hand we affirm that such an education does place the man who has enjoyed it in vital communication with the thought of the world, and qualify him to take his place as a civilized man and citizen, and if it can be shown that the state ought to furnish to every citizen at the expense of the taxpayer, an education more extensive than this, the proof of that obligation must surely be found elsewhere than in the economic relations of the question. There is no pretense that persons thus educated are not well-fitted so far as schools can do anything for them, to meet all the competitions of trade and industry.

§ 188. Philanthropists to whom public education is a comparative novelty, are in danger *of placing too much dependence* on it alone, as a means of elevating depressed and degraded classes. You cannot educate a people without the stimulus of hope. The reason why popular instruction has always been so powerful in this country is to be sought in the fact, that hopefulness is the most powerful element in the life of our people. The very child at school sees that all the prizes of life are free to his competition, and that all the paths of prosperity are open before him. Remove from American society that element of hopefulness, and our system of popular education would cease to yield its beneficent fruits. It would languish and die. We do not believe "National Education" can do much for the English agricultural laborer, till the possibility of becoming the proprietor of the soil is given him. You cannot make him aspire to become an educated drudge. For his elevation our observation would lead us to repose far more confidence in free trade in land without public education, than in public education without free trade in land. A people with the avenues to every species of prosperity open before them are far more likely to educate their children without the aid of the state, than a class of persons against whom the avenues to a prosperous life are obstructed, are to receive an education when gratuitously tendered them. The experience of this country everywhere teaches the efficiency of self-help rather than of government help.

§ 189. The history of our country furnishes one example of the combined influence of free trade in land and a system of public education substantially such as that defined above, in qualifying a farming community for the vicissitudes of life, which deserves to be recorded. *We refer to the history of the farming population of New England.* Free trade in land existed there from the origin of the Colonies, and it has always been the glory of New England, that through her system of public schools every child was taught to read and write his mother tongue. The consequence is that New England never contained a degraded and wretched class, unless brought there by foreign emigration, and that a greater proportion of her sons have not only received the education of her common schools, but have been liberally educated at her colleges for professional and public life, and have become men of national and some of them of European reputation, than in any other community on the globe. This has been true not only of the sons of her wealthy families, but of the hard-handed farmers, that have forced a subsistence out of her rugged and unfriendly hill sides.

Nor is this all. The soil of these states is for the most part barren and its cultivation very laborious. Its winters are long and very severe, increasing the cost of living, and rendering the rearing of domestic animals very expensive. Early in the present century the farmers of these states began seriously to feel the competition of products procured from much better lands. Within the last fifty years, the products of the great interior of the country have found their way to the markets of the Atlantic coast by great lines of easy communication, and by their ruinous competition have driven most of the products of the New England farmer quite out of the market. Lands in New England have declined in price in many cases to one-half and in some cases to one-third the rates at which they were sold at the beginning of the century. In most cases in the history of the world, the falling of such disaster upon a numerous farming population has produced great distress and pinching poverty. The New England farmer has had the intelligence and energy to pass through the trial without any such experience. Some have remained at the homesteads of their fathers, and bought the lands of their neighbors at the reduced prices at which they were offered, and found the means of making a good living from the few products which could still be reared with profit. Others have disposed of their farms, and accumulated wealth by making the mountain torrents that rush down their valleys drive machinery of almost every variety. Others still went to the cities, engaged in commerce and often found their places among the merchant princes of the land. By far the greater number however traced back the lines along which that superabundance of agricultural products came that ruined their New England farming, made new homes amid the boundless fertility of the Great Valley, and became wealthy landowners. Give a farming population freedom of exchange and migration, and the self-reliance which is nurtured by high intelligence, and they will be equal to any emergency. The history of New England farming is worthy of the study of the economist.

§ 190. We mentioned at the beginning of this chapter a third underlying condition of equal competition—*moral integrity*. We do not propose dwelling on this topic. It is necessary to do little more than to name it. *Competition in the economic sense assumes the truthfulness of both parties to the transaction*, that each party is offering for exchange that which he professes to offer, and not something else. Whenever this ceases to be the fact competition between the parties ceases, and the struggle between them is no longer an effort of each to obtain the true value of his commodity, but a succession of cunning tricks to outwit each other. Prosperity means successful villainy, failure unsuccessful effort to defraud another. If any honest men come to such a market they are but too likely to fall victims to the arts of deception that are practiced all around them. Let no one imagine that such a scramble of knaves, each endeavoring to appropriate to himself the greatest possible amount of dishonest gains, bears any resemblance to that competition which is the pervading law of our science, of which truth is ever the fundamental element. The transaction of a people's business in the manner just characterized is the sure symptom of social decay and rottenness. The struggles of unprincipled men in the gold market, the stock market and the grain market to outdo other men in the arts of deception, sustain the same relation to honorable competition, that the ostentatious prayers of the hypocrite do to the genuine devotions of righteous God-fearing men.

## CHAPTER XI.

*Population.*

§ 191. It has been made evident in our previous discussions that population is an indispensable element of our science. We have seen how it is related to wages, to rent, and to the cost of living. It is necessary therefore next to inquire into the economic laws by which the movements of population are controlled. Toward the close of the eighteenth century, the celebrated Mr. Malthus published his theory of population, which has since exerted a prodigious influence on the economic writers and thinkers of the English school. It was originally in the mind of Mr. Malthus a powerful reaction against the day-dreams of the enthusiast Godwin, about the perfectibility of human nature. But its influence on the speculations of economists since its publication have been perhaps scarcely less injurious, than the prevalence of the theories he opposed would have been. As Professor Bowen very justly remarks, "the whole subject of Political Economy is colored with it," and we will add that coloring is a deep tinge of melancholy, which has rendered the whole subject repulsive to all minds of a cheerful and hopeful turn. It is our intention in this chapter to show that a true view of the subject gives no countenance to any such sombre and melancholy conclusions.

*The fundamental principle of Mr. Malthus' theory is, that the natural fecundity of the human race is such, that the population in all countries constantly tends to outrun the means of subsistence*, and therefore to keep the lower stratum of population always on the verge of starvation. English economists especially have accepted this doctrine without due consideration of the checks and modifications to which natural law subjects it, and have laid it so much to heart, that they often seem to regard it as the foremost duty of the economist, to point out methods of preventing the too rapid increase of the laboring classes. Scarcely any theme is dwelt on with more copiousness and eloquence, than the imprudent marriages of the laboring poor ; and we will add, that it seems to us, that on no subject have more eloquent words been wasted. The increase of population in a given country or in a given class depends on natural laws which will have their course, with very little respect to the eloquent words of economists.

§ 192. We have already shown, that in the long course of human events, the fundamental principle enunciated by Mr. Malthus would prove true, provided the whole world can be brought into such a condition of peace, prosperity and civilization as to permit both capital and population to increase according to their own laws, till all the resources of our planet are developed to the utmost, that is till the entire food-producing power of the whole earth has been brought into active use and development. But we purpose to show that in the long interval which must intervene before the human family can make any sensible approach towards such a consummation, *the doctrines of Mr. Malthus are to all practical purposes worthy of no consideration*, and that even at that distant day when if ever there shall be an approximation to that completed order of things, *there are ample provisions in the very nature of the case against the sombre conclusions to which the followers of Mr. Malthus would conduct us.* The safety of the human race in all the changes through which it is to pass in the progressive development of civilization is to be sought where, in the progress of this treatise, we have so often found it, in the full application of the law of competition. The operation of that law will afford the assurance we need through two consequences which will flow from it.

*I. It will disseminate by a regular and necessary process civilized communities over the whole earth, or at least where there are natural resources to sustain them.*

*II. Faithfully applied this law will always derive each succeeding generation from the soundest and healthiest part of the generation that precedes it.*

§ 193. We are first to consider the influence of competition in securing the gradual dissemination of civilized communities wherever they can find sustenance. This, like many other laws of our science, has only within very recent times sufficiently emerged from the confusion of the long conflict which has existed between civilization and barbarism to be capable of being distinctly discerned. But for the last two centuries it has been becoming more and more apparent, and can now be established as a permanent law of human progress. It takes effect both upon labor and capital. We must first consider its relations to labor. If the laborer is only a barbarian, hewing wood and drawing water for a civilized employer, he will be too ignorant to know that there is any place to which he can emigrate and find a better lot, and too stupid to make the effort. Such classes of laborers are almost as immovable as though they grew to the soil. But if the laborer has the intelligence and energy and self-reliance of a developed manhood, whenever the conditions of his life become hard; the government of his country oppressive, or the wages of his labor inadequate to the support of his family, he will seek a new home in some region of virgin fertility of soil and abundant unappropriated resources. And he will carry civilization with him. He cannot do otherwise. It is inwrought into the very texture of his soul. Wherever he makes his home, the institutions of civilization and freedom will spring up spontaneously. From the emigration of such a people civilized communities are as sure to spring up in any wilds where they make their home, as the fruits of the earth are to spring from the seeds which they sow. Such communities can not spring from any migrations of laborers who are not themselves civilized men, and consequently no nation can become the parent of such young offshoots of civilization, whose laborers are degraded and uncultivated.

Perhaps *the first manifestation of this law occurred in the English colonization of North America.* The magnificent results which have come from the settlements on the eastern coast of our country by emigrants from England, as compared with all else that has been achieved by the European colonization of the fifteenth, sixteenth and seventeenth centuries, can be explained only by the peculiar character of the population that planted those colonies. They were composed of farmers, artisans, merchants and scholars from the middle classes in English society, and bore with them to the new world the best elements of the civilization of the mother country, and transplanted them to their new homes, and the eminent success of England in planting colonies in all parts of the world is due to the fact, that she sends out emigrants that unite labor with culture. No nation can plant civilized colonies in the wilds of the earth, unless she has within her own bosom a working population which is imbued with her civilization. It is a great blessing to the world, that in the seventeenth century England had no Mr. Malthus to advise her to bring her birth-rate and death-rate as near to equality as possible, and that when he did appear, she was too wise to follow his advice, and that of the men of his school. Her population is still increasing at home, and widely diffusing her civilization in both hemispheres.

§ 194. We have said that this law of diffusion *was not apparent in the ancient world, or until comparatively recent times.* Several of the civilized nations of antiquity sent out many colonies, but none of them manifested much power to transplant and reproduce their own civilization in the lands which they colonized. It was for the want of that very element of which we have been speaking, laboring men, artisans, tillers of the soil, who could colonize and carry the civilization of the parent state with them. The reason why the Egyptians did not follow the Nile to its source, as the American emigrant does the Mississippi and its branches, and plant their civilization upon the fertile lands of Central Africa, and around the magnificent lakes which recent travelers have made known to the world, was that her civilization was confined to the upper strata of society, and her toiling laborers had no share in it. They did not know how to seek a better lot in other lands, and escape the competition that crushed them at home. They had no cultivation, and if they emigrated could not carry it with them.

There are some of the most cultivated nations of our own times, that seem to be in conditions in this respect very similar to theirs. The birth-rate and the death-rate are very nearly equal, and consequently they neither send out colonies to transplant their civilization, nor increase in population at home. They are as stationary as the followers of Mr. Malthus could desire. Such a nation may exert influence upon the world by its literature and science, its arts, its diplomacy and its arms, but that higher prerogative of reproducing itself under other skies by its colonial off-shoots is denied it.

§ 195. The power which a nation possesses of transplanting her civilization to unoccupied or sparsely occupied portions of the earth, *depends far more on the quality than on the quantity of her emigration.* There are at the present time several countries of Europe which swarm with emigrants, and yet the emigrating population of these nations shows very little power to lay the first foundations of civilized settlements. Their places of destination are colonies founded by men of other nationalities, and already in a prosperous condition. They are mingled with populations of strange language and institutions, and in a generation or two lose their own, and nearly all traces of their national origin disappear. Nations will be successful in transplanting their civilization, just in proportion as the civilizing forces have reached those middle and lower strata of society, in which the pressure of competition is most felt, and the impulse to emigration strongest. Even England herself would be far more powerful in this way than she is, if in any way her agricultural population could be brought up to the position of intelligent, cultivated, self-reliant men. A far less number of such men could do all the work of English agriculture than are now employed in it, and do it much better than it is done, and English economists, instead of uttering fruitless lamentations over the imprudent marriages of their laboring population, would exult in a still wider extension of the English language and English freedom in new regions of the earth than ever before. No doctrine can be more directly at war with the true prosperity of the world under its present conditions, than that of Mr. Malthus and his followers. The true economic lesson of the nineteenth century is not that of the Malthus school, but that given to our first parents, "to *be fruitful and multiply and replenish the earth.*" But we must remove from the generations that are coming all the oppressions of feudal and class legislation, and open to them all the blessings of free thought, free exchange and free locomotion, and then we shall have no reason to stand in fear of the " natural fecundity of the human race."

§ 196. Free competition will not only disseminate civilized labor over the earth, but *it will equally tend to send abroad the surplus capital of civilized nations.* We have seen that by an invariable law, the interest and profits of capital decline with the growth of wealth and civilization in any country. As the rate of interest declines, capitalists naturally become dissatisfied with the small gains they receive, and look abroad for more profitable investments. If there are other countries where the risk is no greater than at home, and the demand for capital so great as to pay a much higher rate of interest, capital is as sure as labor to yield to the force of competition, and go where a higher rate of interest can be obtained. Such opportunities of safe and profitable investment will be sure to be found in those new settlements which civilized labor is building up. The surplus capital of the country will therefore follow the emigrant laborer, and render him its powerful aid in founding and rearing up new free states and nations. As this process goes on, the safety of capital in the remote lands of the world will be constantly growing more and more assured, and capitalists will become less and less reluctant to trust their capital abroad. The consequence will be that the market for capital at home, relieved of a surplus, will be more buoyant, and accumulation more rapid. Surely then it should be the ambition of every civilized nation to secure for itself such a condition of its social and economic forces at home, that it may be able to bear its part in extending the blessings of civilization to the rest of the world.

§ 197. The other consequence which will result from

the application of competition to the problem of population is, that *it will always derive each succeeding generation from the soundest and healthiest elements of the generation that preceded it.* It is not denied that the law of competition honestly applied to society must produce great inequalities of condition. It is now necessary that we should examine these inequalities analytically, and endeavor to understand how they stand related to human well-being on the whole. Any observant man may easily satisfy himself that any civilized society, under the influence of competition, will present four classes of persons.

1. *A considerable number of persons will be found, who are not able to perform a sufficient amount of labor for their own support.* The persons who belong to this class have partly been reduced to it by disease, or misfortunes which they had no power to avoid, partly also by their own vices, or the vices of their natural protectors, and partly they have been born with natural endowments so inferior that they are incapable of self-support.

2. Another class is composed of those who, *though able to labor for self-support, are not able to support families.* These persons also have come into their unfortunate position through the same causes just enumerated.

3. A third class is composed of those, who by a life of labor and frugality *are able to support a family in plenty and substantial comfort.* In this class, in the best conditions of civilized society, are comprehended the great majority of the people.

4. The fourth class is composed of those *who are able to command an income that surpasses all that is needful for the sustenance and substantial comfort of a family.* This class is small in numbers, but controls a large portion of the capital of the community.

As civilization advances, competition has never failed in any country to develop these four classes; and, in respect to the problem of population the division is one of great importance.

§ 198. From the nature of the case *the two lower strata of society as just defined can contribute nothing to the capital of the future, and little to its population.* If marriages occur in these two classes and children are born, they will be born to conditions of poverty and want, and will either perish in infancy or be reared by charity. To a great extent the former will be the fact. Charity may do what it can for them, but their ordinary conditions will be so unfavorable, that few of them can survive those violations of the laws of life and health to which they will be exposed. These results will follow, not only in those advanced states of society in which population is approximating its greatest possible density, but in all stages of society. The difficulty in these cases is not the scarcity of the necessaries of life, but the inability of this class of persons to earn the support of a family. It is simply an application of the fundamental law that one owns nothing, except what he produces by the exertion of his own powers. These classes of persons do not own the means of supporting a family, because they do not produce them by their labor.

The persons included in these two lower strata *will not therefore be to any considerable extent parents of the coming generation.* Just in proportion as society is permeated by intelligence and high moral principle, the marriages of persons of these classes will be few and rare, because everywhere discountenanced and disapproved. They will for the most part spend their lives under the protection and in the families of those who belong to the more prosperous classes, and will not suffer the inconveniences and privations of poverty. Thus competition fairly applied will clearly draw the line between those who should marry and those who should not, and to a great extent prevent the marriage of the latter.

§ 199. The upper stratum or fourth class is, as has been remarked, small, and *does not contribute to the population of the future in proportion to its numbers.* For various reasons the self-indulgent spirit which is apt to prevail in the homes of the rich is proved by experience to be unfavorable to the rearing of children. *The ranks of population for coming generations are therefore chiefly filled from the third class.* It is also obvious, that for the most part in this class only are found the conditions most favorable to a sound, healthy and vigorous humanity. In all the other three classes they are in some degree wanting. In the higher, there is too little of self-denial, self-control and self-government. Both physical and mental energy are apt to be impaired by the absence of any felt necessity of exercising them. Humanity in the homes of the rich is too often like a hot house plant, sickly and delicate, because not inured to the trying varieties of experience which must be met in the open air of ordinary life. In the two lower classes the conditions are still more unfavorable either to physical, mental or moral soundness and health. But in the third class all the conditions of a perfect manhood may be more reasonably expected to exist, physical and mental vigor, a sound body and an active and instructed mind. If in this class the standard of domestic morality is elevated, marriage will be the almost universal condition of life, and large families will be apt to be reared.

§ 200. From the stand-point we have now attained, *we can discover the relation of the law of competition to the reproduction of the race.* It is simply and only a great natural provision for propagating the race from its soundest and most healthy specimens. Every intelligent farmer knows the necessity of providing for this, in order that his domestic animals instead of deteriorating, may improve in their successive generations. The law of competition secures the propagation of the human race in accordance with such a provision. Any other mode of distributing the products of industry than that which results from competition, would defeat this beneficent design, and propagate the race indiscriminately from the best and the poorest specimens, or even give preference to the poorest. For example that system of involuntary servitude which but lately existed in this country propagated the laboring population in the portions of the country where it prevailed, from a race of barbarians, retaining its barbarism in the midst of us. The master encouraged the breeding of his slaves, and reared their offspring as a matter of profit, precisely as in the case of his domestic animals. For the most part slaves were the only available laborers. The system therefore contained a provision for raising up an inferior humanity, a race of barbarians, to be depended on to do the work of the country in all the future. It artificially and in violation of nature's law provided for the propagation and perpetuity of barbarism—a barbarism as devoid of all the ornaments and beauties of life, of every thing except strictly necessary food and clothing, as the beasts of the field.

*The foundation principle of all free society is every man's ownership of himself*, resulting by an inevitable logic, in the law of competition. The law of competition gives us the law of wages, and draws the future succession of the race precisely from that portion of the community that is most favorable to health of body and soundness of mind, and all the noblest attributes of humanity, and thus places the race on an ascending and not on a descending plane for all the future.

One cannot fail to notice the agreement of the law of

population as thus developed *with that struggle for exist ence, that survival of the strongest,* which Mr. Darwin has shown to be very widely prevalent, both in the animal and vegetable kingdoms. We have by no means accepted the extreme inferences which Mr. Darwin draws from his very acute and philosophic observations. We do not think them justified by his facts. But he has shown that the principle above referred to has great influence in modifying a species within itself. We are not however in the least indebted to Mr. Darwin for the application of the principle to the human species in the law of population above stated. In the year 1863, years before we had any knowledge of Mr. Darwin's observations, we developed this law of population in an essay published in the Continental Monthly, then edited by Hon. Robert J. Walker. We have not since seen any reason to call in question its soundness.

§ 201. We come therefore to the conclusion that the law of competition in the distribution of the products of industry, applied to a people however numerous, and spread over however vast a portion of the earth, provided that people is thoroughly pervaded in all its classes with a sound and true civilization, *will secure its propagation on an ever progressive course of growth and improvement;* but that if there is an understratum which is excluded from the benefits of its civilization, poor, ignorant, stupid, vicious, that fact will entail upon it hereditary disease, which it will be exceedingly difficult to eradicate, when society has reached its maturity. We admit of course that the time must come, even on the supposition that all the social and economical laws of human well-being are strictly obeyed, when the population of the world will press hard upon the means of subsistence which can be derived from its soil. But the law of competition, applied under its necessary and natural conditions, affords the means of meeting that exigency as easily and with as little inconvenience, as it daily regulates the supply of breadstuffs or butcher's meat to the population of a great city. The supply is so accurately adjusted to the demand, that on the one side there is no lack and on the other no loss by excess. Precisely in the same manner, give competition unobstructed course, and give it freedom, rationality, intelligence and moral integrity to act upon, and it will adjust the population of the globe to the full productive power of the planet, without giving any occasion of anxiety or perplexity to the economic philosophers. There need be no fear of the too rapid increase of the laboring classes.

## CHAPTER XII.

### *Economic Conditions of General Peace.*

§ 202. It has been made apparent in the two preceding chapters, that it is an important condition of the healthful working of the economic forces, that intelligence and all the higher elements of civilization should reach and permeate that portion of the community that is composed chiefly of laborers possessing little or no capital. It was also shown incidentally, that the fulfillment of that condition is greatly facilitated by such an extension of free, stable and just government as will enable both labor and capital to avail themselves of the resources of the whole world. Such an extension of civilization over the whole world is the ultimate result toward which the whole system tends. In order to this *the prevalence of peace among all civilized nations is of prime importance.* It is our intention in this chapter to turn a little aside perhaps from the direct line of our argument, to show that this also is greatly dependent on the extension of the benefits of civilization to the laboring masses. Nations will not live in peace with their neighbors, while they maintain within themselves such misadjustments of economic forces, as have been all too common in the past history of the world.

In a former part of this treatise, it was shown, that there is such a natural adjustment of man's power to labor to the supply of his wants, that if the necessaries of life only are sought and enjoyed, a large part of his power to labor will find no employment, and remain perpetually useless. The same results will follow to a considerable degree, if the civilizing forces are applied only to a part of society. Doubtless the fund which the Creator has provided for the comfort, culture and ornament of human life is sufficient, if entirely utilized, to confer these blessings in some degree on all parts and portions of the community. When this end fails to be accomplished, when a small portion of society only enjoy these benefits to any degree, and the larger remainder live in disgusting squalor and rudeness, the beneficent designs of the Creator are not accomplished. A large portion of the fund which he has provided for human culture and development is wrapped in a napkin and buried in the earth. For example, we do not believe that the philanthropic and enlightened Englishmen who have reflected deeply on this class of subjects, would for a moment hesitate to admit, that the cultivation of the farms of England might be much better accomplished than it is, by a much smaller number of laborers than are now employed, if those laborers were stimulated by the hope that they and their families were to enjoy the comforts of civilized life. There is at this moment in the economies of England a vast waste of productive power, which might be developed and utilized for the elevation of those degraded masses. The same number of laborers under the influence of proper stimuli might not only produce the food which they consume, but very many comforts and beauties of life, which they never enjoy. The same must be true wherever vast masses of people labor throughout life, stimulated by no hope, but that of continuing a little longer their wretched existence.

§ 203. The point insisted on in this chapter is, *that the existence in any of the nations of the world, of such a vast amount of unused and wasted power is and always must be a destructive element.* In all constitutions of society, it threatens sooner or later to break out into insurrection and anarchy. If you reduce large masses to the helpless and dependent condition of domestic animals, you do not thereby impart to them quiet and unresisting instincts. You cannot so subjugate the human soul to power, that it will not retain a consciousness of manhood, and an intuition of the rights of manhood. It is always a thing not only to be apprehended, but expected that, perhaps after generations of passive subjection, millions of these degraded men will at length find a common expression of their sense of injured humanity, and give vent to their long pent indignation, by laying waste and destroying that wealth for which they and their fathers have labored, but which they have never enjoyed. That tranquillity and social order which are indispensable to the development of the great economic forces of the world can never be assured, indeed must always be in great peril, while the mighty nations that have the peace and prosperity of mankind in their safe keeping, embody within themselves vast masses of men that are doomed to these unnatural conditions. Perhaps there is not a nation on either side of the Atlantic, that has not occasion to look well to its ill-conditioned and suffering masses, lest a cancer should be fastening upon the body politic, destined at some time to prove fatal to the nation. Such phenomena are a violation of nature's intention wherever they exist, and cannot be perpetuated in any country without imminent peril. We ask for no revolutionary reforms. We have shown that all which can be done for such neglected classes is, to give them the full benefit of free competition for the acquisition of any species of capital by the possession of which their labor may be rendered efficient, and the opportunity to acquire that sturdy substantial intelligence, which fits men for success in the practical affairs of life.

§ 204. The object however for which this chapter was especially designed, was to point out the *danger to the peace of the world, which results from the existence of such degraded masses*. If the government of a nation is largely concentrated in the will of one man, or of a limited privileged class, the peace of the world is always endangered by the existence of unused labor power, out of which armies may be constructed. Any one who will attentively consider the character of ancient civilization, will be easily convinced, that the reason of its warlike aspect is chiefly to be found in the fact, that the masses of the people were in a degraded condition. They enjoyed nothing, they hoped for nothing but the bare necessaries of life. There was therefore at all times a vast unused labor force. It was disposable and could be thrown now in this direction and now in that, at the caprice of powerful rulers. They had a better prospect of enjoying in plenty those necessaries of life to which only they aspired, in the service of the state, than in any private employment which was open to them. They were therefore always at the command of despotic rulers, and could be used for any enterprises on which their hearts were set. They might sometimes be employed on such works as the pyramids, the temples of the gods and the massive walls of cities. But they generally were employed in those great military enterprises, which made the history of antiquity one long struggle for universal dominion, till it was finally won by Rome. All the great empires of antiquity were conquered and held together by armies made up of such material. It was this partial character of all ancient civilization, which made military prowess the only title deed by which any nation of antiquity could hold one foot of earth's surface as its own.

§ 205. Just in proportion as modern society embraces in its bosom this same element, it is in similar peril. Free governments that are thus conditioned are in constant danger of anarchy and military despotism. Governments that are strong and concentrated in the hands of one man or a small class, if a large portion of their subjects are in the condition of which we are speaking, constantly threaten the peace of all their neighbors. It is not enough that by book education the people be instructed in the reading and writing of their mother tongue. *They must acquire a standard of civilized living*, which will render them no longer content, for themselves and their families, with the bare means of sustaining existence, and lead them to aspire to something like the true and proper life of rational manhood. When such a standard of living pervades the entire people, its whole labor power will be in demand, to supply its own conscious wants. There will be no disposable hordes of half-civilized men, fit material out of which to construct great conquering armies, to fill the world with terror. All continental Europe is to-day a sad testimony to the truth of what we are saying.

*A people thus internally conditioned will be strong to repel invasion.* Any foreign power will trespass on its territory at its peril. But it will be *incapable of disturbing the peace of the world* by any efforts at foreign conquest. It is not to the shame but to the glory of Britain, that within the last half century her peaceful industries have been so greatly extended, and her labor power so absorbed in them, that she can no longer plunge into foreign wars and dictate terms to the nations of Europe at the cannon's mouth, as she did in the end of the last century and in the beginning of the present. It would be greatly to the honor of her continental neighbors, if they were in this respect much more like her than they are. It is glorious to any nation on earth, that it is too intent on the pursuits of peaceful industry, too much occupied in providing for all the wants of all its people, to have any labor power to waste in meddling with the affairs of its neighbors, and too much love of country and of liberty, not to defend itself against all invasions of its soil, and of its rights among the nations. It would be still more to the honor of Britain if she could so modify her internal economies, as to lift up into the light those classes of her laboring population that are now deprived of the benefit of her civilization, and make the law of competition as efficient to protect them as it is under her present arrangements to degrade and crush them. Till she does solve this problem, the future of her freedom and prosperity will be in peril.

§ 206. Many of the finest intellects and the most philanthropic hearts in the world are employed in earnest endeavor, to devise some method by which for the ages to come, *the peace of the world may be preserved.* All good men in all lands must sympathize with their aims, and devoutly desire their success. But we must express our undoubting conviction, that their radical and permanent success is impossible, except on condition of first finding a complete and satisfactory solution of the problem presented in this chapter. The disease is internal, though its manifestation is external, and an internal remedy must be applied, before the external manifestation will cease. The root of the evil is in the internal economies of society, and until those are brought into nearer conformity with nature's laws, Europe will as now bristle with bayonets. "I made war on Maria Theresa," said Frederic the Great, "because I had men and money and wanted to hear myself talked about." Any powerful monarch who has unused material out of which he can make powerful armies, will be very likely to make war on his neighbors for no better reason, than that he desires the celebrity and the fame of a warrior and a conqueror. The one only reason why an army of more than one million of men that our country had in the field at the close of our great civil war mingled with the people and disappeared forever from view in the short space of three months, is to be found in the fact, that that army was composed of men who longed to return to civilized homes and peaceful industries, from which they expected to derive prosperity and happiness for themselves and their families. Employ the whole labor power of a nation with such efficiency as civilized and enlightened men can attain, in such pursuits as these, and with such hopes, and there will remain nothing out of which to construct permanent armies, or any armies at all, except to meet the urgent necessities of national defense and preservation. For these purposes armies may be made quickly, and will be as quickly dissolved when the end is accomplished. The rulers of nations whose internal economies are thus adjusted, will be powerful still to protect and bless the people, but powerless to disturb the peace of the world. Such nations cannot be warlike, they will "beat their swords into plowshares and their spears into pruning-hooks."

## CHAPTER XIII.

### *Substitutes for Competition. Socialism.*

§ 207. WE think it has been made apparent in the progress of this treatise, that competition is no device of man, but a permanent law of nature; and that it as naturally bears sway in all the transactions of exchange, and in the distribution of wealth between the parties concerned in producing it, as the law of gravitation controls the movements of the planets in their orbits. From this it would seem to follow, that all those who are dissatisfied with the working of competition have their quarrel with human nature itself. We think also that it has been made apparent, that this law of nature is, like every other, beneficent, that it provides for the protection and well-being of all classes of men, in all the conditions of life, and for the steady progress of the race as a whole, in all that is useful to man.

But there are still not wanting those who are dissatisfied with the results of competition, and are earnestly looking around them in the hope of discovering some other and better system, according to which the economies of the world may be constructed. It must be admitted, that there is much in the present condition of the world to excite disgust and heart-sickness at the things that are, and a vague and indefinite longing for something better, of which however few minds seem to have formed any definite conception. Perhaps the long and painful conflict which seems to be everywhere raging between capitalists who employ labor, and laborers who work upon other men's capital, has more influence in producing this mental anxiety than any other cause. It has produced wide-spread distrust of the present order of things, and a vague longing for the re-adjustment of capital and labor on some other principle than that of competition. *Coöperation* is the word which many persons and many schools of social reformers have chosen to express that unknown new order of things for which they are seeking, much as $x$ and $y$ are used to denote unknown quantities in algebra. The word can not be defined till the problems in the statement of which it is employed shall have been solved.

Some use this word and *socialism* almost interchangeably, meaning by it a new organization of labor and capital, by which *capital shall be controlled by communities, not by rich individuals, communities shall be reckoned the owners* of the wealth created by their individual members, and the individual, being absorbed in the community, shall rely on the community for support. *This is socialism pure and simple.*

Others are aiming at a *modified socialism*, in which the capital of all the members of the community shall be managed and their labor directed by the society; but each member on the other hand shall be credited with the capital he has furnished, and with the labor which he performs. All labor is to be classified by the officials of the community, and rated according to the degree of skill it requires. Every member is to have the necessaries of life from the common fund, and if profits accrue from the industry of the community, they are to be distributed among the members, in proportion to the capital furnished, and the relative value of labor performed by each.

Another conception of coöperation is that of an arrangement for *dispensing with the services of the middle men*, and enabling many consumers, by combining in their purchases, to obtain commodities directly, either from importers or manufacturers, at wholesale prices. Coöperative or union stores are of this character. So far as we are informed, little success has attended such efforts in this country, but a good deal of success has been attained to in other countries.

Others still intend by co-operation such an arrangement as will *enable the laborer in some form to share the profits of production.*

There are also some other conceptions of the organization of labor for the purpose of protecting the laborer from competition, which will require consideration.

§ 208. The first of these modes of organization, which we have characterized *as socialism pure and simple*, will require but little space here. It proposes to treat what we have throughout this treatise assumed to be a fundamental law of human nature, as a nullity. If the ideas upon which such a system of social organization must be founded are true, then there can be no such science as that which we are endeavoring to expound. No man who accepts the fundamental law which we enunciated at the outset, and appreciates the irresistible force of such a law can for a moment think the experiment proposed by these men worth trying. Man is no more adapted to such a life, than the barn fowl is to live on the water. He is formed for individual self-care, self-support, self-reliance, self-direction. The desire for individual possession and the sense of individual rights are in every man strong, clear and irrepressible. The attempt to place such a being in a community, which, by its united or corporate will and judgment, is to supercede all individual will and judgment, and reduce each man to a machine to be impelled and guided in the application of his powers by a personality not his own, and patiently to accept through life and for his children after him such results of his labor as the community may allot,—such an attempt cannot succeed. The incorrigibly lazy, the men without enterprise, without high purpose, or any sense of personal dignity, may be satisfied with such a life as a convenient way of living on the products of other men's labor and other men's wits. The artful and unscrupulous demagogue may be delighted with such an organization of easy-going enthusiasts, as furnishing him an excellent opportunity of getting other men's earnings entrusted to his care, and profiting by the credulity of the simple. But upright, honorable, intelligent, industrious men will neither be willing to work for the support of the indolent, nor content, for any great length of time, with the results which will come to them from a life of toil under the direction of others. This is not human life. This is not human society. The perfection of human development cannot be obtained under such conditions. Investigators however sagacious will search in vain in human nature for the "attractions" by which such communities can be organized and held together. They must, in the future as in the past, soon fall to pieces and come to nought. It is the law of human nature, and must be the law of all human society, that the individual man is responsible for his own support, and the owner of all which he produces. Nature herself has provided a modification of this law in domestic society, human ingenuity can devise no other. At all events as economists we need pursue this matter no further. It is quite outside of that fundamental law which we accepted at the outset, as the germ from which our science must grow. If such experiments can succeed, it must be by finding somewhere in the world a human nature with which we are quite unacquainted.

It should also be borne in mind, that no temporary success of a community founded on this principle can prove the soundness of the theory. Such an experiment is made in the midst of the civilization which has been growing up for ages on the principle of competition, and must use a thousand advantages and helps which have originated from that very competition which the advocates of this theory reject. It is necessary to prove more than that a community of socialists can live amid the sustaining influence of the civilization of the nineteenth century and guided by the light of ages. It must be shown that it can stand alone, grow from its own roots, and mature a civilization by the development of its own laws.

§ 209. That scheme of socialism which we have just considered *seeks to eliminate the idea of individual ownership* from the human soul, and treats all competition, not as a law of nature, but as a mean and mischievous selfishness. The *modified form of socialism* of which we are next to speak does not wholly discard individual ownership, but *denies to the individul any appeal to competition for the protection of his right to the results of his own labor.* The officials of the community must grade all labor, and assign to each class its relative price. It is impossible they should do this with any pretense of justice in any other way than by reference to the current wages of labor as fixed by competition. A community organized to protect its members from all competition is therefore dependent, in adjusting its most important and delicate arrangements, on results which never could have been attained to, except under the free competition of that society at large, against which its existence is a perpetual protest. It is not therefore a system within itself.

While it rejects and condemns as oppressive that organization of industry which free competition produces, it is glad enough to guide its own way in the darkness which its negations have created, by the light which that hated and rejected system emits. It refuses competition to its own members. But it is still compelled to settle the property rights of its members by rules which that very competition has established. Such a community has surely very little reason to boast of the progress it has made in organizing a new system for the coöperation of labor and capital. How would it settle matters among its members, if all the rest of the world should be converted to its "new system?"

In other respects this form of communism is liable to nearly the same objections which have been urged against socialism pure and simple, though perhaps in a less degree. The lazy, the stupid, the careless of the future, are made sure of support by the labor, the skill, the foresight of others. The crafty, the cunning, the unscrupulous have still an inviting chance of practicing on the easy credulity and unsuspecting thoughtlessness of enthusiasts ignorant of human nature, and too good naturedly indolent to take care of themselves. It is an admirable device for enabling those who will not or cannot work, to live by the skill and pains-taking industry of those who will. Such a system is in open conflict with human nature, and we need not be at the trouble of arguing against it. Those laws of nature against which it has arrayed itself are quite strong enough to vanquish it without any help from us.

§ 210. Those organizations of consumers which are formed for the purpose *of dispensing with the services of retail dealers*, and deriving supplies directly from the importer or the manufacturer, with little or no addition to wholesale prices, need not detain us long. They violate no economic principle. It is of course desirable that the consumer of a commodity should obtain it from the original source of supply through as few hands as possible, for he must pay a profit on each transaction of exchange. The question, for example, how the products of the great manufactory may be most advantageously distributed to the consumers is a fair and open field for the exercise of ingenuity and skill. The economist will not hesitate to pronounce that plan the best, which on the whole accomplishes the distribution most cheaply. An examination of the methods which have been adopted for this purpose under the name of coöperation, will show that none of them are complete in themselves. They are not solutions of the problem for universal use. For example in many of them many consumers unite in furnishing the capital. Commodities are then purchased of the manufacturer or importer at wholesale prices as regulated by the general law of competition. They are then sold out to the combined consumers at customary retail prices, and the net profits are divided in proportion to the capital furnished. Of course both the price at which the goods were originally purchased, and those at which they are disposed of to the consumer are determined in the ordinary method of competition. The whole system is therefore founded on unmodified competition, and is no solution of the general question. This is no reason why individuals should not resort to such methods when they find they can be benefited by them. But it does suggest a doubt, whether they are likely to prove extensively and permanently applicable. The present system of retail dealers is the result of long experience, and it is very probable that many and unexpected difficulties will be encountered in the attempt to dispense with it. We see no reason however for making any show of those difficulties. We shall rejoice in any success which may attend experiments of this sort, as in all successful applications of labor-saving machinery. Such it would really be.

§ 211. Coöperation as a means of *giving to the laborer the advantage of an interest in the results of his own labor*, deserves more attention. We have already remarked, that the most perfect system of labor is that in which, to the greatest extent, the laborer owns the capital which he uses. As all which he produces is then his own, the stimulus which impels him to labor, and to use all his powers both of mind and body in rendering the results in the highest degree abundant and excellent, is as strong as possible. A man acting under such a stimulus will invariably accomplish more, than the same man would accomplish if he had no interest in the matter, except to obtain his daily wages. Any constitution of society either by law or custom, which tends to divide men into two classes, a small class owning all the capital and under no necessity of performing any labor, and a large class having no capital and doing all the work of society, is economically bad, and on economic grounds should be reformed if reform is possible.

We have already indicated *what the needed reform in respect to agricultural labor is.* In every country under heaven the true coöperation of agricultural labor and capital is the ownership of the land by the men that till it. The true movement towards such coöperation is not the compulsory equal division of estates practiced in France, but absolute free trade in land. We do not believe that any scheme which philanthropy can devise will reach far towards the so much to be desired improvement of the condition of agricultural laborers, without the abolition of land monopoly. Some land owners may be humane and wise enough to try and to succeed in the experiment of giving their laborers, in addition to living wages, an interest in the products of the farm. Such an arrangement would no doubt be as wise as philanthropic. Any employer can afford, on the simple principles of gain and loss, to pay to a laborer who knows that he has an interest in the profits of his work, more wages than to one who feels no impulse of hope of a future better than the present. But it should not be forgotten, that such a boon is no compensation to the laborer for being perpetually excluded from the proprietorship of the land, nor is even this small boon likely to be often extended to the laborer under the present system.

*Something may be done for the laborer by education.* Of that we have spoken in a previous chapter. Those who are well acquainted with our great system of public education will not be very sanguine as to what mere book education can do, except under favoring circumstances in other respects. Few of us will believe, that the laborer can be educated into comfort, while he still remains the hopeless drudge, deprived of all prospect of ever becoming the lord of the soil.

As to such coöperation as we are now speaking of, in other modes of production than agriculture, there is no natural obstacle in the way of applying it to any desirable extent. But it is entirely at the option of employers to adopt or reject it, and we have not much hope of obtaining a general reform from the philanthropy of employers. We do not deny that they are as philanthropic as other men, but most men are slow to carry philanthropy into business arrangements. They are much more apt to construct them according to the cold, hard laws of profit and loss, than to take any philanthropic considerations into the account. If it can be demonstrated by experiment, that to admit laborers to a share of profits is the most profitable mode of management, we should then hope, that, like any other new and useful invention, it would be adopted into general use; and if so adopted we should believe it would greatly increase the profits of the manufacturer and the thrift and comfort of those who live by labor. The subject is certainly worthy the diligent study both of the philanthropist and the capitalist. Perhaps nothing would tend more powerfully to bring to a happy termination the conflict which has been so long raging between capitalists and laborers without capital, and unite as friends those who now so often regard each other as natural enemies. The continued prosperity of all branches of industry, the peace of society, as well as the comfort and happiness of all who work with other men's capital, imperatively require, that in some way coöperative and friendly relations should be established between these two parties as speedily and as widely as possible.

No reason exists in the nature of the case, *why at least a portion of the capital of a joint stock company should not be thrown open to the competition of operatives*, thus enabling them, if disposed, to invest their savings in the stock of the company. Of course those who have supplied the larger portion of the capital would reasonably wish to retain the control of its management. But this is no reason why operatives might not be permitted and encouraged to purchase a minority of the stock. Such an arrangement would greatly benefit the operatives, by affording them a desirable investment for all their savings, and their employers also by insuring the good will of employés, and a deep personal interest in the prosperity of the company. Such experiments are eminently worth trying in the present relations of employers and employés to each other, and both capitalists and philanthropists have a very deep interest in them.

§ 212. Such modes of coöperation as the last two we have considered *are not at all kindred to socialism.* They leave the ownership of all property intact. In the case of the co-operative store, competition is only removed one step farther back, from the retail merchant (whose services are dispensed with) to the wholesale merchant. Prices are determined just as in the ordinary method of obtaining supplies through the retail merchant. In the case in which employés become sharers in the profits of trade, it is only another method of paying wages. The wages paid are not a fixed amount, but depend in part on the profits realized. Should any company succeed in so establishing this coöperative system, that it should be seen to give to its employés a decided advantage, other operatives would be anxious to be employed by that company, and other employers would be under a necessity of adopting the same system, in order to compete successfully for laborers. This consideration encourages the hope, that if co-operation is really practicable and capable of being made beneficial, it may come into general use. It has the same chance of being generally adopted as any other really good invention. It will prove true in this case as in so many others, that if tried and found to be good, competition will compel everybody to adopt it.

We cannot leave this subject without saying emphatically, *that there can be no more mistaken philanthropy than that which assails the law of competition in the interest of the laborer.* There are but two possible methods of dividing profits between the laborer and the capitalist. One is the method of competition, the other the method of force. If the latter is to be resorted to, it must be done either by enforcing the will of the laborer or the will of the capitalist. *If the laborer is to enforce his arbitrary will, capital will cease to be accumulated,* the capitalist can gain nothing and will therefore have no motive to employ his capital, or to save his gains if any were acquired. Capital will decline, production will languish, and the laborer will be without employment.

*But if the will of the capitalist is to be enforced, the laborer will be a slave.* The only hope of the laborer is in meeting his employer on equal terms, and entering into a contract with him with the free consent of both parties. This is the freedom of labor and the freedom of capital, and there can be no other freedom of either. Philanthropy and economy are perfectly at one in so organizing labor and capital, that in all cases these two parties shall meet each other under such conditions, that competition shall have its free and unobstructed course.

§ 213. Two so-called reforms have been proposed in the interest of socialism which merit a passing notice, more as an illustration of the utter anarchy which has taken possession of the minds of that class of men, than because they are really worthy of any serious consideration. We shall first consider the entire land revolution which has been proposed. The scheme is, *that private ownership of land shall be abolished, and the state itself shall become the sole land-holder,* and that it shall assign the use of particular portions of land to each cultivator, according to rules prescribed by law. The first question which presents itself to the mind in view of such a proposition, respects the method by which the state is to become the owner of the land. The more respectable of those who advocate this theory would deny that they have any thought of depriving the owners of land of their property without compensation. If this is so, then a nation situated as ours is must, by a single act of legislation, incur a debt equal to the entire value of all the lands of the United States now owned by individuals. The owners of the property must be divested of it, and compelled to receive in compensation for it the promises of the government to pay. The first step therefore in the execution of this scheme must be a *forced loan*, equal in amount to the value of all the landed property in the United States.

One is impelled next to ask, *how is the interest of this loan to be paid?* If we are told that it is to be by the rent of the land, then we ask, in what manner the land is to be rented? If it is to be thrown open to free competition, rents will be as dear as now, and it is impossible to see what benefit the landless cultivator of the soil can derive from this stupendous revolution. And yet if the state has stipulated to pay to the divested owners the full value of their land, full rents must be obtained, or the state will not receive enough for rents to make its annual payment of interest. A constantly increasing deficiency of income must involve the state in inevitable bankruptcy. If the intention is to assign lands to the cultivator at a reduced rate of interest, then national bankruptcy is inevitable. On that supposition competition in the assignment of lands would be out of the question. That is the enemy which the scheme is intended to crush. How then is it to be determined who are to enjoy the most desirable parcels of land? Evidently there are only two methods by which it is possible that this should be determined. Either they must be allotted to those who will pay most for them, and in that case this whole revolution will be a failure, or else they must be assigned to the favorites of the government, than which nothing more odious and tyrannical can be imagined.

§ 214. We must believe that *this wild scheme of iniquity and folly is a very natural offshoot from the almost equally unsound principles which have underlain the land-tenures of Europe for ages.* To a very great extent, those land tenures have been, it is sad to say are even now, in flagrant violation of the only economic law which can be defended on strict principles of natural justice. When the legislation of the nation violates fundamental economic law, the wildest confusion of thought will get possession of the minds of men, and anarchic ideas will prevail more and more till the abuse is corrected. The insane theories in relation to the nature and functions of money, which have gained prevalence since the passage of the Legal Tender Law of 1862, afford a striking illustration of the truth of this remark. Had the legislation of Europe for centuries recognized the simple truth, that the ownership of land differs not at all in its nature from the ownership of any other species of property, and permitted the exercise of that right of free exchange in respect to it, which is implied in the very nature of ownership, such theories could never have gained possession of even a portion of the national mind. There is little hope of successfully meeting such theories by argument, till the land tenures of the several countries are brought into conformity with natural justice. Even in France, the existing order of things is far from satisfactory. The owner of land has a right to bestow it at his death according to his own will and judgment, and the law requiring the equal distribution of it among his heirs is an assumption, on the part of the state, of a right to interfere in the matter, which could not exist or be supposed to exist, if the proprietor was admitted to have the same absolute ownership of land as of any other property. The right to interfere in one way with the matter, implies the right to interfere in any other way, at the discretion of the state. Free trade in land is the only weapon by which tendencies to such anarchy can be eliminated from the public mind.

§ 215. The other proposition of the socialist reformers on which we purpose to say a few words, *is the claim that it is the duty of the government to provide employment and pay wages to all unemployed laborers.* This claim has been more insisted on by these reformers than any other. It has cut an important figure in some of the great revolutions of Europe, and there probably is no country in Christendom, in which it has not at times been asserted with so much energy and show of force, as in some degree to endanger the public peace. It is the most radical and the most subversive of all social order of any of the wild schemes of the sect. It is in principle *an utter negation of the right of private property.* When it is asserted that the state is bound to provide employment and wages for every unemployed laborer, it should not be forgotten, that the state is not a producer and therefore not an owner of property, except so much as is needed for its public uses. What therefore it gives to one, it must take from another. If therefore the state is bound to see to it that every man has a living (and this is what the claim amounts to), the meaning is, that the state is a personality charged with the right and the duty of taking from those that have, and giving to those that have not, just so much as their necessities may seem to require. The property which the state will protect for any citizen is not that which he has earned and therefore rightfully owns, but what the state may see fit to leave him, after taking from him what it may think necessary to supply the wants of his neighbors. Every man is freed from all apprehension of want. If times are prosperous and wages high, one has on the one hand no fear of want however prodigal he may be, for if times become hard, and he is out of employment, the state will provide for him ; and on the other hand he has no motive to accumulate, for if he does the state may at any time take it away from him, to supply the wants of those who waste all their earnings in reckless prodigality. If he becomes discontented with his wages, he has no fear of losing his place by engaging in a strike, for if he finds himself unemployed, the state is bound to employ him and pay him wages. It needs no argument to show that such doctrines as these are destructive of all rights of property, all social order, and of civilization itself.

It becomes every honest statesman and true philanthropist to turn a scrutinizing eye upon our whole system of legislation, to discover if possible any trace of the recognition of these anarchic teachings. Socialism is a madness, but there is much method in it; and if we allow ourselves to admit into any part of our system, and retain there any germ of socialism, it will be developed rapidly, and bear fruit after its kind. Our poor laws, our public charities, our system of public education at the expense of the state, and all our legislation in respect to the relations of laborers to their employers should be carefully examined, and in every particular placed upon a basis of sound economic principles. It is the business of the statesman and the moralist and not of the economist to pursue this investigation. The signs that this leaven of mischief and anarchy is present and working upon the masses of American society, are painfully apparent to every thoughtful observer of the passing scene.

## CHAPTER XIV.

### *Taxation.*

§ 216. SHOULD the suggestion be made that this is not the proper place for the discussion of this subject, our answer is, that perhaps the suggestion might have been equally appropriate, if it had been introduced elsewhere. *The relation of taxation to economics is not logical but accidental,* and therefore a treatise on that science has no logical place for it. And yet it is so connected with all the economies of society, that it cannot be passed by in silence. The science must at all points assume, that those natural laws which it would construct into a system must have free action, without being turned aside from their natural course either by fraud or violence. The fact however is apparent, that in all communities there are men, who are not disposed to respect those laws, but will utterly disregard and violate them, unless restrained by force. The only agency which can effectually exercise such restraint upon the lawless is government, acting in the name of society, and able to command the whole physical force of the community to execute its will. In the performance of this important function, civil government becomes quite indispensable to all production and all exchange. It may be regarded as a laborer whose services can nowhere be dispensed with, like a watchman that guards our premises by night, and this service it cannot perform, any more than any other laborer, unless it receives its appropriate reward. And yet its wages are not determined by economic laws. It receives whatever it demands. In some cases it takes the position of a partner, and accepts for its compensation a certain per centage of the profits. But that share of the profits is not determined by agreement between all parties, but by the will of this one partner. The state furnishes no capital, because it has none to furnish, but it cannot perform its function unless it is supported by the contributions both of the capitalists and the laborers whom it protects.

We cannot therefore apply to the consideration of this subject those economic forces with which we have had to do in our whole previous discussion. As economists we have really nothing to do with taxation, except to point out those functions for the performance of which the economies of society are necessarily dependent on the state, and to protest against the assumption on the part of the state of any functions which do not legitimately belong to it. The first duty of the state to the economic interests of society we have already indicated,—protection of every citizen in the enjoyment of all his personal rights,—protection against all enemies threatening to assail those rights, and most of all against any species of tyranny or injustice from the state itself. No people can be prosperous that does not habitually live in the conscious security which the ever-present protection of such a civil state affords. There must be an assurance that the laws are just and will be justly and efficiently executed, that the judiciary is pure, enlightened and righteous, and that the police force is energetic and unceasingly vigilant. Such a government is always cheap at what it necessarily costs to sustain it, and such a government will never place unnecessary burdens on the people. Exorbitant and unnecessary exactions always prove that the government itself is unfaithful to its most essential function.

§ 217. It is sometimes asserted, rashly and thoughtlessly we think, *that protection of person and property is the only function of government.* It is certainly not true. In addition to this function civil government must be the agent of society for providing certain conveniences and comforts which are necessary to all, but cannot well be provided for by private enterprise. *One of these is the postal service*, by which intelligence is rapidly, safely and cheaply conveyed to every part of a great nation. Indeed under the present peaceful relations of the nations to each other, and those improved international postal arrangements which modern statesmanship has devised, it provides for cheap and rapid communication between any one individual in the civilized world however humble he may be, and any other.  Every little post-office in Christendom is in easy and certain communication with every other.  Nor is this limited to Christendom.  The present postal system of the world is as cosmopolitan as our science itself.  It is a grand practical recognition of universal fraternity, and a striking illustration of the vastness of the benefits which enlightened governments at peace with one another can confer on mankind.  The benefits which it confers on the economic interests of society are simply incalculable.  It renders the negotiation of exchanges not only possible but easy and cheap, between any two individuals dwelling in any portion of the civilized world.

The expense however of sustaining this magnificent system should not fall either in whole or in part on the taxpayer.  It should be and may be self-supporting.  That nation whose postal service is a burden upon the general revenue may well be suspected of a lack of statesmanship.

Another very important service which the government renders to the economic interests of society *is the construction of the great thoroughfares of the country, and the roads by which every man communicates with every other.*  This also includes the care and improvement of the streets of cities and the numerous arrangements which are necessary for the health, comfort, convenience and safety of their inhabitants.  It is not possible to point out any agency by which these necessary arrangements could well be provided, except that of the government.  In such a system of government as ours, all these wants, except the construction of great national thoroughfares, should be provided for by local taxation.  Each local community should in these respects take care of itself

It is also worthy of very serious consideration, whether the resources necessary for such objects of local improvement should not be raised and appropriated by the votes of taxpayers only. Excessive municipal taxation is at the present time one of the greatest burdens of the American taxpayer, and we will add one of the greatest dangers of the future. The rights of property cannot be safe in any country, where men who pay no taxes and bear none of the burdens of society have an unlimited power of imposing taxes for other men to pay, and where the hope of obtaining a profitable job from the public will induce multitudes of men who perhaps never paid a tax in their lives, to vote for some costly public work, without any proper consideration of its utility or importance, and quite regardless how inconvenient and oppressive may be the burdens which it will impose on the taxpayers. If we are told that under our system there is no remedy for such an evil as this, our answer is, that only shows that the system greatly needs reforming. We believe in liberty, but liberty which works constant injustice will not be of long continuance. Men who pay no taxes are not well qualified to impose taxes on those who do.

§ 218. We have already explained *the necessity of providing at the expense of the state certain opportunities of education to all the people.* In so far as this has not been sufficiently provided for by the munificent school funds which many of the states received from the general government, or other funds for school purposes which the states may have acquired, the means necessary must also be raised by taxation. Under our system they should be raised by local taxes. To what extent of costliness public education at the expense of the state should be carried, it is not within our province here to inquire. It is proper however to lay down a principle which, if we are right in the conclusions to which we have come in the course of this treatise, must be fundamental to the whole subject. That principle is, that the only reason why provisions for gratuitous education should be made at all at the expense of the state, is that the health and safety of society require it. It is a reason of the same kind as that which justifies and requires such police regulations as are necessary for the prevention or removal of local nuisances dangerous to the health of the community. It is to prevent the growth upon the body politic of cancerous tumors and fatal gangrene. The doctrine that it is the duty of the state to provide gratuitously for every child of every resident on the soil the means of an accomplished education in every department of literature and science, rests on no better foundation than the doctrine that the state is bound to furnish employment for all unemployed laborers, or to render the ornaments of dress equally accessible to all men whether rich or poor. Aside from what is necessary for the safety and health of the community, the state is under no more obligation, and has no more right, to undertake the education of every man's children, than to feed and clothe and house them. The same fundamental law which makes a man the owner of all which he produces by his labor, also throws upon him the burden of supporting himself, and that family to which he gives existence by his own voluntary act, and the support of a family includes education, as truly as food and clothing and shelter. The more we scrutinize the phenomena of human society, the more apparent it will become, that the family and not the individual is the constituent unit.

It may perhaps be urged, *that the well-being of society requires* that facilities should be furnished at the expense of the state for the complete education of all the people. If this were granted, it would not hence follow, that the benefit derived to society from such an arrangement would justify the cost of it. It might be a fine thing for the community, that every man should have a railway station directly in front of his own door, but the levying of a tax sufficient to accomplish it, would be the confiscation of all property. The same would be true to no small extent of the attempt to provide for the gratuitous education of the entire people by taxation, provided that education was extended to the whole circle of literature and science. Nothing can realize that conception of public education which is entertained by many minds, and is deeply affecting our school legislation, short of a severity of taxation which will be found insupportable to the taxpayer. There may be good things which a householder cannot afford to provide for his family, and so there may be good things which the state cannot afford to provide for the people, because it will cost more than the people can afford to pay.

It has however *never been proved that a provision for the universal gratuitous education of the people would be beneficial to society.* It is a question which lies quite outside of our science, and we cannot therefore permit ourselves to enter on the discussion of it here. We can only state it, and leave the discussion of it to others. Can it be shown that the constitution of the state is such as to qualify it to devise and carry into execution a complete system of education for all the people? Does any sane man believe that it would be wise and safe to entrust that entire interest to political bodies and political action? If not, then surely it is time for thoughtful men to begin to search in earnest for the limit, beyond which state provision for the education of the people ought not to go, and at which the burden ought to be thrown upon individual parents, of educating their own children. The whole subject is left in the recent legislation of the country at loose ends, and no limit can be discerned to the burdens which are liable to be thrown upon the taxpayer in the interest of gratuitous education.  The subject requires, not popular declamation, of that we have had too much already, but discrimination, definition, thoughtful statesmanship.  We are convinced that to a certain extent gratuitous education ought to be provided for the people at the expense of the taxpayer.  But there is a limit beyond which it is not possible to carry that provision, without ruinously severe taxation, and beyond which the interests of education are much more wisely left to the fathers and mothers of the nation, than controlled by the state.  The time has fully come when this limit ought to be determined by wise, sound statesmanship, and legislation be made to conform to it.

It is surely not difficult to see that the principle which we asserted in respect to taxation for local improvements equally holds here.  A greater injustice can hardly be conceived of, than that men who pay no taxes should have unlimited power to vote taxes upon all the property around them to educate their own children.  The men who pay the taxes should surely have the right of deciding by their own votes, how much shall be appropriated to the gratuitous education of the whole community.  To deny them that right, is, so far as it goes, to take the disposal of their property out of their hands and commit it to the hands of others who have no interest in it, except to obtain as much as possible of it for their own uses.  This cannot be a sound and righteous system of taxation, and if persisted in it will sooner or later result in disaster.

§ 219. *Provisions for the care of the unfortunate constitute another important part of American taxation.* We cannot conceive that a government representing a Christian people can fail to make some provisions for the education of the deaf and dumb, the blind, and the feeble-minded, and for the care of the insane. The only questions which can be raised with reference to such provisions must respect the scale of costliness upon which they shall be constructed, and whether the benefits of them should be given to all gratuitously. It is evident that if such interests are provided for with unthinking prodigality, considering only what is desirable, and not at all what burdens may be thrown upon the taxpayer, it is quite possible that these provisions may become far more costly than the real necessities of the case require, more costly too than a regard for the well-being of these unfortunates demands or permits. Such provisions should certainly be made in a spirit of generous liberality, but not without the frugality of the true statesman, who will incur no greater cost than is necessary to accomplish the substantial ends at which he aims. That there has been much of this statesman-like frugality of late in our outlays for public charity, we think will hardly be pretended. If burdensome taxation is an evil at the present time, this subject will bear examination.

Provisions for the care of the unfortunate *must necessarily be to a certain extent gratuitous*, otherwise the poor to whom they are especially important would not be able to enjoy the benefit of them. But it is impossible for us to conceive of any good reason why the state should assume the entire burden of the education and care of all these unfortunates, however affluent their condition may be. The burden upon the taxpayer would be greatly relieved, if all persons in affluent circumstances were required to make fair compensation for the benefits which they receive from these institutions, and we believe such persons would prefer to pay the full value of the service rendered them, rather than to receive it as a gratuity.

Under the present tendency to burdensome taxation of which all taxpayers are sensible, the state ought to study every honorable method of diminishing the burden as much as possible. Of taxation for the relief of the poor we shall speak in a chapter especially devoted to that subject.

§ 220. There is one claim of the government not only upon the capital but upon the labor and the life of the citizen, which is in the nature of the case unlimited. A government which is the defender of the peace of society and of all the rights of the citizens, not only has the right but *is bound in duty to protect its own existence*, and its power to perform its proper function, against any enemy that may assail it. When thus assailed, the government may claim the property and the personal service of every citizen, to whatever extent and at whatever hazard may be needful for its own preservation. To preserve the life of society is more important than any individual person or private interest can be, and the less must give way to the greater. On this principle only can national existence be preserved and prolonged.

When a nation has incurred obligations however great in such a struggle for self-preservation, those obligations are to be regarded as a mortgage on the entire labor and capital of the nation, from which they can never be released, except by the full performance of all the promises which the government has made. National indebtedness binds the conscience of an entire people. Nations should be very cautious of incurring such obligations unnecessarily, and scrupulously faithful in their performance.

§ 221. There are some uses to which the tax-levying power is often applied, against which it is the duty of the economist to enter his protest. *That power should never be used for the purpose of diverting either capital or labor from those modes of employment to which they would resort if left to themselves.* A legislature is destitute of nearly all those qualifications which are necessary to fit it for judging in what way capital ought to be invested, in order to be most profitable to the community. Bring such a question as this before an American Congress for decision, and there is not one chance in a hundred that it will be decided correctly. The members are not practically acquainted with the real elements of the question. They do not view it from the stand-point of the man who is about to lay out his own labor, or invest his own capital. They will be open to the influence of any man who may approach them for the purpose of accomplishing his own selfish purposes. Many political considerations which are quite irrelevant to the case will influence their minds and their votes. To draw a correct decision of the question out of the midst of such influences is seemingly impossible. Yet these men after such a deliberation come to the conclusion that American capital is too largely invested in some one branch of industry, and ought to be withdrawn from it, and invested in some other, in which these sages have been made to believe that more of it should be employed. They immediately look around themselves for the means of accomplishing what they think desirable. The power of taxation is chosen as the instrument, and a heavy tax is imposed on all those who use certain foreign products, not for the legitimate purpose of taxation, to bring revenue into the national treasury, but only for the purpose of compelling labor and capital to leave one mode of investment in which they are profitably employed, and seek another in which our legislators think it would be better that they should be invested. This is a two-fold abuse; it is the exercise of the legislative function for a purpose for which it was never intended, and is quite unfitted; and it is ap plying the power of the legislature to impose taxes to an end quite foreign to its legitimate uses. The power of taxation is frequently used for the purpose of discountenancing modes of using capital which are regarded as immoral or injurious to society. The propriety of such a use of it involves moral and religious questions which, though very interesting and important, cannot be appropriately discussed in this treatise. But the cases of which we are speaking are not of this sort. Both the mode of employing capital which is encouraged, and that which is discouraged, are admitted to be legitimate and proper, and conducive to the general good; and the legislator assumes to encourage the one and discourage the other in the comparison, because he claims in his capacity of legislator to be a better judge how capital ought to be invested than the capitalist does, and uses his power of levying taxes to compel such a use of capital as he judges best. This is a usurpation. The fit reply of the capitalist to such intermeddling of the legislator is,—that, sir, is none of your business; I am a better judge of it than you are.

§ 222. This introduces the consideration of the *mode of taxation*,—a subject which lies outside the limits of our science, and of which we had therefore purposed to say nothing. But more reflection has convinced us, that it so nearly concerns the subject matter of which we must treat, that its consideration cannot be entirely omitted. Our views of imposts levied for the purpose of fostering certain industries, by protecting them from foreign competition, have been freely given. *But our science enters no protest against imposts levied for the purpose of raising necessary revenue.* It cannot be denied, that that mode of taxation is recommended to the legislator by many important advantages. But instead of being in his hands a fit instrument to be employed in diverting trade from channels in which it tends to run, into others which he regards with more favor, the greatest objection against the use of it lies in its liability to exert such an influence.

Let us suppose, for example, that a duty is imposed for the purpose of revenue only, on some commodity, the supply of which is partly produced at home, and partly imported. A duty levied on the importation of that commodity must, to all appearance, raise the price of that portion of the supply which is produced at home, and give a relative advantage to those engaged in that industry, to which they are in no way entitled. No true statesman, seeking revenue only, would sanction such an impost. He would either levy imposts upon commodities that are not and cannot be produced at home, or he would balance the foreign imposts by a precisely equivalent internal tax on the home production, so that the home and foreign product would meet on terms of equal competition in the home market as before. Otherwise the price of the commodity would be raised to the consumer by the whole amount of the duty, and yet, so far as the supply was produced at home, the producer and not the public revenue would receive the benefit of it. In the free trade system of England, this point is carefully guarded. Her policy is to raise her revenue from commodities not produced at home.

It may be objected to this, that it would often bring the burden of taxation on the poor as well as on the rich; since, for example, such articles as tea and coffee must be taxed, because they are not produced at home. To this we reply, first, that these are luxuries rather than necessaries of life, and therefore very properly subject to taxation; and second, that the most efficient revenue duty is shown by experience to be a low rather than a high one. The tax which it would be necessary to levy on those articles would be so low a percentage, that its effect on a pound of tea or coffee would be but barely perceptible, and could not be a ground of just complaint. A demagogue might be disposed to magnify it, but a statesman would hardly regard it as a matter of serious importance. In a country where the vote of a poor man is just as weighty as that of a rich man, a small tax on an article of luxury, which presses with absolute impartiality on every voter, should never be complained of. A man who cannot pay a tax of five to ten cents per pound, on the few pounds of tea and coffee which any poor man would use in a year, can hardly be fit for a voter. No man of any spirit, whether rich or poor, would permit such a plea to be made in his behalf.

§ 223. The question is much agitated at present, *on what forms of property taxes may be properly levied.* One of the most important points in this discussion relates to the adjustment of tax levies, in respect *to debtors and creditors.* A definition of property has been proposed, according to which debts due any one are not property, and are therefore not taxable. All property, it is claimed, has materiality and a local situation. Debts due to any one have neither, and are therefore not property. The reader need not be told, that we cannot accept this definition. According to our definition of wealth, skill and power to labor are property. Yet they have no materiality. An invention is a mere conception of the mind, yet it is property. But in the case under consideration, the definition of property proposed, even if admitted, would not avail. A man may be to-day the owner of one hundred thousand dollars in gold. To-morrow he may lend it, and receive for it real estate security. He has not by that transaction divested himself of all his property, or of any of it. Indeed it matters not whether he has taken security on real estate, or relied on the bare credit of the borrower. The moment that loan is made, he owns the property of the borrower to the amount of one hundred thousand dollars. The evidence of indebtedness which he holds is the proof of his right to such an interest in the property of the borrower. It is his title deed. The borrower may use the gold as he pleases, but the creditor is the owner of that amount of property which is in the present possession of the borrower.

The question is certainly a fair one, *how the transaction as thus described, should affect the two parties, in respect to their liabilities to taxation.* By the laws of some of the states, the tax assessor disregards this transaction entirely. He estimates the property of the debtor just as if the debt did not exist, and the property of the creditor as though the gold was still in his hands. It is only necessary thus to state the case, to convince any candid mind of the unreasonableness of the law. That item of one hundred thousand dollars is doubled in the assessment and twice taxed. A state that makes out its tax lists on that principle estimates the property of the people of the state at an amount immensely greater than it is in truth. Such an assessment is a delusion, and a tax levied on it is a public oppression. It would be easy to show that, if taxes are assessed on this principle, the same property is not only liable, as in the case above given, to be reckoned twice over, but to be repeated any number of times. It is wonderful that any legislator should fail to notice the bald injustice of such a system of taxation. Nothing can be plainer than that the same property should be taxed but once.

§ 224. The question will rise *whether the debtor or the creditor should pay the tax.* The answer cannot be difficult. Who is the real owner of the property in question? No one can be at a loss for an answer. The property of the debtor is the amount of all which stands in his name, minus the debt. The property of the creditor, in the case supposed, is one hundred thousand dollars, the amount of the debt due him. Then let each of the parties be taxed for the property he really owns. Let the amount of the debt be subtracted from the property of the debtor, and assessed to the creditor. No injustice will then be done to either party. An assessment conducted on that principle would give the nearest possible approximation to the real value of the property of the people, and a tax levied upon it would be as near an approach to equity as is attainable.

In case of *a debtor and creditor residing in different states*, the question would arise in which state the tax should be paid. A very clear and simple principle seems to be at hand to settle this question. All capital should contribute to the support of the government that protects it. Property should therefore be taxed in the state, to the courts of which its owner would resort, to enforce his rights. A mortgage must be foreclosed in the courts of the state in which the mortgaged property is situated. To that state therefore the creditor should pay taxes, no matter where he himself resides. The same principle will hold, when no real estate security is given. The creditor should still pay the tax to the state in which he is to bring suit, to enforce his rights.

The construction of a system of taxation on these principles would greatly *facilitate the discovery of all property rightfully subject to taxation.* If the person in whose name any taxable property stands, is required to make an exhibit of his property, he will of course, for his own protection, make known any indebtedness which can be offset to it. Let him also be required to give the creditor's name and residence. Let the neglect of the creditor to pay the tax, work a forfeiture of his claim against the debtor; in which case, the debtor being released from his obligation to pay the debt shall become liable for the tax. The effect of such a law would doubtless be, that in the original contract for the loan, the debtor would agree to pay the tax, as a part of the consideration for the use of the money. In such a case the property of the borrower would be estimated without reference to the debt, and the creditor would be unknown in the assessment, and would simply receive a lower rate of interest on account of his exemption from taxation. This arrangement, so perfectly equitable between the parties, would secure to the state precisely the amount of revenue to which it was entitled. For such a debt, the creditor should of course not be taxed in the state in which he resided. The adoption of these principles of taxation in all the states, would greatly facilitate the free movement of capital over our whole country, according to the law of supply and demand. It would secure equity everywhere, and work injustice no where.

§ 225. It needs no argument to prove that the rapid increase of taxation for purposes of local improvement, gratuitous education and charitable provisions for the unfortunate is *one of the great dangers which threaten the future of our country*. The entire amount of taxation borne by the citizens of many of our towns and cities, exclusive of all charges levied by the federal government, ranges from three and a half to seven per cent on an assessment of property at its cash valuation, and that at a time when the current rate of interest cannot be said to exceed eight per cent per annum. It surely needs no argument to prove, that such taxation must be very oppressive to the industries of the country, and a great obstacle to the accumulation of capital, especially when it is farther considered, that to the figures given above must be added all the charges of supporting the federal government, and for paying interest and principal of the national debt.

If any one thinks there is nothing burdensome and alarming in such taxation as this, we must be excused from believing that he is either a financier or a statesman. Such burdens laid year after year on the industry of the country do not indicate statesmanship, but recklessness such as disqualifies one for any position of public trust. These are plain spoken words, but the gravity of the case requires it.

## CHAPTER XV.

### *Pauperism.*

§ 226. *There is no logical place in the science of economics for such an anomaly as pauperism.* That science has to do with a society made up of units, each one of which is a personality endowed on the one hand with power to labor, and capable on the other of supporting itself by its own labor. Each one is expected to be, not only self-supporting, but to be capable of adding something to that great human patrimony, which is constantly being acccumulated for the benefit of all. In each of these units may be embraced all the individuals of a family. There may be a mother whose entire power to labor is absorbed in the care of children. There may be children who will not yet for many years be able to bear the burdens of the laborer, or adequate for self-support. There may be decrepid age whose task is already done. There may be the invalid whom disease has prematurely disqualified for labor. But the unit is the family, and that unit with all embraced in it is expected to be self-supporting, and if possible accumulating. "If any one will not work neither shall he eat," is sound economy and sound morality.

But this theoretic economic world is not in all respects the real world in which we live. There are frictions in the workings of our economic machinery, which we must not refuse to consider. Some are never endowed with powers of self-sustentation. Others are deprived of those powers by disease or by the inevitable providence of God. Others through sheer indolence refuse to work that they may eat. Others still are disqualified for self-support by their vices, or are deprived of the means of subsistence by the indolence and vices of their natural supporters and protectors. Any of these cases of disability are liable to occur in respect to persons who are not embraced in any self-supporting unit, and are therefore entirely unprovided for.

Over and above all this, it has been true in all the past history of the human race, that in the progress of society in wealth and population, large numbers of men have fallen out of the current of general prosperity, and spent their lives on the very verge of starvation. No civilization has ever existed for any considerable length of time, which had not a lower stratum of extreme poverty and wretchedness. Perhaps nowhere in the world's history has this phenomenon put on more shocking and revolting aspects, than in some of the most cultivated and wealthy modern nations. To this hour we are provided with no effectual antidote or remedy for this disease of the body politic.

§ 227. *What then shall be done for these masses or with them?* As economists we cannot refuse to consider this question. We have pointed out the laws by which ample supplies of human want are created, exchanged and distributed. But here are vast masses belonging to our common humanity, that perform no such service in the creation of wealth as would give them an available claim to a share in the distribution. Is there no possible readjustment of economic laws, by which these wants may be supplied? Must not our laws of distribution be made in some way to bend, or relax their tension, so as to give bread to these hungry mouths? All agree in maintaining that the bounties of the Creator are intended impartially for all, and that the system should be so constructed as to give to all a fair opportunity to supply their wants by their own labor. All would equally agree that it is the province not only of Christian charity, but of humanity, to supply the wants of all those who are incapacitated to labor, either by natural imbecility or inevitable calamity. All these cases are easily disposed of, not only in theory but in practice. If the sufferings of the poor could be confined within the limits which we have just defined, the humane impulses which are native to the human heart, and still more the charity which is deeply imbedded in the very foundations of our religion, would be entirely adequate to provide for every exigency of the case, without any interference either of the economist or the legislator. But when all these cases have been provided for, there still remains a vast amount of uncomforted and unmitigated wretchedness. What shall be done with and for it?

§ 228. At this point it seems to us the question should *first be referred to the consideration of the Christian, the moralist and the statesman.* We have already indicated the economic causes, which we think tend to increase and perpetuate these evils, and earnestly insisted on the necessity of their entire removal. We have insisted on such a construction of all our economic machinery as will give to every man a fair chance in the race of life. Our science can do no more. Are there misadjusted moral forces, are there social customs and arrangements which increase the temptations to vice and multiply the number of its victims? Can any change in our laws and police regulations remove dangerous temptations out of the way of the young and the unwary? Are our towns and cities collecting revenue from branches of traffic which deprave the morals and waste the substance of the people, and which therefore ought to be utterly prohibited instead of being made sources of revenue? Is there any possible application of moral forces in the power of the moralist and the Christian, whereby men may be lifted out of these morasses of society, and restored to virtuous self-control, self-support and self-reliance? There is no good citizen who is not deeply interested in every one of these questions, and the man who passes by any one of them, saying this is no concern of mine, is not a good citizen.

§ 229. There is nothing in the past history of the world to justify the expectation that any immediate and effectual remedy of these evils can be secured by the application of social and moral forces, and we are forced back upon the question how will the economist deal with them. Our answer is, he can deal with them only in negations, but those negations are very grave and imperative.

1. *We must not repeal or disregard the great fundamental law of the science, that every man owns himself and all which he produces.* To over-ride that law under any pretext, is not to relieve the poor, but to make everybody poor and all poverty hopeless. That law is the gravitation of the economic universe. Repeal it, and the whole falls to pieces. Repeal it, and no man will work except for the supply of immediately pressing want. Why should a man work, when his neighbor who will not work is as likely to enjoy the fruits of his labor as himself? Under such an order of things there can be no

accumulation, no civilization. Just in proportion as you weaken one's sense of security in the enjoyment of the fruits of his industry, you diminish the stimulus to labor, and weaken all the forces that impel society onward in a career of prosperity. In helping a few you bring all into peril.

2. Another prohibition which science lays on us is, that *we must not remove from any man the fear of suffering want, as a consequence of neglecting labor and frugality.* We have shown in the first part of this treatise, that all that originally induces any man to work, is the seen necessity of working, that his wants may be supplied. Take from any man or any class of men all sense of this necessity, and they will cease both to work and to save. We do not at all hesitate to say, that it is better that some, nay that many should suffer want, and even perish, than that these two prohibitions should be disregarded. If the laws and the government cannot provide relief for the poor without weakening the force of these two fundamental principles of our science, it is far better that they should abstain from any interference, and leave the poor to the care of individual charity. If in our efforts at public philanthropy, we weaken these great natural forces, we make ten paupers in relieving one. We take food from the mouth of him that has labored for it, and give it to him that is living in idleness on the fruits of other men's toil. Remove the hope of gain and the fear of want from men's minds, and you have no other motive by which you can induce men to exert their powers either for their own or for the common good, and all must go down together into the common wretchedness of savage life. To insist on these two prohibitions is nearly the whole which our science has to say of pauperism.

§ 230. *Still the ear of humanity cannot be entirely deaf*

*to the cry of suffering, perishing poverty.* It is to be hoped provisions may be made for relieving the extreme necessities of the poor, without any dangerous violation of fundamental laws. The first principle which we shall enunciate as the result of experience and philanthropic inquiry is, that relief should be furnished if possible only at establishments provided for the purpose. Experience shows that relief granted at public expense to the poor at their own homes or on the streets, is always demoralizing. These establishments should always be provided with the means of furnishing employment for all who are aided, and all should be required to work to the full extent of their ability. "By the sweat of thy face shalt thou eat thy bread," is a divine law, and men must not repeal it. Such houses for the relief of the poor may with suitable management be made nearly self-supporting.

The greatest care should however always be taken, *not to throw the products of such establishments on the market at rates which are below the price as determined by general competition.* It is quite ruinous to producers in any line of industry, to be liable to be undersold by the products of the labor of those who are not working for a living. It is the case of the needle-woman over again in another form. It is better to support either paupers or prisoners entirely at the public expense, than to ruin the business of honest and industrious men by such an unnatural competition. Indeed it is no competition. True competition is a struggle for life on both sides. In this case life is at stake on one side and not on the other. For this reason it is always best to employ the labor of paupers in producing those great staples, the demand for which is so large, that their competition will produce no appreciable effect on price. Such a public provision for the poor or the unfortunate should never be permitted to underbid independent individual labor.

§ 231. *The reason for confining the relief of the poor to public establishments is*, that multitudes would apply for and accept relief at their own houses or in begging from door to door, who would never ask for it if they could receive it only at the poor-house. We would be glad to be considerate of the feelings of the poor. Christian charity will find innumerable cases, in which the duty of soothing and sparing the feelings of the sufferer is just as imperative, as the duty of supplying food and clothing. But we are speaking of public provisions for the relief of paupers, and in constructing a system for this purpose, the poor must consent and be content to receive aid in ways consistent with the greatest good of the whole, and not in disregard of it. Society must not make such provisions for the relief of the poor, as to take from poverty all its terrors. The sufferings of poverty are nature's penalty for idleness, and no community has any right to repeal that penalty. Out-door relief, that is relief of the poor at their own homes removes all limits, and speedily introduces into practice the vicious principle, that every necessitous person, no matter how his necessity may have been caused, has a right to be relieved. This is the fundamental principle of The English Poor Law, and it is admitted by economists and philanthropists to have fearfully extended the area of English pauperism, and to have produced a state of things which sometimes occasions serious apprehension for the future of English society. Let the principle once be established, that every one who is really necessitous has a right to be relieved at public expense, and may obtain the relief he needs by simply making his necessities known, and disastrous consequences are inevitable. As soon as the times are hard and the procuring of the necessaries of life becomes difficult, application will at once be made for aid at the public expense.

This application once made and granted will be repeated and urged as long and as often as the difficulty of living continues. Having found a source of supply easier than industry and frugality, a man will cease to depend on these or to practice them, and his demands on the public treasury will be more frequent, larger in amount, and more urgent. Soon he is a pauper for life with his family. If there had been no relief short of the poor-house, he would have increased his efforts, and gotten by the hard place without ever becoming a pauper at all.

The influence of every such case is very bad upon neighbors, whose circumstances are about equally hard. Seeing one neighbor relieved at public expense they inquire why they should not have such help as well as he, especially seeing that their labor is taxed for his support. One such seed of pauperism dropped in a neighborhood soon yields a large harvest. We do not desire to swell this volume with the statistics of English pauperism. But we advise every one to look into them and take warning. English pauperism sometimes puts on aspects so grave, that it seems to threaten to engulf the wealth of England, great as it is. The subject is regarded with solemn apprehension by all thoughtful Englishmen. English poor relief has not only tended to increase the number of paupers, but it has actually increased it on a vast scale. It is an experiment which ought not to be lost sight of in this country. It is better for all, rich and poor, that some should perish of want, than that such a cancer should fasten itself upon the nation.

This view of the subject assumes peculiar importance and seriousness in a country which is governed by universal suffrage. In many of our states, perhaps in all, a man does not cease to be a voter by becoming a pauper. He not only contributes nothing to the support of the government, but his daily bread is drawn by taxation from the fruits of other men's labor; yet his vote has just as much weight as that of the most industrious, frugal and thrifty citizen. He votes the appropriation of other men's earnings to his own maintenance. We suspect any intelligent foreigner, on first becoming acquainted with this fact, would regard it with astonishment. It is humiliating to acknowledge, that in some states at least our poor laws are so constructed, as to admit of and favor the distribution of bribes to the voter under pretense of relieving the necessitous. It cannot be denied, that there are some cases in which municipal authorities incur the just suspicion of administering the poor laws in this manner, for the purpose of securing their own reëlection. It needs no prophet to foretell, that under poor laws so constructed and administered, pauperism will be likely to increase with alarming rapidity. This evil has not as yet, in most parts of our country, grown to alarming dimensions. But principles have found their way into our legislation, which are producing serious inconvenience in some localities, and are fitted to awaken grave apprehension as to what may happen, when our population shall become dense and the means of subsistence difficult to be obtained. The law should surely be so constructed, as to set no temptation before public officers to encourage pauperism by bribing voters, and the time to arrest such an evil is while it is yet in its infancy.

§ 232. *Establishments for the relief of the poor should be public reformatories.* Vice is incomparably the most fruitful of all the causes of poverty. So soon as any one throws himself upon the public for relief, no time should be lost in resorting to all known appliances tending to moral reformation and self-government. No one should continue to receive either public or private charity while persisting in the practice of those vices and self-indulgences which have reduced him to poverty. A great deal of poverty is caused by indulgences of the appetites, which are so common as hardly to be considered criminal. Many a man who has spent his life in comparative plenty, will find on examination, that if he had added to his necessary expenses the unnecessary expense of tobacco, he must have spent his life on the very verge of want. Houses for the relief of the poor should be so conducted, as to cultivate in the highest degree habits and principles of frugal self-government.

Nor is this enough. *The men who are obviously living such lives of vicious self-indulgence as must necessarily reduce them and their families to want, should be arrested in the midst of their career, and placed at once under such restraints* as will save the living of their families from further waste, and under such reformatory influences as may tend to restore them to the paths of virtue. The most common and perhaps the most destructive of all the vices which are multiplying and aggravating pauperism among us is drunkenness. For half a century the best portion of American society has been well aware of the prevalence and destructive character of this vice, especially of its tendency to increase the amount of hopeless poverty. Many plans have been proposed and many experiments made, to restrain and eradicate the evil. These efforts have certainly not been without some success, but it must be admitted that the degree of success which has attended them has fallen far short of the wishes and even of the hopes of the philanthropist. We suggest that in one very important particular, they have been fundamentally defective. They have not held the inebriate himself to a due responsibility for the consequences of his life. We have no wish to screen from censure the men who obtain their own living by knowingly selling to their neighbors the means of ruining their families and bringing destruction on themselves. But after all the primary responsibility is on the inebriate himself. No community should allow its members to waste their earnings and destroy their own power to labor by lives of vicious sensuality, and then throw their families and perhaps at last the miserable remnant of themselves upon public or private charity for support. The men who are living such lives should be arrested in them at once by the friendly hand of society, pronounced by a legal process incapable of self-care, and placed under a conservator with power to protect and restrain them, save their property from waste and apply it for the support of their families. Any prohibitory legislation which treats the inebriate as a mere victim to be pitied, and throws the whole responsibility of the evil upon the seller, is radically defective. A community that allows inebriates to go unrestrained, till they have reduced themselves and their families to pauperism, should bear the burden of supporting them without a murmur. We place the men who have become insane through the inevitable providence of God under effectual restraint, so that they may neither harm themselves nor others. How much more then should we impose restraints no less effectual, upon persons who are almost daily making themselves insane, objects of disgust and terror to the families they ought to protect.

§ 233. The aspect of the subject just presented suggests another, the consideration of which must not be omitted. Society often, by its toleration of vices which it ought to prohibit, by lending its countenance to practices on which it ought to frown, *becomes responsible for their existence, and incurs a moral obligation to relieve the poverty which they occasion*, even though in affording such relief it violates public policy. If the community deals with a traffic in spirituous liquors or with incitements to any other vice by legislation that tends to countenance and encourage it, instead of discountenancing and restraining it, that community becomes thereby morally bound to support the widows and orphans that have thus been reduced to poverty. Let every such traffic receive from the community the frown of indignant rebuke, and feel the hand of rigorous restraint and repression. Exterminate such a traffic if you can ; if you cannot, restrain it as much as possible.

This consideration has a special force in relation to all those systems of legislation which construct society on a false principle, and place large classes of men in conditions so disadvantageous, as necessarily to reduce them to hereditary pauperism. We regard for example the English system for the relief of the poor, with extreme disapprobation, as dangerous to all her future. But we should grieve to see provisions for the relief of the poor abolished, while the agricultural laborer remains in his present unfavorable condition. We should say, abolish your poor rate if you must, but in the name of humanity abolish your land monopoly at the same time. If the land monopoly is to be retained and perpetuated, surely those interested in its perpetuity should not refuse to support the agricultural poor.

Before leaving this painful subject we must remind the reader, that the mere economist cannot deal with it in its totality. Its deepest roots are not in our science, but in the sister science of ethics. Men are pressed down into the morasses of society far more by moral than by economic causes. And even when some maladjustment of the economics of society is the primary cause of the evil, the cure must still be chiefly moral. Adjust and re-adjust our economic machinery as we may, it is still morality that makes and unmakes humanity.

## CHAPTER XVI.

*Wasteful Expenditure.*

§ 234. It has already been remarked, that the laws which regulate the application of the products of industry to their appropriate uses belong rather to the department of ethics than of economics. Yet there are two topics the consideration of which perhaps more properly belongs to the moralist than to the economist, but which are so related to the whole economic system, and so vitally important to it, that we cannot with propriety neglect all consideration of them. They will therefore form the subjects of the two concluding chapters of this treatise.

§ 235. From what has already been said it is obvious, that all the uses to which the products of human labor can be applied are *divisible into two classes.* One class is composed of all which is expended for the necessaries of life. This class we shall call *necessary expenditure.* The other class consists of all which is devoted to the gratification of desires, the satisfaction of which is not necessary to the preservation of life and health and the continued power to labor, and the preservation of the race. This class we shall call *disposable expenditure.* All expenditure of the first class is so determined and fixed by the natural laws of life and health, that it is little dependent on human intelligence or choice. There is indeed opportunity for the exercise of much wisdom in the selection of materials, and of much skill in preparing them for use. But food, clothing and shelter must be enjoyed alike by rich and poor, noble and peasant. The rich may incur much expense in the preparation of necessaries which the poor cannot afford, but the necessities of the case are universal and poverty itself is no exemption. But in the use which is made of that portion of the products of labor which we have called disposable, men differ very widely, and on the use which they make of them the prosperity and happiness of society very largely depend.

§ 236. Almost immediately after the strictly necessary wants of men are supplied, we find in almost all communities a vast demand for a few articles of diet, which certainly *are not necessaries of life, and of which some appear to be in ordinary circumstances injurious*. They do not minister to nutrition, but produce their effect on comfort and happiness, by operating directly upon the nervous system, by exciting, tranquilizing and narcotic influences. The demand for them, in a great number of cases, is so imperative and urgent, that for the sake of obtaining them men will often sacrifice the food and clothing necessary for themselves and their families. The proportion of all the results of human labor, in all the civilized countries of the world, which is expended for *spirituous liquors, tobacco, tea, coffee and opium* almost surpasses belief. It is hard for science to demonstrate what beneficial influence they exert on the human economy. Some of them are certainly employed by great numbers in such a manner as to be destructive of reputation, impair health, shorten life, render men incapable of labor or self control, waste property and wreck the whole man. These sad phenomena are exhibited not in a few occasional instances, but in great numbers, in all classes of society and in all the conditions of life. Yet the expenditure of our country for these articles nearly approaches if it does not equal or exceed the cost of bread or necessary clothing. Those substances belonging to this class which are most in demand, and most open to the charge of being far more injurious than beneficial are, under our present revenue system, subjected to a tax which, if enforced against almost any other article not a necessary of life, would be prohibitory, without any perceptible diminution of the demand. Many of the most enlightened, virtuous and philanthropic men among us believe, that at least the traffic in intoxicating liquors is destructive of public health and morals, and ought to be suppressed as a public nuisance. Yet under all these discouragements and burdens, the traffic is openly pursued, and the consumption seems to be increasing with all its evil consequences.

§ 237. It is not our business to deal with the question of the relation of these substances to the human constitution, and to the laws of life and health. That question belongs to the chemist, the physiologist and the physician. But the existence of an expenditure so vast, and in some of its aspects so destructive, *for which science can render so little account, and furnish so little justification*, is not creditable to our civilization. The same remark may be made with very little modification in relation to the whole civilized world. Civilized men should surely act more intelligently and reasonably in relation to a subject of such importance. If intoxicating drinks render some service to the human constitution, which justifies the enormous expense incurred by the use of them, and the risks encountered, certainly science should be able to demonstrate it, and relieve the conscience of the nation, which evidently at present is ill at ease on the subject. If these substances, especially intoxicating drinks, have no such beneficial relation, the whole energy of a civilized people should be exerted, to arrest so wasteful and destructive an expenditure. If we can place any reliance on statistics, a very few years of the consumption of intoxicating drinks alone at the present rate, will equal the whole cost of the four years war of the great rebellion. We think this a field of inquiry, in which scientific research should be prosecuted with utmost earnestness. Whence this craving for stimulus? Whence this appetite, not for food, but for destruction? The life we are living as a nation in relation to this matter, and to a great extent the same is true of other civilized nations, is more brutal than human. We are obeying the blind impulse of appetite instead of being guided by enlightened reason.

§ 238. There is another branch of expenditure, which, though less destructive, is scarcely less wasteful or more rational. We refer to the passion *for excessive personal ornamentation.* It has already been clearly shown, that a true economy enters no protest against the love of the beautiful. The resources of the world and the powers of man are evidently so adjusted to human want, that ample provision has been made for the ornamental as well as for the necessary; and the latter must be cultivated or a large amount of human power must be quite useless to mankind. Beauty is a real good, and humanity fitly adorned is a far nobler thing than if unadorned.

But the methods in which the ornamental is pursued and applied deserve attention. Every one knows that in the real world around us, *the use of ornament is not regulated by any permanent canons of beauty,* and that in this whole department *fashion* rules with an undisputed supremacy. We are not going to attempt a scientific definition of fashion, yet it is obvious that a certain capricious thing known by that name has, in respect to all that is designed to be ornamental, more influence than reason. It is our duty here as everywhere to hear the voices of nature, and there are teachings of nature in this department, which lead to the regulation of the ornamental on principles which perhaps we could not have anticipated. There is a natural taste for rank,

Society tends to arrange itself in grades one above another. Against the aristocracy which intrenches itself in legislation, all Americans protest. But after all we are not less devoted to the conventional aristocracy of custom than other peoples, and the classes esteemed the higher are not less jealous than other aristocracies of the peculiar privileges and honors which they claim for themselves. They cannot be, in such a society as ours, permanent, but are as changing as drifting masses of sand. Men go up to-day and down to-morrow, but this makes them by no means less desirous to render the boundary lines of the high rank to which they claim to belong as clearly drawn as possible.

§ 239. In this social rivalry there is a constant endeavor *so to employ personal ornament, as to make it distinctive of that rank in which one claims a place.* The style of dress and equipage which is for the time being the badge of the highest social position, is eagerly emulated by all that are below. No costliness is spared by the prosperous merchant, mechanic or farmer, to array his household, especially his wife and daughters, in the style that is recognized as the badge of high society. In a short time any style that is thus emulated will cease to be a badge of distinction; it will have descended to the multitude, and the leaders of fashion must invent some new mark of distinction. This soon shares the same fate. Thus new costumes of gentility follow each other almost with the rapidity and capriciousness of the changes of the wind, and a burden of expense is brought upon the community almost unlimited. The love of the beautiful is to a great extent supplanted by the love of the fashionable, and the expense of living is increased beyond all reasonable limits.

§ 240. This cause of the expensiveness of living operates *even more powerfully in a democratic community* than any other. In aristocratic communities, the social pyramid is divided into portions quite definitely distinguished from each other by parallel planes, and those in the lower strata accept rather contentedly the social position assigned them, and do not so much emulate the style of ornamentation which is the badge of a rank higher than their own. Rivalship in dress is in some degree limited to those in the same rank. But in a democratic society no such recognized social planes exist. Those in every social condition emulate, to the best of their ability, the external symbols of the highest gentility, and will spare no expense in their power to incur, to attain to them. An element of expensiveness is thus introduced into the whole life of a democratic people, more burdensome to many families than the entire cost of necessary food and clothing, far more burdensome than the taxation imposed on us by our national debt. When we were bearing the burden of the income tax, exemption was made, even in our time of extreme necessity, for all whose income did not exceed six hundred dollars. But this is a tax that knows no exemption. It is levied on a father's and a mother's pride in the social position of their daughters, and is therefore sure to be paid, even at the expense of bankruptcy at no distant day, and not seldom of a widowhood and orphanage of uncomforted want and poverty. This picture will be found to be true to the life in instances sadly numerous. If we are to have, at no distant day, a mass of pauperism as fearfully vast and hopeless as older civilized countries, the cause of which we are speaking will bear a most important part in bringing it upon us, and in pressing down our own sons and daughters into it.

We are not denouncing fashion. We have admitted *that it grows out of certain principles in human nature, which cannot be eliminated.* But it is well for us all to be aware of the *destructive excesses and perversions* to which those principles are liable, and to be put on our guard against them. It is not beneath the dignity of science, to point out the influence of this cause on the expenditures of a community, and to show how much safer guide to true prosperity is found in the cultivation of a taste for the really beautiful, the fittingly ornamental, than in following the ever shifting caprices of fashion. Is the elevation of a free community to this nobler standard of life a thing to be despaired of?

This subject is worthy of grave consideration, not only in the homes of those whose resources are scanty, but in the mansions of the rich. The latter may be able to bear the exactions of fashion without being distressed by them. But they might easily learn, that these fashionable follies render their lives much less dignified and honored than they might be, and that the sums that could easily be redeemed from this waste could be devoted to the accomplishment of objects which would afford them much more rational and enduring happiness. Perhaps they are not aware of the profound pleasure which many cultivated persons experience in visiting an attractive home of wealth, where good taste has dictated everything, fashion nothing. If such persons will break away from this bondage, they will not only have a delightful sense of freedom, but they will do a great deal to protect those in less favored conditions of life from the destructive fascination of fashionable folly. If the canons of taste instead of the canons of fashion can once make their authority respected in the homes of the wealthy, there is hope we may yet be a truly economical people.

§ 241. The prevalence of this unwise style of expenditure is the more to be deplored, on account of its *powerful tendency to prevent the formation of a taste for the really beautiful.* There are a great many homes in which fashion exacts an untold amount of costliness, where there is yet a sad lack of almost everything that is really beautiful, or even convenient and comfortable. Costly gentility in public and before the world, the merest humdrum in their ordinary routine in private, make up life. Such a tendency is unfavorably affecting our national character. Of course expenditure imposes its law on production. Labor and capital can only be made to yield profit, when they are employed in producing what the people desire to purchase. If the people are disposed to expend their resources chiefly upon the latest fantastic productions of the tailor, the milliner and the dressmaker, little will be left for the genuine artist. True art must be expected to languish very much in proportion as the arts which fashion patronizes are encouraged and rewarded. The question has been much discussed, whether the fine arts are likely to flourish in our country. That must depend, not upon our political institutions, but on the dominant ideas and prevailing tastes of our people. The character of our people is to make this country great, or to belittle it. Art did prevail in democratic Athens more than among any other people on earth, and prevailed most when she was most democratic. If a democratic people loves beauty and has a true taste for it, cities and villages and rural homes will be full of the productions of true art. But if it loves nervous stimulation and follows blindly the caprices of fashion, its public gatherings may be full of meretricious magnificence, but both its public and its private places will be dolefully barren of all the grandest productions of genius.

§ 242. To give the law of competition free course is to make the people *the arbiters of their own destiny.* Men who are really free to buy and to sell, to employ and to be employed, to own land and to sell land, will also be free to expend their disposable resources according to their own tastes; and by their folly to make themselves mean, or by their wisdom to make themselves great and renowned in the earth. We have unequaled advantages for accumulating wealth, and unlimited freedom in expending it. By the very abundance of our resources and the freedom which we enjoy, it is placed in our own hands to become the greatest or the meanest of nations. That momentous question turns on the single hinge of private expenditure. If our prevailing tastes are low, vulgar, and sensual, the world will minister to our gratification and our ruin. If our tastes are pure and rational and wise, the world will no less contribute to our gratification, and to our growth in all that is noblest in manhood, and worthiest of our privileges and our freedom.

§ 243. The question how men expend their power to labor, is no less interesting, than the use they make of its results. The common human patrimony is equally affected by the waste or misapplication of the one or the other. It has been shown in its proper place, that the increase of human power by the use of labor-saving machinery does not, as might have been anticipated, minister to idleness, by dispensing with the necessity of labor, but on the contrary greatly increases the demand for it in every department. But while this is true, it does nevertheless tend to the rapid increase of capital, and by increasing capital increases the number of those who are not compelled to labor by any necessity. Will it not then diminish the amount of labor actually performed? That it does to some extent relieve the rich from the pressure of necessity to work is certainly true. But if the rich man himself would remain rich, his life must be pretty industriously employed in managing his estate, with a view to its preservation, enlargement and right use. It must however be admitted, that there are not a few deriving their subsistence from the incomes of the rich, who do spend aimless lives, devoted only to the enjoyment of each gratification of desire which for the present moment seems most attractive. In just so far as the possession of wealth induces those who subsist by it to lead such lives, it is ruinous in its influence. It makes those lives worthless, which it was intended to render more efficient and useful. The conception with which we began this treatise, that every human being is a laborer, is accordant with the only true manhood. He who in the enjoyment of wealth leads a life without any aim to achieve something worth living for, falls out of the true human life into the life of an irrational animal. His wealth has deprived him of his manhood. All who are entrusted with riches should use their utmost endeavor, that they be not thus perverted to the injury of any who subsist by them. There are innumerable ends which a rich man may pursue, which greatly ennoble and adorn life, and yield an abundant reward. It is the privilege of those who are relieved from the necessity of toil, to aim at and achieve results which are beyond the reach of the utmost endeavors of those who must labor for their daily bread. That is a very unfortunate rich man, who on being relieved from the necessity of toiling for subsistence, knows not how to employ himself in anything which will be of service to mankind.

## CHAPTER XVII.

*Public Liberality.*

§ 244. IN the view of many, this topic is entirely outside of our science. Several recent writers have accepted the definition of the science proposed by Archbishop Whately,—The Science of Exchange,—and have thus reduced the science to a mere "quid pro quo." Our readers are already well aware that we by no means accept this definition. We believe that the word wealth may be so defined as to be accurately expressive of the whole group of phenomena of which the economist is to treat, and comprehensive of all the uses of the thing defined. In this view of the case *all the original desires of man which impel him to labor are natural forces with which the science is concerned.*

One of these *is the love of social prosperity and wellbeing.* It is one of the noblest impulses of humanity, and an exceedingly important element in the economic system of the present age. Man's power to render the universe helpful to human well being by the exertion of his labor was designed to minister to the gratification of every natural desire of the human soul. Man may not only exert his powers to procure what he desires by exchange, but for the production of beauty which all may enjoy, and none can appropriate, and for that perfected civilization which is the common inheritance of mankind.

*There are common wants of communities, which the desire of gain and the direct expectation of profits will never sufficiently provide for.* Men will build machines, railways and ocean steamers under the influence of the hope of gain, and they will realize the profits the hope of which stimulated them to these undertakings. But there are some of the very highest wants of men of which they never become in masses sufficiently conscious to provide for them on principles of exchange. Of this character are hospitals for the sick and suffering stranger or unfortunate, monuments appropriately to record the great events of a nation's history, and to honor the memory of the founders of states, the discoverers of science and art, and the benefactors of their race, colleges and universities for the highest culture in all the various departments of knowledge, and libraries in which the thought and wisdom of the ages shall be garnered up for the instruction of successive generations, and made accessible to all the curious and the studious.

*Governments cannot be relied on to supply these wants* of society. In no country has the government, as a general rule and in the long course of its history, embraced within itself the highest thought and the most perfect culture of the successive generations. Force, not thought or argument is the weapon of a government, and it can therefore never be relied on for quickly and keenly appreciating those moral and spiritual forces, which are most of all potent and beneficent in the formation of the character of a people ; and of course it cannot safely be trusted, promptly and efficiently to apply such forces. The sword is in all ages the emblem of civil power, and an agency adapted to wield the sword with effect can hardly be expected to be eminently fitted for the intellectual, moral and spiritual culture of society. Certainly the experience of the ages has shown that it is not. Here then is a wide field for the exertion of beneficent influence on all the future of society, which must always invite individual effort. Here are most important wants of communities, nations and the race that can be supplied only by individual liberality.

§ 245. It has been shown in the foregoing treatise, that with the increase of capital, its rate of profit constantly declines. With this decline the motive to accumulation is diminished also, and some have their apprehensions, that in the wealthier countries of the world, this motive may become sufficiently enfeebled to arrest the increase of capital. Should the whole civilized world approach such a plethora of capital, there would be a liability to rash and hazardous speculation, in which much capital would be wasted, and the rate of profit of what remained would be thereby raised. But the same state of things would also be *favorable to the investment of capital in enterprises of public liberality* without any direct expectation of profit in return. When capital is superabundant and profits are small, it may be expected that the owners of capital will incline more toward the side of prodigality than of frugality. All their desires are likely to be more freely gratified. But if the moral culture of society has not been neglected, it is to be hoped that all would not be swept along on this current of self-indulgent folly. Many we might reasonably hope would gratify the highest impulses of our nature in the enjoyment of their wealth, rather than the lowest and most debased. As a true civilization attains to a more abundant supply of capital, it may be expected, that as there will be increased ability, so there will be increased disposition, to perform acts of generous liberality; and that men will find more pleasure in expending their accumulations for the benefit of mankind, than for sensual or even esthetic gratifications.

Men of wealth *can never afford entirely to neglect such outlays of capital*, even if they have regard only to their highest prosperity in trade. The sound and healthy condition of trade always depends much upon the intelligence of the community, and especially of men of leading influence in it. Men of wealth are in their own private affairs *deeply interested in the higher education—* that education which forms the character of the leaders of society. For example the doctrines of currency and freedom of exchange which are defended in this treatise are either true or false. If they are false it is exceedingly desirable to all the capital of the country, that our schools for the higher education should not favor them, nor give them currency among the leading minds of the nation. If they are false, science can demonstrate their fallacy, and effectually guard our young men that are growing into public influence from adopting them. But if they are true, it is more important than can well be expressed, that all nations as well as our own people should as rapidly as possible be persuaded to adopt such freedom of exchange in all things, and between the inhabitants of all countries, as will give to the labor and capital of the world all the advantages to which they are naturally entitled. According as men of wealth believe these doctrines to be true or false, they should vie with each other, in securing for the hopeful young men of our country, a true knowledge of the scientific principles which underlie all production and all exchange of values. It is the present misfortune of our country, that many of our public men have never considered these matters at all, and are discharging public functions of the gravest importance to all the interests of trade, without having received any education in the scientific principles which underlie all such questions. This cannot be a healthy condition of affairs. It is impossible in such a country as ours to detach individual prosperity from public intelligence.

§ 246. Apart however from all considerations of personal interest, it is fit *that the hope of achieving something for the lasting benefit of one's country and of mankind* should be a powerful stimulus to an industrious and frugal life.  The man who seeks to obtain, by the use which he makes of wealth, the exalted pleasures of beneficence, will insure for himself, in addition to that deference which wealth itself is apt to inspire, that affectionate reverence while living, and that grateful remembrance in after years, which men are accustomed to accord to eminent wisdom and goodness.

It has been shown elsewhere that by the very law of ownership, *the rich are made the treasurers of a portion of the common patrimony of the race.*  Of this relationship men are apt to be entirely unconscious, and to live just as they would if they only were interested in the capital which they control.  Their lives would be much wiser and happier if *they would recognize this fiduciary relation in which they stand to the rest of the world,* and seek to promote, by wisely directed effort, that general well-being to which they cannot help ministering by their efforts to increase their own wealth.  They would thus become public benefactors, as well by intelligent purpose as by the necessity which is imposed on them by the law of ownership.  We cannot forbear the suggestion, that when capitalists show themselves to be in spirit and intention what the very structure of the economic system compels them to be, they will accomplish much towards putting an end to that dangerous feud between capital and labor, which is awakening so much just apprehension in the minds of all thoughtful men.  When all men see that capital is, not only by a necessary law of nature, but with voluntary intention and purpose, held in trust for the general good, the laborer and his employer will feel themselves to be in fraternal and not in hostile relations to each other.  The employer will feel that the laborer is a natural partner in the business in which they are co-operating, and will gladly recognize his rightful claim to considerate regard. The laborer on his part will feel that he has an interest in all the products he is helping to create. We do not believe this unnatural and ruinous conflict ever can be terminated, except on such terms as these. All must come to recognize that community of interest which has been shown to pervade the economies of the world.

§ 247. Great care must be taken that such acts of public liberality should be performed in such a manner and under such conditions, *as to violate no economic law.* For this reason *no public institution of charity or education should be permitted to hold lands by an inalienable tenure.* We are aware that the great universities of England largely owe their present magnificent endowments to the fact, that centuries ago they were endowed with lands which they could not alienate, the rent of which has steadily increased with the progress of the nation in wealth and population. It may be asked why we should not provide our public institutions in the same manner with permanent and ever increasing resources. We answer, because such endowments would interfere with that free trade in land which is most fundamental to American, and it seems to us to all truly free society. One great obstacle which stands in the way of the speedy abolition of the English land monopoly will be found to lie in the vast landed estates held by great, permanent and noble institutions of learning and beneficence. All those who are most intimately related to those institutions would be apt vehemently to resist the change. But the permanent prosperity and beneficent power of those institutions would not be really at stake; to us on the contrary it seems, that the change would be very happy in its influence on them, so far as they are really rendering important service to the society. Endowments in land held by inalienable tenure, acquired while society was yet in its infancy render such institutions independent of the thought and progress of each living generation, and too often blindly conservative of an antiquated and dead past. Public funds will always produce greater present income at interest, than in real estate. If therefore all real estate held by such institutions is made alienable at the discretion of trustees, they will be under a strong inducement to dispose of it in order to obtain a greater revenue available for immediate uses. Thus the freedom of exchange will not be interfered with, and the immediate productiveness of the fund will be increased. But the farther increase of the fund from the rise of real estate will be arrested, and for its growing necessities as wealth and population increase, the institution will be thrown upon the liberality of each succeeding generation. As capital is rapidly increasing, if the institution is performing well its high function, the experience of this country shows, that that liberality will be adequate to all exigencies as they arise. Institutions founded on such a basis may always be expected to stand abreast, not of the whims of capricious faction, but of the sound thought and healthful progress of a living civilization. Funds thus invested in public institutions of beneficence are not withdrawn from the active capital of the future. It makes no difference to one who wishes to borrow money, whether he obtains it from a private capitalist, a bank directory, or the trustees of some fund devoted to an object of public munificence. Such funds are far more likely to be preserved from loss or waste than they would be if transmitted to uncertain heirs, and are always available for the practical use of the age, by the payment of the current rate of interest. Institutions thus endowed will represent the highest culture of the present, as they should do, if they are to educate the leading minds of the generation that is to succeed.

They will still be conservative rather than radical in their tastes and tendencies; but they will not be rockbound islands in the stream of progress, which the current has no power to shake or to wear away, bringing the cultured intellect of each passing age into hopeless and perpetual conflict with its living practical thought.

§ 248. A government so purely democratic as ours *will always represent the average thought of the nation*, and never its highest and *most cultured thought*. Yet it is evidently most desirable, that such a nation should have an efficient system of culture, representing its highest thought, and controlled by it. Such a system it can hardly be expected to have under purely popular control. Our own country is at the present time and in its past history able to furnish ample illustration of this. It is for the most part through the liberality of the wealthy, that such a system of liberal culture has been originated and sustained. The most cultivated intellect of the nation, coöperating with its liberal capitalists has a duty to perform, and always will have, which cannot be neglected without imminent peril. Thus far in our history such an alliance between the intellect and the capital of the country has always existed, and has produced results most eminently satisfactory. They seek no alliance with the state, they ask no privileges from the state, they desire to lay no burden upon the taxpayer; they only ask freedom of opportunity, to found and to perpetuate the highest civilization, by the exertion of intellectual and moral forces only. It is greatly to the honor of our free institutions, that the public liberality of individuals acting only on the voluntary principle has laid foundations so ample, and reared superstructures so creditable to our civilization. Nor is there any reason to apprehend, that the voluntary principle will be inadequate to the much larger necessities of the future.

§ 249. In another point of view this subject seems invested with very important relations to interests which are directly economic. It is obvious to any one, that in such a country as ours, *there is a liability that the accumulation of capital may be prematurely arrested.* We have spoken freely in the foregoing chapters of land monopoly, and have very earnestly deprecated it. We have no intentions of retracting or modifying anything which we have maintained on that subject. But we wish to deal fairly with the whole question. There is but one known way in which the name and honors of a family can be handed down through successive generations. It must be done, if done at all, through a landed estate, which descends inalienably in the family and bears its name. When such facilities are afforded by the laws for perpetuating a great family interest, men are induced to accumulate wealth not only for themselves and their children, but for their remote posterity. Under such circumstances there will always be a strong motive to acquire for the purpose of founding and improving a family estate, and adorning a family mansion. But under such a law of descent as ours, no such motive can exist. One may lay up for his children, but there can be little hope that any estate which he can accumulate will reach his distant posterity. The temptation therefore is to live more for the present and less for the future. It cannot be denied, that one of the dangers of American society is, that each generation will live for itself alone, and that we shall be characterized alike, by the greed and rapidity of our acquisition, and the profusion of our expenditure. We seriously ask the thoughtful, if there are no indications of the development of such a national character. Have we not some real reason to apprehend a growth of sensuality and fashionable ostentation, limited only by our success in the prosecution of gain?

It is then eminently desirable on grounds purely economic, that in the absence of the possibility of men's calling their lands by their own names, they should *seek to perpetuate their names by the permanent public institutions of learning and philanthropy* which they found and foster. The names of Yale and Harvard and Phillips are not likely to be forgotten. It is also not improbable that foundations which have been laid in the great interior of our country may confer a like honor on their founders. A prevailing disposition among the capitalists of this country to employ their capital for such purposes would do much to arrest these tendencies towards wasteful prodigality, to raise families above a life of sensuality and fantastic display, and would redeem from waste a great amount of capital to be securely held at the current rate of interest, and just as available to assist and reward labor, as though it was still owned by a private capitalist. This subject is worthy of the most serious attention, on account of its economic relations, over and above all its relations to the higher culture. It is the natural and proper substitute for that ambition of family, which can only be gratified by the aristocratic tenure of land. It is by far the nobler sentiment of the two, it is in perfect harmony with democratic institutions, and can be freely indulged without any interference with the helpfulness of capital to labor, or with that perfect freedom of exchange, which must sooner or later pervade the economies of the world. All capital thus disposed of will fall into a succession in which it will probably have the best chance that can be devised of being protected from waste and loss, and preserved for the distant future. In presenting this topic, we therefore believe that we have not at all overstepped the limits prescribed to a grave scientific treatise.

www.ingramcontent.com/pod-product-compliance
Lightning Source LLC
Chambersburg PA
CBHW032046220426
43664CB00008B/884